Class
Reunion

The *Critical Social Thought* Series
edited by Michael W. Apple, University of Wisconsin–Madison

Class Reunion

The Remaking of the American White Working Class

Lois Weis

ROUTLEDGE

NEW YORK AND LONDON

Published in 2004 by
Routledge
270 Madison Avenue
New York, NY 10016
www.routledge-ny.com

Published in Great Britain by
Routledge
2 Park Square
Milton Park, Abingdon
Oxon OX14 4RN
www.routledge.co.uk

Routledge is an imprint of the Taylor & Francis Group.

10 9 8 7 6 5 4 3 2 1

Library of Congress Cataloging-in-Publication Data

Weis, Lois.
  Class reunion : the remaking of the American white working class /
Lois Weis.
      p. cm. — (The critical social thought series)
  Includes bibliographical references and index.
  ISBN 0-415-94907-6 (hardback : alk. paper) — ISBN 0-415-94908-4 (pbk. : alk. paper)
  1. Working class whites—United States—Economic conditions. 2. Working class whites—
United States—Social conditions. 3. Working class—United States—Longitudinal studies.
  4. Social classes—United States. I. Title. II. Series: Critical social thought.
  HD8066.W45 2004
  305.562'089'09073—dc22
                            2004005186

For Tereffe Asrat, my husband

FREEWAY STEEL'S RETIREES
LEFT SCRAMBLING FOR BENEFITS

FREEWAY—Some of them went to work in the blast furnaces when they were just 18, then spent half a lifetime handling molten slag and inhaling steel dust in some of the most dangerous jobs on earth.

But for the tens of thousands of Freeway Steel workers who stuck it out, retirement brought a rich reward: A healthy pension and a lifetime of almost free health care for themselves and their families.

"It was capitalism's version of socialized medicine," said John Von Mason, a retired Freeway Steel vice president. "And it was an implied contract. It was the company and the workers saying, 'We are going to take care of each other.'"

It may go down in history as a promise unfulfilled. Bankrupt and only a shadow of its former might, Freeway Steel announced last week it was seeking bankruptcy court approval to terminate health and life insurance benefits for 95,000 retired workers March 31.

Freeway News, February 11, 2003

CONTENTS

SERIES EDITOR'S INTRODUCTION

I recently took a trip back to the city on the East Coast where I was born and raised—and where I worked as a printer and teacher for a number of years. One of the earliest heavy industrial cities in the United States, known for its textile mills and manufacturing base, the city seemed even poorer economically than I remembered it. It also still had enclaves of white working-class communities abutting neighborhoods populated by people of color from all over the world. In fact, like many "rust belt" cities, it was now a city where European-Americans were in the minority. Always a remarkably diverse city because of its textile mills and status as a destination for large numbers of immigrants, it may have been very poor, but it also now had a vibrancy that was even more visceral than before.

Yet, it was also still a tense city. Declining industrial jobs, increasing rates of impoverishment, high rates of immigration by diaspora populations and by economic and political refugees from Asia, the Middle East, the Caribbean, Africa, and so many other places had created hybrid cultures and a good deal of interethnic solidarity. But it had also created a defensive white working and middle class.

I passed by the elementary school and high school I had attended. The high school had been made notable when a popular film was made about its principal who had "cleaned up the school." (He did so by throwing out a large number of difficult-to-reach and alienated students, many of whom wound up on the streets and ultimately in jail because there was nothing to replace the school—no social and youth services, no respectable jobs, no alternative forms of education; just the realities of the oppressive economic conditions that are even worse in these communities now.)

As I went by the high school, a wash of memories came back. Questions arose about what had happened to the students with whom I had gone to school. I did know that, unlike me, most had stayed in those poor and working-class communities in which I, too, had grown up. I unfortunately had lost touch with nearly all of them.

Reading *Class Reunion* immediately brought all of these memories and questions to the very forefront of my mind. It is a fascinating and illuminating book, one that cannot fail to direct our attention to the questions surrounding "What happened to ... ?" and to so much more. Lois Weis is the author of the justly well-regarded book *Working Class Without Work* (1990), a powerful and provocative analysis of the lives of students in deindustrializing America. Among the things that set that book apart was its subtle examination of the ways gender differences worked ideologically in the creation of political identities. She revealed that while working-class young men might be integrated into rightist ideological positions and identities, the lived culture of young women provided "unconscious" resources that made it harder for them to be fully integrated within rightist ideological projects.

Does this hold true as time goes on, as capital continues its radical restructuring of people's presents and futures, and as gender and racial dynamics get more complex? In *Class Reunion*, Weis returns to the same community and the same people. What she shows is crucial to our understanding of some of the most important social and ideological trends in the nation as a whole.

Her picture of what has happened to the students with whom she spent so much time is evocative. It illuminates both stability and sea changes that have occurred and are continuing beneath the surface of communities that have suffered the effects of capitalism's constant search for lower costs for labor and for higher profits. At the same time that the book points out disturbing continuities between then and now, it also points out progressive possibilities that are constantly bubbling up in the lived culture of the women and men in these communities. Finally, Weis provides a model of how engaged scholarship can and should go on.

While the complex reality of class is the primary focus of attention for Weis, as she so clearly recognized in her earlier book, classed actors are always sexed and raced as well. One of the most striking insights in this volume involves the transformations that have occurred in patriarchal relations within these communities. Some of the most influential books in the history of working-class youth (e.g., Willis, 1981) showed the integral relationship between class and masculinity. *Class Reunion* recasts this and demonstrates that changes in men's and women's working lives have had very real, indeed sometimes even momentous, effects on class and gender relations. Because of the often harsh changes in the economy and the destruction of the (always weak and insufficiently funded) government programs and the safety net that such programs and benefits provided, men are doing much more of the work of domestic labor. Cooking, cleaning, child care—all of these are taken up as natural, as "things we all have to do to get by." Thus, as odd as it may seem at first glance, the closing of factories, the loss of industrial jobs, the growth of low-paid service sector jobs, and similar things may have had the paradoxical effect of bringing about changes in working-class male identities in partly progressive directions.

Do not misinterpret either my or Weis's points here. The destruction of economic livelihoods that has laid waste to entire communities is never good. But it may also set loose dynamics that can alter daily life and can change other power dynamics such as gender in unintended, and even partly positive, directions (see, e.g., Arnot, David, & Weiner, 1999).

Issues of race also provide a key building block of Weis's analysis. She understands a fundamental dynamic that underpins all too much of American life. In times of economic insecurity and constant worry, whatever hard-won gains the working class has made can be easily washed away. In the face of these insecurities, race often plays a powerful role. This of course is nothing new. As Charles Mills argues, much of political and economic life of societies like our own rests on an unacknowledged "racial contract" (Mills, 1997). However, as Weis documents, one of the things that binds men and women together within particular fractions of the working class is a disturbing kind of solidarity: a defense of neighborhood and community against the racial Other.

Whiteness has always required an Other, a "constitutive outside"— usually but not always African American, Latino/a, or Asian. In the case of the people whose lives are insightfully illuminated here, however, it is not only, say, the black Other who enables whites to maintain their identity. In this community it is also the "Arab" who is positioned as the danger to hearth and home. Thus, even before the horrible events of 9/11, anti-Arab sentiment was growing in many

xiv • Class Reunion

communities. After 9/11, the conservative nativist backlash could and
did build on this, often with deeply disturbing consequences (see
Apple, 2004). Weis's discussion of the place of race in the lives of this
particular group of white working-class people is exceptionally
perceptive.

Lois Weis writes about these issues in such a way that critical theoretical resources and the richly detailed portraits of real people are
blended together seamlessly. This shows a real talent. It is hard work
to write in such a way, and few authors are as good at it as she is. This
is not to say that all things can or should be written about in "simple"
ways. As Terry Eagleton puts it, "Not all wisdom is simple and spon-
taneous" (Eagleton, 2003, p. 77). But as he goes on to say, "There is
something particularly scandalous about radical cultural theory being
so willfully obscure" (Eagleton 2003, p.77; see also Apple, 2001).
Class Reunion is an antidote to this. It is filled with the kind of
portraits of real people, and complexities and contradictions of their
lived experiences, that are compellingly honest and that enable the
reader to rethink stereotypes about class, gender, race, and age. And
it provides important critical cultural, economic, and political tools
that enable the reader to make even greater sense of what these
portraits may actually mean in the context of the radical transformations we are witnessing all around us. This is quite an achievement.
Because of these attributes, this is a book that makes a lasting contri-
bution to all of us who are concerned with what has happened and is
happening in schools and communities throughout the nation in a time
of severe economic and cultural crisis.

Michael W. Apple
John Bascom Professor of Curriculum and Instruction
and Educational Policy Studies
University of Wisconsin-Madison

References

Apple, M.W. (2001). *Educating the "right" way*. New York: RoutledgeFalmer.
Apple, M.W. (2004). *Ideology and curriculum* (3rd ed.). New York: RoutledgeFalmer.
Arnot, M., David, M., and Weiner, G. (1999). *Closing the gender gap*. Cambridge, U.K.:
    Polity Press.
Eagleton, T. (2003). *After theory*. New York: Basic Books.
Mills, C. (1997). *The racial contract*. Ithaca, NY: Cornell University Press.
Weis, L. (1990). *Working class without work*. New York: Routledge.
Willis, P. (1981). *Learning to labor*. New York: Columbia University Press.

ACKNOWLEDGMENTS

Numerous individuals were involved in the production of this volume, and I am deeply grateful for the participation of so many. Individuals in Freeway invited me into their lives, first as teenagers in 1985–1986, and again as adults in 2000–2001. Struggling to situate themselves amid a rapidly changing social and economic context, they are worthy of our respect. The Spencer Foundation and the Baldy Center for Law and Social Policy at the University at Buffalo funded portions of the research over the past four years; while not responsible for any aspect of my analysis, I trust I do justice to their sponsorship. Ilene Kalish originally signed the volume and, upon her departure, Catherine Bernard took over the project. I am indebted to Ilene for her initial sponsorship of the book, and especially to Catherine for offering painstaking feedback and seeing the volume through the production process. I could not have asked for a finer editor. Michael Apple, as series editor, has been enormously supportive of my scholarship over the years, and I am grateful for his unwavering faith.

Michelle Fine, Catherine Cornbleth, and Greg Dimitriadis read a draft of the manuscript and offered extraordinarily helpful comments on this earlier version. Cathie and Greg forced me to continue to look below the surface of what I thought I saw, and I am grateful for their smart read and sheer persistence. Michelle, my coauthor on so many projects, underlined the importance of this particular volume. Our collaborative work of so many years is written into the pages of this book in innumerable ways. Craig Centrie, an artist in his own right, continually encourages me to view ethnography as an art form, one deeply rooted in technical skill, yet thoroughly dependent upon deep imagination. Graduate students Michelle Meyers, Catie Lalonde, Touorouzou Hervé Somé, Carrie Freie, Susan Ott, and Tina Wagle worked steadily on this project. Somé read all of Bourdieu in the original French, encouraging me to work off the original corpus of work rather than rely solely on published English translations; Michelle Meyers worked with the economic data; Susan Ott and Tina Wagle acted as coders; Catie Lalonde brought a wealth of knowledge with respect to representations of the working class in the media; and Carrie Freie engaged the broader literature on white working-class men and women. Michelle and Somé also read a draft of the manuscript and offered invaluable critique. Amy Ferry is, once again, responsible for the final product; her speed and thoroughly professional orientation have been invaluable to me over the years.

My final thanks are reserved for my family. Tereffe Asrat, my husband, has stood by me as I have moved from one project to another. His respect, coupled with his searing analytical mind, is woven through this manuscript in ways too numerous to count. It has been my privilege to be married to Tereffe for twenty-one years. I could not be prouder of our two daughters, Sara Asrat and Jessica Asrat. Sara pushed me (nagged, really) until I wrote the prospectus and offered much-needed help with census data as well as additional data generated by the County Commission on the Status of Women. A fine writer in her own right, Sara promoted this project from its inception. Jessica's keen analytical mind and intense focus on her own writing continue to inspire me. Her unwavering commitment to aspects of social justice stands as testimony to the potential power of the next generation. To Tereffe, Sara, and Jessica: You've made my life enormously fun and most definitely worth living.

I leave *Class Reunion* knowing that the zest with which so many engage the world can only serve to make it a better place. You have my respect and my profound thanks.

Lois Weis

INTRODUCTION
In the Shadow of the Mills

I remember the grit on the windows. And on the cars. And all of a sudden it wasn't there anymore. We had a pool; the pool would be dirty from the soot in the air. The colors in the sky were amazing; it was just the stuff they were dumping in the lake, you know, yellows and greens and purples, and [we said] "Look at the sky." And I remember picking up my dad at three o'clock and all the hundreds and hundreds of men coming out at that time. You know the bridges—I crossed through five, and there he was, standing, waiting for us.

Rhonda, age 16, interviewed in 1985

My dad is a machinist. He needs one more day in the plant to get his twenty years [thus getting his pension]. He's fighting now to get one more day. Me, I want to go to college 'cause I see what happened to him. He's working for like seven/eight dollars an hour. Like, what he used to get in the plant, compared to that, it's nothing. To get a better chance, you got to go to college.

Bill, age 16, interviewed in 1985

In 2001, Rhonda is a registered nurse, married to a state trooper. They have one daughter, ten months old. Bill was recently fired from his job as a tollbooth collector for engaging in a fight with a motorist. He is not married, lives with his mother, and has no children.

It is fifteen years since I first interviewed Rhonda, Bill, and thirty-nine additional third-year white students as part of a full-scale ethno-graphic investigation of a white working-class high school located in

Freeway—a then rapidly de-industrializing town in the northeastern United States. Based on a form of what I call *ethnographic longitudinality, Class Reunion* is the 2004 story of the individuals who first appeared in *Working Class Without Work* (Weis, 1990). More than just a story of thirty-one individuals whom I reinterviewed in 2000–2001, however, *Class Reunion* is an exploration, empirically and longitudinally, of the re-making of the American white working class in the latter quarter of the twentieth century. Arguing that we cannot write off the working class simply because white men no longer have access to well-paying laboring jobs in the primary labor market (Edwards, 1979), jobs that spawned a distinctive place for labor in the capital–labor accord (Hunter, 1987; Apple, 2001), I track and theorize the re-making of this group as a distinct class fraction, both discursively and behaviorally inside radical, globally-based economic restructuring (Reich, 1991, 2001; Rogers & Teixeira, 2000; McCall, 2001).

In this context, Bill's and Rhonda's stories are not unique, but rather are suggestive of what has happened to a large portion of the white industrial proletariat in America, a proletariat that has been remade and, simultaneously, has re-made itself in the face of massive changes in the global economy. Reconstituting itself on a daily basis in homes, bars, hospitals, donut shops, gas stations, schools, warehouses, and the like, the white working-class fraction is effectively staging its own "class reunion"—a class reunion which, given the fundamentally altered world economy and the particular place of the industrial proletariat inside this new economy, embodies deep restructuring along gender lines, the outcomes of which are markedly unclear. Demands for, and the very necessity of, women's independence in this newly minted class fraction exist inside a highly traditional patriarchal culture, one laced with and maintained at times by physical beatings. Ironically, though, it is this uneasy gendered realignment that is a necessary condition for the newly articulated "settled" white working class. As men and women of the new white working class simultaneously and collectively assert whiteness in relation to familiar groups of color in the United States, such as African Americans, as well as new key groups, such as, in this particular community, Yemenites, men and women reconverge. Splitting along gendered lines as shaped and ultimately propped up by heterosexuality, white working-class men and women reunite along race lines, producing, for the moment at least, a working collective which, paradoxically, serves in part to challenge increased globally driven demand for the neoliberal subject.

Beginning with my 1985 ethnographic investigation of Freeway High and culminating with intensive follow-up interviews with these same students in 2000–2001, I track the sons and daughters of the workers of "Freeway Steel" and similar industries, returning after fifteen years. Exploring identity formation among American white working-class male and female students in relation to the school, economy, and family of origin, *Working Class Without Work*, my original volume, captures the complex relations among secondary schooling, human agency, and the formation of collective consciousness within a then radically changing economic and social context (Bluestone & Harrison, 1982). I suggest in this volume that young women exhibit what I call a "glimmer of critique" regarding traditional gender roles in the white working-class family, and that young men are ripe for New Right consciousness, given their strident racism and male-dominant stance in an economy that offers them little.

Now, fifteen years later, I return to these same students as they, and we, meet in *Class Reunion*. Through a careful look at the high school and young adult years of the sons and daughters of the industrial proletariat in the northeastern "rust belt" of the United States, I capture and theorize the reshaping of the white working class *as a distinct class fraction*, tracking this rearticulation through careful and explicit attention to issues that swirl around whiteness, masculinity, femininity, representations, and the new economy. Reflective of the triplet of theoretical and analytic moves that Michelle Fine and I put forward as signature of our work (Weis & Fine, 2004)—deep work within one group (over a fifteen-year time period in this case); serious relational analyses between and among relevant bordering groups; and broad structural connections to social, economic, and political arrangements—I argue in this volume that the re-making of the American white working class can be understood only in relation to gendered constructions within itself, the construction of relevant "others" as uncovered ethnographically—in this case African Americans and Yemenites ("Arabians")—as well as deep shifts in large social formations, most particularly the global economy. Amid cries of "farewell to the working class" (Gorz, 1982) and assertions of the complete eclipse of this class, given the lack of "direct representations of the interactions among workers on American television" (Aronowitz, 1992), *Class Reunion* suggests, in contrast, that the American white working class is very much alive, having re-articulated itself as a distinct class fraction in the last quarter of the twentieth century.

Class Understandings

This rearticulation can be understood only in relation to a particular formulation of social class. Like Walkerdine, Lucey, and Melody (2001), I understand social class to be the "social and psychic practices through which ordinary people live, survive and cope" (p. 27). This involves understanding "the practices of living, the process of subjectification and the formation of subjectivities." Unlike celebrated prior investigations of the working class, that tag social class fundamentally to the male giving of labor power in a capitalist economy (Willis, 1977), I, like E. P. Thompson (1966) and other more culturally driven theorists, stretch understandings of class so as to include the practices of everyday living—practices that are both engaged in by, and simultaneously encircle, men, women, and children on a daily basis. Under this formulation, class is "lived as an identity designation and not simply as an economic relation to the means of production" (Walkerdine et al., 2001, p. 13). Rather than conceptualizing class as linked primarily to men who labor in particular relation to the capitalist economy, then, class becomes lived at a much broader level and as a specific location "at a particular time and in a particular place" (Walkerdine et al., 2001, p. 13). Such an altered understanding of social class enables a distancing from raging debates that circle around the degree to which working-class people (read white working-class men) exhibit a change in consciousness that will ultimately lead to the toppling of existing power arrangements.

This renders analyses such as those of Andre Gorz (1982), perhaps brilliant but limited in scope. He, like Paul Willis (1977), conceptualizes the working class as related wholly to masculinist confrontation with the work world. While Willis pries open a sociology of gender analysis with respect to youth culture (Arnot, 2002, 2004), and certainly must be given credit for this, he, like Gorz, concretizes the working class in terms of its relationship with wage labor, wherein the male wage packet becomes the primary means of self-definition, particularly when the wage is secured through enactment of a valued form of hegemonic masculinity.

Academics have done a great deal, whether consciously or not, to center the working class as white and male. Stanley Aronowitz (1992) traces what he calls the displacement of representation of the working class among workers on prime-time American television (Bettie, 1995). "Working men," he suggests, "are seen almost solely in police shows and in beer commercials with working-class representations disappearing for the most part with Archie Bunker." For Aronowitz, class has been eclipsed "ideologically and politically from the politics of subalternity," resulting in a form of "cultural homelessness," which makes it virtually impossible for working-class men to forge a class identity. Although Aronowitz suggests that he does not mean to ignore gender and race formations, there is, as Bettie points out, "consistent slippage between this hopeful statement and the ensuing analysis which reveals that we are to read 'workers' as white men in industrial occupations" (Bettie, 1995, p. 125). Joining Andre Gorz, Paul Willis, and others, then, Aronowitz centers the working class wholly in its relationship between white men and the industrial economy.

Working from a different perspective and pressing for a less exclusive formulation, Bettie stretches the composition of the working class itself, arguing that this class no longer can be read solely off white men:

> What we see then on prime time television and embedded in other popular culture venues may be less an ignoring of white working classness in an obvious or not so obvious attempt to fracture the class, but rather, the possible evocation of actual social changes in class structuring and of the related family revolutions of the twentieth century, social forces which render the very term working class anachronistic . . . .Class, race and gender become more visibly entangled as the working class is increasingly composed of people who do not represent the unmarked categories of whiteness and maleness. (1995, p. 126)

Bettie correctly argues that any assertion of the eclipse of the working class depends on a very specific definition of this class—one which centralizes and encodes the white male worker in a particular confrontation with capitalist production. Broadening our understanding of social class along the lines suggested earlier catapults us into wholly new territory both with respect to what the working class is and to how we study class configuration and reconfiguration more generally. Once we move off the space of working class as defined thoroughly in relation to place-bound industries and associated union activity, it is certainly true that large numbers of men and women across race and ethnicity are members of what can be called a broader working class. This, however, begs the question of the trajectory of the former industrial proletariat—a class fraction which is, by and large, white, male-dominant, and linked intergenerationally in particular ways to the industrially based capitalist economy.

In this book I maintain that the sons and daughters of the white industrial proletariat are engaged in the ongoing process of reshaping a new white working class *as a distinct class fraction*, one distanced in key ways from other parts of what might be considered a broader working class. This does not mean that there are no forms of working-classness in the United States (and elsewhere) that are not white. On the contrary, I believe there are segments of this broader class that can be classified and identified as such, even in the United States. What it does mean, however, is that a *new* white working class is shaping itself along very particular lines under radically different structural conditions than those that gave rise to the industrial proletariat, both as object and as subject. It is this reshaping that lies at the heart of *Class Reunion* and, as I will argue throughout this volume, it is privileges historically associated with whiteness, as well as continuing struggles around gender roles and definitions, that are key to the ongoing struggles of the white working class as it redefines itself as a continued distinct entity amid radical economic restructuring. It is the remaking and subsequent reconfiguration of this *specific* class location in a particular locality that provides the central "problem" of this volume.

The generalized nature of the shift in the global economy, as well as deeply based particularities embedded within the American context, must be addressed here. Dramatic changes in the global economy may be experienced worldwide, but are lived out in particular locations— locations that exhibit and manifest distinct histories in terms of, among other things, relations between and among groups as well as the definition of what constitutes a group to begin with (Cornbleth, 2003; Omi & Winant, 1994). In the United States context, the fact that the white working class, particularly white men, emerges as a group *fundamentally* in relation to constructions around and with African Americans is absolutely essential to any understanding of the continued elaboration and struggles of this class fraction. Working-class whites, both individually and as a designated and simultaneously lived collective category, emerged discursively and materially in relation to black Americans, working off of deeply rooted constructions of "blackness" in the white imagination, a point which Toni Morrison (1992) and others have taken up with great clarity. While whiteness emerges in relation to constructed notions of "other" (Said, 1979) in a wide variety of contexts and, within the United States, across social class and ethnic/race configurations, the historically embedded relationship between white working-class Americans and black Americans is particularly salient. More than any other group, the identity and material position of white working-class Americans is carved historically in relation to blacks, both discursively and materially.

This historically rooted connection between blacks and working-class whites (stemming from their proximity) is unique to the United States. The situation is not precisely duplicated in Canada, Britain, Australia, or New Zealand, for example, where although there are populations of color and certainly a history of colonial domination in some cases, there is no long-term on-site history comparable to that of slaveholding America, with its subsequent legally sanctioned apartheid and the ongoing and widespread struggles of black Americans in relation to continued institutional and representational racism. Again, this is not to argue that the white working class does not emerge in relation to any significant "other," or even an "other" of color in myriad national contexts. Rather, I am pointing out that the American white working class, and white America generally, quite simply *cannot be understood* without reference to blacks. This is unique to the American context, rendering elements of *Class Reunion* fundamentally entrenched in the United States. It does not mean, however, that key points embedded within my analysis, including those around race and raciality, are not useful in other contexts, but simply that the particular significance of a certain kind of whiteness production and the ways in which such whiteness plays out historically in relation to this particular class fraction is specific to the American context.

Additionally, there has been a virtual explosion of educational opportunities in the United States and, as I shall suggest throughout this volume, for a variety of reasons white working-class women have been poised to take advantage of these opportunities. While this may be true in other contexts as well, recent work by Arnot, David, and Weiner (1999) and Walkerdine, Lucey, and Melody (2001) suggests that the situation in Britain, for example, is somewhat different. Tertiary-level education in the United States is not reserved for the middle class or higher, nor does class necessarily predict whether one will obtain a *form* of tertiary-level education or not. To be sure, the United States system of education is highly stratified (Karabel, 1972; Olivas, 1979), with working-class students largely in community colleges and comprehensive colleges (mid-level state schools) rather than Research I universities (top-tier state universities such as the University of Michigan or the University of Wisconsin-Madison, or top-tier private universities such as Harvard or Princeton) or competitive liberal arts colleges (such as Swarthmore), which are both more difficult to get into and, in the case of private colleges, substantially more costly. In spite of this deep stratification, however, given the thousands of colleges in the United States, a significant number of the sons and daughters of the former industrial proletariat can and do enter, and ultimately complete, postsecondary education, particularly women—an artifact, perhaps, of the massive tertiary-level educational system across the United States. For these reasons, the ways in which social class "predicts" the future for working-class and middle-class women in Britain, for example, will not necessarily play out exactly the same way in the United States. While class may bear the same long-term imprint, it will not necessarily do so in the same way. Indeed, as I argue here, the American white working class stages its own "class reunion," but a class reunion that meanders along a rather complicated and circuitous path.

Beyond the particularities of the United States context lies a broader shift in the global economy, a shift which plays out in the United States in locally specific ways, although ways shared in many respects with other first-wave industrialized nations such as Britain, Australia, Canada, France, and Germany.

In terms of local specificity, however, American corporations dominated world markets at the end of World War II. The American steel industry, for example, was virtually the only major producer in the world. By the 1960s, Germany, Japan, Italy, and Britain had rebuilt their steel industries, using the most advanced technology, and had become highly competitive with America. By the 1970s, the American steel industry was in sharp decline relative to that of other nations (Bluestone & Harrison, 1982), a decline reflective of what American scholars in the 1980s referred to as deindustrialization. As Barry Bluestone and Bennett Harrison argue, "when the employment lost as a direct result of plant, store and office shutdowns during the 1970s is added to the job loss associated with runaway shops, it appears that more than two million jobs were destroyed. Together, runaways, shutdowns and permanent physical cutbacks short of complete closure may have cost the country as many as 38 million jobs" (p. 26).

What was referred to as deindustrialization by American economists in the 1980s is now understood to be a fundamental shift in the global economy, one which represents a radical break with past practice. Robert Reich, clearly one of the nation's most brilliant and original labor economists, argues:

All Americans used to be in roughly the same economic boat. Most rose or fell together as the corporations in which they were employed, the industries comprising such corporations and the national economy as a whole became more productive—or languished. But national borders no longer define our economic fates. We are now in different boats, one sinking rapidly, one sinking more slowly, the third rising steadily. (1991, p. 208)

As Reich (1991) describes it, that boat holding routine production workers is sinking most rapidly, as the old corporate core is being replaced by "global webs which earn their largest profits from clever problem-solving—identifying and brokering. As the costs of transporting things and of communicating information about them continue to drop, profit margins on high-volume, standardized production are thinning because there are few barriers to entry. Modern factories and state-of-the-art machinery can be installed almost anywhere on the globe" (p. 209). As a consequence, the former working class is in competition with routine production workers all over the world, most of whom will work for a fraction of what the American, British, or Australian worker (even nonunionized worker) demands. Given this situation, the old collective bargaining agreements (what we can call the "capital–labor accord") are useless—leaving routine production workers without a stable foothold in the new economy:

> About three decades ago the American economy began to shift out of stable large scale production toward continuous innovation. The shift has been accelerating since then. Technology has been the driving force. New technologies of communication, transportation, and information culminating recently in the internet and so-called e-commerce, have dramatically widened customer choice and made it easier for all customers (including business customers) to shop for, and switch to, better deals. Wider choices and easier switching has intensified competition at all levels—forcing every seller to innovate like mad, cutting costs and adding new value.
>
> In the old industrial economy, profits came from economies of scale—long runs of more or less identical products. Now profits come from quickness to innovate and attract (and keep) customers ... As technology gives all buyers more choice and easier ability to switch, it makes all sellers less secure. The dynamism and innovation that rewards buyers also subjects sellers to less certainty, more volatility, higher highs and lower lows. Almost all earnings are becoming more volatile and less predictable. (Reich, 2001, pp. 106–107)

While Reich's "reprise" centers primarily on those who sell, the implications for men and women of the old industrial working class are profound. If sellers must constantly "court buyers" through innovation and accompanying cost-cutting mechanisms, this leaves the working class (and the poor, obviously), who primarily still have only their labor to sell, at the mercy of an increasingly competitive and mobile, yet, in contradictory ways, dynamic economy. The very impersonal dynamic that Reich describes is the dynamism which renders the working class not superfluous in the sense that they are not needed, but increasingly expendable, given the vagaries of the new business climate: let go when they are not needed and/or are too expensive, only to be picked up again when the next, and thoroughly different, "opportunity" comes along. Although it is arguably the case that industrially based workers were *always* similarly expendable, the current situation differs substantially from dynamics embedded within the old industrial economy, where the "bargain" between capital and labor was such that a noteworthy segment of labor, after much struggle, was able to win a living wage and a set of accompanying benefits in return for raw labor power in a thoroughly place-bound economy. Given that production was embedded within a specific non-mobile site, and assuming a relatively finite number of workers, the working class, even under conditions of mobile scab labor (often the racial "other" in the United States), had some power to bargain. There are no such bargains being struck today, as the new economy demands wage labor at the lowest level possible in order for business to thrive (Apple, 2001; Hunter, 1987).

Under such conditions, business is not hamstrung by local labor power at all; if any given enterprise, no matter how temporary, does not obtain labor at an acceptably low cost, it seeks labor elsewhere (a wide variety of tasks can now be outsourced) and/or owners simply relocate the business. Nationally based and/or owned U.S., German, French, or British business is tagged to work that can now be done almost anywhere, given high-speed fiber optics, new and quicker modes of transportation, and the Internet. The old working class, tied to an industrial economy under which plants are expensive to build, maintain, and move, is not a collective player in this new economy at all, rendering the sons and daughters of the former industrial proletariat exceedingly vulnerable—perched at the competitive edge of new global economic arrangements. Indeed, the new economy demands, under the politics of the "third way" and the demise of the "concept of jobs for life" (Giddens, 1998), "forms of subjectivity" in which "self-management and self-invention are to be celebrated" (Walkerdine, Lucey, & Melody, 2001, p. 211).

I focus here on the American economy, but writers in Britain and elsewhere comment similarly, although the particular ways in which the class structure is both being realigned and simultaneously is realigning itself will undoubtedly differ by context. Quoting Walkerdine, Lucey, and Melody (2001):

> We are confronted with huge changes in the global labour market, changes that have caused the British economy to become dominated by the service sector, the technology and communications industries and a huge and powerful financial sector. In the new global economy the stable Fordist model of manufacturing has given way to downsized industries that are shadows of their former selves. Many of the new manufacturing industries are not even British owned and products are assembled in different places, with capital, production processes and workers now being much more mobile. (p. 1)

Paul Willis similarly admits that he "caught the lads of *Learning to Labour* (1977) at the end of what is perhaps the last great golden period of working-class coherence and power in a fully employed Britain. At least the lads all got jobs. That is not so for their counterparts now, both in the U.K. and for their counterparts in other industrial societies" (2000, p. 86).

Habitus

Given my argument, it is tempting to suggest, as others have, that class has all but disappeared, particularly the working class. As I suggested earlier, though, this argument rests upon a particular (male-centered) understanding of the working class, one which I do not find useful as a way of unpacking class configuration under the new economy. Pierre Bourdieu's concept of habitus, in contrast, enables an analysis of social class that goes far beyond materiality and, in the case of the former industrial proletariat, men's connection to wage labor. As Diane Reay (1997a) notes, "Habitus … includes a set of complex, discursive dispositions. It involves understandings of identity premised on familiar legacy and early childhood socialization. As such, it is primarily a dynamic concept, a rich interlacing of past and present, interiorised and permeating both body and psyche" (p. 227).

Jean-Francois Dortier offers the following definition:

> It is first the product of a learning that has become unconscious, that translates itself into an apparently natural aptitude to move freely in a given milieu. The musician can ... freely improvise with his piano only after ... acquiring the rules of composition and harmony. (as cited in Thérion, 2002, p. 2)

In brief, habitus encompasses all of the general dispositions (ways of doing things, of reacting, of being) which result from the internalization and accumulation of past learning; a form of "know-how" inculcated by the family, the school, and the broader social environment as part of the generalized process of socialization.[1] We become aware of our habitus (socially acquired dispositions) when we are immersed in a totally different milieu, a milieu whose rules of the game we do not know. Even in middle- and upper-middle-class occupational positions, for example, the "comfort level" may not be there due to class-embedded habitus if one is born of working-class parents, a phenomenon written about at length by British and American scholars of working-class background (Reay, 1997b, 1998, 2002; Charlip, 1995; Overall, 1995; Langston, 1993).

Wacquant (1992) argues that the dynamic quality of habitus stems from its interconnection with Bourdieu's concept of field: "a set of objective, historical relations between positions anchored in certain forms of power for capital" (p. 16). Picking up this point, Reay notes that the existing dialectic between field and habitus "produces a relationship of conditioning in which the field structures the habitus but, at the same time, the habitus can influence perceptions of the field in which it finds itself and generate a relationship of cognitive construction" (1997a, p. 227).

Under Bourdieu's formulation, there can be many fields and forms of habitus, but *power* is inextricably and continually woven through both the field and the dialectical relationship between field and habitus. Thus social class *must* be understood as both objective location and, simultaneously, what individuals and/or groups do with this location, whether consciously or not (Lareau, 1987, 2004; Horvat, Weininger, & Lareau, 2003).

Working off Bourdieu enables us to accomplish, theoretically speaking, two important things. To begin with, the site of the economy, although critical, is not the *only* site around and through which social class identities emerge, thus moving us away from the notion that social class must be read off men and can be best understood through men's connection to the wage labor process. Rather, the family, the school, and so forth are as fundamental to the habitus as is the wage labor sector, paralleling E. P. Thompson's (1966) understanding of social class. Second, given the fluidity and flexibility of identity production under Bourdieu, we cannot fall victim to the assumption or assertion that identities are stable or even "real" (essentialist).

Having said this, while identities may not be stable, coherent, or homogeneous, the categories of social identity *become* "real" inside institutional life, leading to dire political and economic consequences. As Michelle Fine and I argue (Weis & Fine, 2004), you cannot spend significant periods of time in poor and working-class communities, an upscale suburban mall, a prison, an elite suburban golf course, or an independent private school in the United States and still believe that categories of social identity—whether race, ethnicity, social class, or gender—are *simply* inventions or "fictions." Embracing categories of social identity as socially constructed and flexible, I nevertheless equally embrace such identities as fundamentally political ways of organizing the world (Carlson & Dimitriadis, 2003).[2]

Class, then, while perhaps a "phantasmatic category," nevertheless organizes the social, cultural, and material world in exceptionally profound ways. The books we read (if we read at all); our travel destinations and modes of travel (bus, car, private jet); the films we see; the foods we eat; the clothes we wear; whether we have orthodontically straightened teeth; where our children go to school, with whom, and under what staff expectations and treatment; the "look" and "feel" of home- and school-based interventions if our children "fail"; the types of plates and cutlery in our home; where we feel most comfortable and with whom; sports our children play and where they play them; where we live and the nature of our housing; and, specifically in the United States, whether we have health insurance and if so, what kind, with what coverage, and for how long, are all *profoundly* classed experiences, rooted not only in material realities but also in culturally based expectations, whether recognized or not.[3] Without ignoring the leveling effects of mass media and wholesale consumer culture, we must recognize that class is, nevertheless, worn on our bodies as it seeps through our minds. Thus, with deep respect for many of my more poststructurally inclined scholar-friends, I analytically embrace categories of social identity while recognizing the ways in which such identities are simultaneously "fiction" and "real."

Compositional Studies: Critical Theorizing on Social (In)justice

Class Reunion explicates what Michelle Fine and I call "compositional studies"—a theory of method in which analyses of public and private institutions, groups, and lives are lodged in relation to key social and economic structures. This theory of method is conceptually akin to what an artist does, leading us to call our articulated method "compositional studies" (Weis & Fine, 2004). A visual artist has no composition without paying explicit attention to both the positive and the negative spaces of a composition. Positive space (the main object) must have a negative referent, and the negative referent, visually speaking, is as important to the composition as a whole as is the positive. It is these "blank" or "black" spaces in relation to "color" or "white" that I pay attention to here. Like the artist, I explicitly explore the negative bridging spaces within the composition, intentionally probing the relations between "negative" and "positive" spaces, understanding at all times that no "positive" exists except in relation to the "negative." As I move to comprehend the remaking of the American white working class, I bear in mind that relevant bordering groups as well as social and economic trends are as essential to the ethnographic composition as the primary group under consideration. Indeed, this is what my work with white working-class youth and adults has taught me—that this group simply cannot be understood without careful and explicit attention to the "black spaces"—bordering "others" as well as the deep context within which this all plays out over time.

The form of *ethnographic longitudinality* as represented by this volume enables us, in particular, to shift our eyes from pieces drawn at one point in time to those drawn at another, prying open the specter of compositional ethnography ever further. Beginning with an understanding of economic and racial formations over time, I focus on the field of relational interactions within this broader context. It is this set of relational interactions inside a profoundly changing economic and social context that encourages/enables me to understand the continued gauze that binds the former white industrial proletariat together as they stake out a distinct class fractional identity in the new global economy.

I draw, in this volume, upon two data sets, the first gathered as part of a year-long ethnographic investigation of Freeway High and the surrounding community, in which I chronicle the forging of white working-class male and female identities under conditions of great economic change in the mid-1980s (*Working Class Without Work,*

1990); and the second, which involves contacting the students whom I interviewed as part of the original ethnography and reinterviewing them fifteen years later in 2000–2001. Of the 41 white cohort students, I reinterviewed 31 (the particularities of this process are elaborated in the Epilogue).[4] Working with these students in 1985–1986 and meeting them again in their early thirties enables me to describe and theorize class re-articulation in relation to—and around—the actual lives of people. Thus I move back and forth between what I know about the world economy and the larger context in which these individuals' lives are playing out; a methodological "diptych" that enables me to shift between larger social forces and lives "on the ground." Drawing upon the recent work of labor economists, I map articulated lives within and against economic and social trends. Rather than talk only about class in terms of broad trends, however, I move between what I know statistically and relationally and what these men and women are telling me, thereby mapping the interrelationships between structure and agency over time. I, like the men and women with whom I work, move back and forth between life on the ground and the structural forces with which they (and we) cope. Unlike "resistance theorists," who read expected long-term oppositional culture off point-in-time analyses, however, I am able, through this form of ethnographic longitudinality, to trace the actual consequences of youth resistance, leading to a far different picture than existing studies of youth "oppositional culture" suggest.[5]

Working with these individuals when they were in their third year of secondary school offers a tremendous advantage as I make sense of what has happened to the American white working class. As such, I organize the chapters as follows: Chapters 1 and 2 are recrafted versions of chapters which appear in my earlier volume, drawing upon ethnographic and ethnographic interview data gathered in the mid-1980s. In contrast to my later chapters, they are largely descriptive, elaborating what I call *modal* cultural form among white working-class male and female adolescents of the time period. In these two chapters I carefully draw a portrait of class-linked identities which these students produced while in high school. Chapters 3 through 6 revisit a subset of these same students, moving carefully between the two data sets so as to understand the remaking of the white working class. Most of the heavy theoretical work is confined to these later chapters, although I render these chapters as accessible as possible while capturing the complexities of the "moment." The tones of the two parts of the book are somewhat different, then, as surrounding ethnographic and theoretically based scholarship, the students/adults with whom I work, and I as the investigator collectively grow older. In addition, my earlier chapters work off a larger number of students, as I use data from numerous students who participate in the original ethnography to draw a picture of emerging white male and female working-class identities. In chapters that are based upon the 2000 data, I employ a different and more targeted technique, focusing on individuals whom I see as *emblematic* of key trends. Using thick data from a smaller number of such individuals enables me to draw carefully and fully both what happens to individuals in this particular class and geographic location and the contours of the social class fraction as a whole. Again, heavy theorizing in relation to whiteness, masculinity, femininity, and the new economy is confined largely to these later chapters, including Chapter 7.

Reflective of ethnographic form, the data themselves push me to consider carefully issues which swirl around whiteness, masculinity, femininity, and the new economy. It is true, of course, that I have a fairly wide repertoire in relation to these debates. However, it is the data themselves as I read them off my interaction with these individuals that encouraged/enabled me to write this volume. I had no particular preconceptions as to the contours of the lived white working class until I looked carefully at the data, always situating these data within broader economic and social trends. Like any good ethnographer, then, the contours of my argument emerge largely in relation to the data themselves.[6]

Freeway

Freeway is an ideal site in which to conduct an investigation of the remaking of the white working class. What attracted me to Freeway in the mid-1980s was the recent closure of the steel plant, a closure that sent shock waves through the community. Examination of data gathered from the Standard Metropolitan Statistical Area (later referred to in the census as a Metropolitan Statistical Area) of which Freeway is a part confirms a number of trends that early economists such as Bluestone and Harrison, and later economists like Reich, discuss. Occupational data for 1960–2000 (see Table 1.1) suggest that the most striking decreases in the area are found in the categories of "Construction, Extraction, and Maintenance Occupations" and "Production, Transportation, and Material Moving Occupations." These two major categories constitute virtually all the traditionally coded "blue-collar jobs." When combined over the forty-year period, the data suggest a relative decline of close to 100 percent of jobs in these categories, with an absolute change of close to 17 percent. "Construction, Extraction, and Maintenance Occupations," which constitute close to 17 percent of available occupations in 1960, come in at just over 7 percent in 2000. Similarly, "Production, Transportation, and Material Moving Occupations," which stood at just over 25 percent of all existing coded occupations in 1960, stand at just over 15 percent in 2000, up slightly from 1990.

Data suggest a related climb in the proportion of workers in "Managerial, Professional, and Related Occupations" during this same time period. Whereas 19 percent of the 1960 workforce is so classified, close to 34 percent of the 2000 workforce falls into this category, representing an absolute change of just over 14 percent and a net percentage change from 1960 to 2000 of 75 percent. Increases in "Sales and Office Occupations" (net percent change 22 percent) and "Service Occupations" (net percent change just over 55 percent) similarly display a shift away from industrially based jobs and toward the availability of service occupations, reflective of Leslie McCall's (2001) argument that the restructured economy is "becoming more high-tech, more international, more flexible, and more service-oriented"—an environment, she suggests, "that lowered the wages and security of most workers even as it created unprecedented concentrations of wealth" (p. xi).

Table 1.1 Occupations by Year for Freeway SMSA, All Persons.

	% of All Occupations					Absolute Change	Net% Change 1960–2000*
Occupation	1960	1970	1980	1990	2000		
Managerial, Professional, and Related Occupations	19.2%	21.9%	21.7%	25.8%	33.6%	+14.4%	+75.0
Sales and Office Occupations	22.8%	25.4%	30.7%	32.7%	27.9%	+5.1%	+22.4
Service Occupations	10.1%	12.9%	13.9%	14.7%	15.7%	+5.6%	+55.4
Farming, Fishing, and Forestry Occupations	1.0%	0.6%	0.9%	0.9%	0.2%	-0.8%	-80.0
Construction, Extraction, and Maintenance Occupations	16.8%	15.4%	12.5%	11.0%	7.2%	-9.6%	-57.1
Production, Transportation, and Material Moving Occupations	25.3%	23.6%	20.2%	14.8%	15.4%	-9.9%	-39.1
Occupations Not Reported	5.1%						

*Absolute Change
1960 figure × 100 = Net% change 1960–2000

Most interesting is the distribution of gender and occupation over this same time period. While it is not my intention to offer an extensive analysis of race, gender, and the occupational structure, data reported in table 1.2 are telling in this regard. Among all whites in the Freeway area workforce in 1960, for example, 22 percent and 19 percent of men and women, respectively, were situated in the category of "Managerial, Professional, and Specialty Occupations." This compares with 32 percent and 38 percent of men and women, respectively, in the year 2000. Service occupations, on the other hand, were held by 6 percent of all working white men in 1960, compared to 18 percent of all working white women; 12 percent and 17 percent of white men and women are similarly situated in 2000. Fifty-three percent of all white men worked in traditional blue-collar jobs in 1960 ("Precision, Production, Craft, and Repair Occupations"; and "Operators, Fabricators, and Laborers"), compared with 37 percent in 2000. Generally speaking, reflective of broader economic trends as well as the entrance of large numbers of women into the paid labor force between 1960 and 2000, men and women converge in terms of the census category sector in which their job is located. In addition, white women have made relatively greater strides toward obtaining managerial and professional positions than white men. This does not map neatly onto equal financial remuneration, however, since widespread gender inequality in pay scale still abounds (McCall, 2001; Anonymous, 2003).

In the Freeway area the restructured global economy is most stunningly symbolized by the closing of Freeway Steel, a phenomenon that led me to the area in the mid-1980s. In 1969, the plant payroll was at a record high of $168 million, topping 1968 by $14 million. The average daily employment sat at 18,500. Production of basic oxygen furnace and open hearth was at a near record of 6.5 million tons.

In the first seven months of 1971, layoffs at the Freeway plant numbered 4000, and the decline continued steadily into the mid-1980s. In contrast to 18,500 jobs in 1979, there were only 3700 production and 600 supervisory workers left in 1983, with 3600 on layoff. At the end of 1983, the plant closed, leaving a city in the shadow of the mills. Despite negotiated buyout deals, 95,000 production workers later lost health and life insurance benefits as the giant steelmaker declared bankruptcy.

Since 1900 three generations of Freeway families had poured and worked steel for American industry. By 1984—one year after the shutdown—the plant lay "ghostlike ... an industrial corpse, a cannibalized

TABLE 1.2 Occupation by Race and Gender for the Freeway MSA: 1960, 1990 and 2000—Percentage within Each Race/Gender Group

	1960				1990				2000			
	Black		White		Black		White		Black		White	
	Male	Female	Male	Female	Male	Female	Male	Female	Male	Female	Male	Female
Managerial, Professional, Specialty Occupations	3.6%	7.6%	21.5%	18.5%	12.5%	19.1%	23.3%	27.2%	19.3%	26.3%	31.5%	37.6%
Technical, Sales, and Adm. Occupations	4.9%	10.4%	15.0%	43.0%	14.7%	33.2%	21.2%	45.6%	17.8%	31.6%	18.7%	38.4%
Service Occupations	9.4%	53.0%	5.5%	18.1%	23.7%	30.7%	10.5%	16.9%	24.1%	29.4%	12.2%	17.1%
Farming, Forestry, Fishing Occupations	0.4%	0.1%	0.5%	0.2%	0.9%	0.1%	1.5%	0.5%	0.2%	0.0%	0.3%	0.2%
Precision Production, Craft, and Repair Occupations	11.7%	0.9%	24.4%	1.3%	13.1%	1.4%	19.3%	1.8%	7.4%	0.6%	14.4%	0.4%
Operators, Fabricators, and Laborers	58.8%	17.9%	29.0%	13.5%	35.0%	15.6%	24.2%	8.0%	31.3%	12.1%	22.9%	6.3%
Occupations Not Reported	11.3%	10.1%	4.2%	5.3%	N/A	N/A	N/A	N/A	N/A	N/A	N/A	N/A
Total	100%	100%	100%	100%	100%	100%	100%	100%	100%	100%	100%	100%

complex of lifeless smokestacks, black buildings, motionless booms and empty rails" (Strohmeyer, 1994). In 2001 the corpse still lies empty, in stark testimony to a world that was, and would never be again. *Class Reunion* excavates the reshaping of this distinct class fraction as Freeway youth who come of age during a time of stunning economic and social upheaval go to school, obtain jobs, negotiate family and community life, and bear and rear children. The industrial giant, and more broadly the infrastructure keyed to the entire industrial proletariat, has shut its doors. But the people do, after all, live on.

Part I

1985

1

A TIME OF PAIN
Young Men at Freeway High

ROB: It's like a dictatorship here [school]. Mr. Smith, Mr.
 Amsdel; Mr. Strong is the worst.... He'd take me out of
 school for being late to class. You woke up late or something, and he comes and kicks you out. He suspended us
 for two days for skipping class ... that just makes you more
 mad and you want to get even with him.... Next time you
 come late again. Put a stink bomb in his office. Walk by and
 throw it in.
LOIS: So, who wins in the end?
ROB: Probably he will. Or we do, when we graduate.

Rob, grade 11, 1985

White male adolescent working-class identity in Freeway is forged
along three primary axes: (1) an emerging contradictory code of
respect toward school knowledge and culture not in evidence in key
previous studies of white working-class male youth; (2) a set of
virulently patriarchal constructions of home/family life which position
future wives in particular kinds of subordinate relationships; and (3)
constructed notions of African Americans and Yemenites ("Arabians"),
which are intensely racist and which split along distinct gender lines.
Here we hark back to 1985, when the Freeway youth are in their third
year of high school, exploring who the young men are as they wind
their way through adolescence at a time of intense reorganization of
the American economy. As they strike out on the road to manhood,
they carve a set of paths like no generation before them—paths strewn
with trashed hopes of working in the steel mill like their fathers and
grandfathers, worn with disillusionment and discontent. Like the lead
character in the BBC serial *The Missing Postman,* or the motley crew

of men in the fully and justly celebrated *The Full Monty* (Walkerdine, Lucey, & Melody, 2001), they and their fathers struggle with what it means to be a man in the midst of a radically changed economic context.

Attitude Toward Institutional Authority and School Meanings

Previous studies of white working-class boys suggest that opposition to authority and school meanings is deeply etched within the class cultural formation, ultimately reinforcing an "us versus them" ideology appropriate to the historic struggle between capital and labor. The most obvious dimension of the lads' culture in *Learning to Labour* (Willis, 1977), for example, is generalized opposition toward authority and school meanings. The lads engage in behavior designed to show resentment while stopping just short of outright confrontation. Unlike the "ear 'oles" (so named because they simply sit and listen), they exhibit extensive absenteeism, signaling their generally oppositional stance: their "struggle to win symbolic and physical space from the institution and its rules, and to defeat its main perceived purpose: to make you work" (p. 26). The core skill here is being able to get out of any given class, thus preserving personal mobility within the school. Personal mobility encourages the preservation of the collective (cutting class means meeting friends elsewhere) and can be seen as a partial defeat of individualism, positioning the group as a collective "we" in the face of anticipated future external control over their labor.

Work by Howard London (1978) in a community college in the United States, and by Robert Everhart (1983) in an American middle school, affirms Willis's findings regarding the rejection of school-based meanings among white working-class students. A common thread runs through these studies: the often overt and sometimes covert rejection of school meanings and culture. In all these studies there is an attempt on the part of working-class male youth to carve their own space within the institution—space that can then be filled with more personal meanings, ones fundamentally anti-school. Such school-based conflict sets the stage for later enacted capital and labor struggles during times of high activity in an industrially based economy.

Comparable resentment toward authority characterizes the 1985 Freeway boys, being linked primarily to perceived institutional control over student attire and the use of time and space. As with Willis's lads, resentment tends to be caged in practice, stopping just short, on most occasions, of outright confrontation.

TOM: I don't like the principals. Most of the teachers are assholes ... They have a controlling power over the kids, or at least they try to. Me, I won't take shit from no one. That's the way I am.... Whatever they do, they can't bother me, 'cause when I get my diploma, I can say what I want to them....

The kids should have some rights. Like, let me say, for one example, I know there's smokers in this school. A lot of kids smoke.... To solve all smoking problems with kids going outside and skipping classes, give the kids at least once a day a place to go to—a room—and have one cigarette or something. Five minutes a day....

They [school authorities] play head games with kids.... They think they can push you any which way they want.

LOIS: If they're pushing you around, why stay for your diploma?

TOM: 'Cause it helps for, like, a job or whatever. It's like a reference for this, this, this. It's like a key that opens many doors.

* * *

BOB: I think Mr. Strong is an asshole. He's an assistant principal. I know he's in an authority position, but he just seems to think he has control over anything that happens in this school at any time.... The way the control is handled [is what I resent]. Mr. Strong, that man has no sense of humor. He's like, blah, and he just starts acting like God or something.... They have to have control somehow. It's their job. It's just the way they're going about it [that is bad]. The way Mr. Strong is going about it bothers me.

* * *

JIM: I'd like to see the students pick what they want to wear.... In the summer it gets extremely hot. You got to wear jeans; you can't wear shorts.

And I think that administration is a little too harsh on students.... A kid skips a class. Three days' detention. School policy. They're going out of their way to look for what's wrong. They're going out of their way! Like they [the principals] go to [the local donut shop] to find the kids.

* * *

JOE: There should be a smoking lounge. Because why should kids get in trouble for smoking? Other schools have smoking lounges. It sounds reasonable. . . . [Also] the detention. The reasons why kids get detention are stupid.

LOIS: Like, give me an example.

JOE: Like being late a certain amount of times. You get a detention. That should be changed.

LOIS: Why?

JOE: Because why should somebody get detention for something that might not have been their fault? A locker that won't open. Reasons like that. Go to the lavatory. If you have to go to the lavatory, you're gonna be late. Teachers don't let you go during the period.

While it is arguably the case that I could find such a group of like-minded male students in virtually any school, the expressed collective resentment of authority, particularly as related to control over time and space, is deeply etched in working-class male culture. Middle-class students may feel the same way, of course, but most accept that school-based knowledge is utilitarian, that it provides an important stepping-stone to a desired lifestyle (Anyon, 1981). What is noteworthy in the Freeway case is that in spite of an expressed anti-authority stance, students by and large adhere to school rules. When overtly challenging the institution, students may skip a class here or there and go to the local donut shop, smoke a cigarette or marijuana, or drink alcohol in the parking lot, but significantly, students generally exit the school building rather than confront authority directly within it. Although they escape to the parking lot (which is directly behind the school) or the donut shop a few blocks away in order to smoke, they inevitably return before the day is over. Such short-term "visits" tend to punctuate the school day rather than the large-scale absenteeism so prevalent among the urban poor. While such grumbling and short-term visits to the parking lot are certainly not seen as positive by the teachers (who often interpret such behavior as not caring, and therefore inhibiting learning), Freeway male challenges to schooling in the mid-1980s are relatively benign.

As I probe further, it is clear that students express a noticeably more positive attitude toward schooling and accompanying mental labor in general, *at least in the abstract*, than students of comparable social class background in previous studies. Students in what is called the advanced curriculum (a specifically college prep curriculum which involves approximately twenty-five students per year out of a possible three hundred) express a desire to attend college more frequently than other students, but virtually *all* students assign value to education, albeit in highly utilitarian terms. This is a distinctly different response than was gleaned from students in previous studies of white working-class males. The wholesale rejection of school knowledge and culture expressed by Willis's students, for example, is not in evidence in Freeway, and it is indeed significant that a group of "lads" does not exist in this school.[1] While a distancing from school knowledge and culture certainly does take place (going to the donut shop, for example, instead of attending class, or attending class stoned), students are nevertheless, by and large, physically present in school and do not generally overtly and directly battle school culture or authorities. In light of the economy, schooling is, for good or bad, seen as the only game in town.

JOHN: College prep [is my major]. It's the only thing to do.

LOIS: What do you mean?

JOHN: Well, around here, 'cause there's nothing else. Everything's going down south. Like any kind of good jobs, a better education's what you're gonna hafta need. Unless you plan to sweep the floors someplace the rest of your life. And that ain't really gonna be my style. . . . Like, I work at the Metro Club [a private club in the city] now, and he'll [dad] pick me up and I'll be complaining and he'll say, "See, get a good education, get a good job."

I'm a busboy. I wait on people. Serve 'em shrimp cocktail. Pick up their dirty dishes, things like that. . . . You're there and you do nothin' but runnin' around. Do this and do that for this person. Get their dishes and bring these people soup. It's a bitch. He [dad] says, "Wouldn't you rather have these people waiting on you? Go to school and get an education." My father never got a high school education. He got a GED [high school equivalency diploma]. He wants me to keep going.

* * *

BOB: Well, I want to go to college. I don't know what for yet. I was thinking of something like biology, something like that. Probably [City Community College] or [Suburban Community College]. Probably transfer [to a four-year school]. . . .

My mother wants me to [go to college]. So does my father. My mother has post-education [at a local hospital]. She was a worker there. But my father quit school in the middle of twelfth grade.

* * *

LOIS: What do you hope to do when you leave high school?
JERRY: College, but I'm still not certain which one. I'm looking around here, but if I get a scholarship, I'll go away. Right now it looks pretty good, whether it be sports or educational.

* * *

JIM: I've got a couple of colleges I've been looking at. University of Maryland or University of Seattle. And I was thinking of pursuing the commercial art field and becoming, eventually, a comic book artist or an illustrator.... I'll probably take out student loans. [I'm] working part-time. I'm a stock boy. I have a bit of money put aside. I've been doing it six months.

* * *

SETH: I'm going to go to college, hopefully an aeronautical school in Chicago. I been thinking to myself, I'm really going to do well in college.
LOIS: What made you decide to do that?
SETH: The greediness. The money. I want a well-paying job.

* * *

LOIS: What do you plan to do when you graduate?
STEVE: Go to college.
LOIS: For what?
STEVE: I haven't decided ... I just wanna go. Can't get a job without going to college. You got to be educated to get a job, a good job: you don't want to live off burgers when you're old.

* * *

LOIS: What do you plan to do when you leave school?
LARRY: Go straight to college.
LOIS: Where do you want to go? What do you want to do?
LARRY: You know, I can't tell you specifically, but I want to make money....
I don't want to end up like my parents. Nothing against them.
LOIS: What do you mean?
LARRY: Well, I want to own a house. I don't want to use the term "make ends meet." I don't ever want to have that in my vocabulary.

Not all the 1985 white working-class males intend to go to college, nor do they discredit manual-labor jobs totally. Nevertheless, of the boys interviewed in the mid-1980s, it is striking that 40 percent express a desire to go to a two- or four-year college, and there is far less celebration of manual- labor jobs than earlier studies suggest, studies that were conducted during the heyday of shop-floor culture—a culture that has, for all practical purposes, disappeared. Where students celebrate traditionally working-class jobs, they are skilled or craft-based positions, such as motorcycle mechanic, electrician, machinist, and the like. In contrast to Willis's lads, not a single boy interviewed in the initial Freeway study expressed the possibility of being a generalized wage laborer.

Freeway boys in the mid-1980s tend to look at schooling in highly utilitarian terms—not unlike middle-class students in Jean Anyon's study (1981). As such, schooling is seen as enabling them to make a lot of money, get a "good" job, stay "off burgers," to forget the phrase "make ends meet," and buy a house. Most (not all) of these young men grew up in small but tidy homes bought with money amassed through their father's work in heavy industry, and they, too, desire a house, the primary symbol of working-class stability (Bensman & Lynch, 1987). While resenting aspects of institutional authority and school meanings as young men in previous studies do, particularly surrounding control over *their* space (dress, smoking) and *their* time (class attendance), most intend to pursue schooling simply because they "have to." We do not have the flavor here of Willis's lads at all: indeed, even those most negative about school concede the importance of the "credential." As Rob states, reflecting upon the low-level battles between students and school officials, "I guess we [win] when we graduate," suggesting the grudgingly conceded utility of the diploma and school culture generally. The other option for these boys, as they see it, is to "sweep the floors."

In spite of the deeply felt sense that schooling is the only way to keep one "off burgers," most concern themselves only with passing, not with excelling, competing, or even doing well. The language of "passing" a test or "passing" a course dominates student discourse around schooling, much as obtaining a union card dominated the discourse of previous generations of white working-class males. "Getting over" is what school is all about in the minds of the vast majority of these young men—passing, so as to gain the diploma and move on to the next, presumably more lucrative, level. Needless to say, in a highly stratified society that is undergoing intense economic re-organization and the phasing out of the formerly well-paid yet underschooled industrial proletariat, "passing" high school will get one only so far.

Office Procedures Class, November 24, 1985

SAM: We're getting our social test back today.
JENNIFER: Do you think you passed?
SAM: Yeah, I copied a couple of answers from you.
JENNIFER: You better not have. I didn't study.

* * *

Social Studies, January 30, 1986

JEROME: [Comes in all smiles.] This is my last day in this class. [He is repeating the class from last semester.]
PAUL: Did you pass?
JEROME: I passed ... I got a 68. [65 is passing.] I passed! [He is very excited.]

* * *

Social Studies, April 5, 1986

[Ed gets his test back. He got a 78 (a C).]
ED: [Smiling] I like to see those passing marks.

* * *

Social Studies, April 5, 1986

PAUL: [Teacher passes the test back. Paul turns the paper over fearfully.] I passed! [With great happiness; he got a 66; 65 is passing.]

The vast majority of students, males in particular, are concerned only with *passing* the course. It is the expressed "getting through" school that drives this group of students, rather than obtaining even minimal competence associated with the substance of education.[2] Grades follow suit here: my analysis of all grades over a three-year time period indicates that grades for white students tend to be in the mid to high 70s. Most, in fact, end up with Cs and Ds, but they do pass. Coupled with low average PSAT and SAT college entrance examination scores, such grades do not allow admission into even the American four-year comprehensive college sector.[3]

The desire to simply "get through" is further clarified with respect to behavior around homework. It is not that homework is done well (pride in craft), that one learns something, or even that it will help one get something that is desired later on (a good grade on a test, for example, which translates into entrance into a college) that is important to these students. Rather, homework is seen simply as something to be completed, and students routinely copy from one another so that they can, at minimum, hand something (anything) in.

Social Studies, September 17, 1985

ONE STUDENT TO ANOTHER: Did you do this [homework]?
OTHER STUDENT: No, I missed it.
[Several others are saying they didn't do their homework.]
SECOND MALE: Fuck. I remember in school and then forget at home. [He grabs the paper of another student and copies it.]

* * *

Social Studies, January 26, 1986

Mr. Antos walked around, checking to see whether the worksheet was completed. They all showed him the sheet. As I [Lois] walked into the class, Charles was copying from someone. He had the two sheets on his desk. Charles showed Mr. Antos, and I said, "Who'd you copy from?" He said, "Sam," and pointed across the room.

* * *

English, January 24, 1986

During the video [of *Macbeth*] everyone was very quiet until the end of the tape, when Mr. Santili requested that everyone who was going to take the exam on Monday come up to the desk to get instructions and to get their corrected homework. When Vern and Chris returned, Chris was disgruntled because Vern had copied her work but got a better grade.

* * *

Study Hall, January 24, 1986

Vern was required to do a writing assignment in English class. He acquired another student's homework, copied it verbatim, and signed his name [the assignment was to write a letter to an admissions counselor at a university].

* * *

Social Studies, September 11, 1985

At the start of class, kids are switching homework and copying from one another.

* * *

English, October 29, 1985

MR. JAMES: Okay, pass in your homework

I [Lois] asked Vern and Chris whether different people did the homework at different times and then they share. They said, "No, one guy always does it [in here] and six of us copy. In chemistry, one guy does it and the whole class copies." I asked if the teachers notice. They said, "Most don't." Chris said, "I don't care if they do."

With few exceptions, students adhere to and absorb the form of schooling with little to no involvement with its substance. Though holding true for both males and females, the pattern is exaggerated for young men. They work less and copy from other students more, exhibiting little relationship with the content or context of school knowledge. Even in the case of the very practical assignment involving the letter to a college admissions counselor, for example, the goal is simply to get it done, rather than construct a letter that can be used as part of a dossier for the purpose of college admission.

An adherence to form but not substance is further apparent in classroom observations. Students rarely cause trouble in school, almost never acting on their expressed negativity and resentment of institutional authority other than to withhold their labor. Nevertheless, while they dutifully attend class on a more or less regular basis (on any given day 94 percent of the high school students are in school) and hand in assigned homework, most hand in homework they have copied from others and/or lifted directly from the book, and the appearance of order in the classroom masks virtually complete nonengagement. Rarely can students articulate what the class discussion or lecture is even about.

English, February 12, 1986

In Mr. Windemere's class, students alternated with Mr. Windemere reading from a poem. Everyone in the class was exceptionally quiet and followed instructions closely, or at least enough so as to give the impression they were following instructions. When Mr. Windemere called on specific students to read, they were [often] unable to pick up at the appropriate place.

* * *

Social Studies, November 26, 1985

Teacher passes out a worksheet on women. He says, "Okay, this is to be done in class today. If you don't complete it here, do it for homework. I'll check tomorrow." [Some chatter.]

TEACHER: There are additional questions on page 193. If you don't have enough to do now, I can add them. [The room is completely quiet.]

* * *

Math, March 7, 1986

Today's class is on processing equations—solving for X. A major portion of the class was spent on isolating X.

The entire class is almost completely engaged in looking down at their desks or writing. Few people are actually watching the chalkboard where the teacher is going through various steps. [The algebra is the equivalent of eighth-grade work; this is an eleventh-grade class.]

Mr. Marks frequently reminds the students to study hard because there is going to be a test on Monday.

In my year at Freeway High, I witnessed only one class "out of control." By this I mean that the teacher was unable to keep minimal order; students were running around the room and being overtly disruptive. Significantly, this was when a substitute was present.

Social Studies, October 29, 1985

A sub is here, an older black male.

On the board was the following: "If you have not finished yesterday's assignment, finish it today and read and answer question number 2 on p. 87."

The word was out on the sub. Three black females and one Hispanic male were there who normally were not. Two black males walked in and then walked out. Four white males were called out, sequentially, to "go to Mr. Strong's or Mr. Smith's office" [the vice principals]. They were called out by their friends.

The place was disorderly, and this was the first time I'd seen this at this school.

EDDIE [a Hispanic male] called out, "Hey, black girls, what did Martin Luther King say before he died?"
MARTHA: I had a dream! [laughter]
EDDIE: Seven black girls in one class, Whoo-ee!
The girls started rapping [singing phrases to the rhythm of a current song]. The sub just smiled.

This was the first and last time I witnessed such a scene at Freeway High.[4] Normally students pay attention by not paying attention, but do not collectively disrupt the class. In fact, this is not ironic at all, since order can perhaps be best maintained insofar as education is distanced from the lived, and thereby excitable, experiences of adolescents. At Freeway High, however, this takes on a particularly vacuous form. If students are told to answer questions 1 through 21, they do so, even though they make no effort to understand the questions. In response to this "homework" assignment, several students copy largely irrelevant paragraphs from the text and share these "answers" with others, who hand them in as their own. Teachers, of course, in accepting this set of negotiations as "homework," collude in this form of education. Yet, even on that contested terrain—that is, when a substitute is present—Freeway students are generally docile, doing what they need to do in order to "pass," but not disrupting what passes as education.

Social Studies, October 23, 1985

A sub is here. Eddie says, "Teacher looks preppie today. [He has on tan slacks, a white shirt, a red tie, and a dark blue jacket with gold buttons.] I like to see the young teachers preppie. [To me] Isn't he handsome?"

[Assignment on board]
   1. Pg. 63–64 #s 1–24. *Write Out* each question and what you consider to be the correct answer.
   2. Pg. 65, #4.

These kids are remarkably quiet. Some chatter. The substitute says, "Quiet down"; they do so.

I spent one year at Freeway High; for three days a week I sat in on classes, walked the halls, had lunch in the lunchroom, and interviewed students and teachers. Only once, in the earlier example of the substitute teacher's class, did I see a class "out of control." For the most part, students did not directly challenge either the pace *or* the direction of classroom activities; rather, they responded passively, doing what they were told but not consciously doing anything at all. They were quiet, but not engaged; they did homework, but didn't *really* do homework. This disengagement coexisted with a more positive valuation of education than previous studies uncovered among white working-class youth, particularly males. The more positive valuation plays itself out, however, largely in terms of student participation in the maintenance of the appearance of order and a willingness to "hand something in," in order to pass courses. In accepting this, teachers obviously participate in and even affirm the negotiated form of the "established" educational paradigm in a largely white working-class school.

The working-class male's emerging contradictory relationship to school knowledge and culture reflects, to some extent, Sennett and Cobb's (1972) observation about the class in general.[5] However,

Sennett and Cobb are talking about adults who, unlike youth, have already experienced the brutality and alienation of working-class jobs. Ironically, what had been perceived as wholly oppressive (schooling) is later seen as a means of salvation and freedom, a point that Willis (1977) also makes with respect to the "lads," as the lads defeat aspects of dominant ideology in school, its "very furnacing in [Pyrrhic] victory" (p. 146). What is interesting in Freeway is that this contradictory code of respect is embedded in the modal cultural form *while students are still in school*—not, as in previous studies, after they enter the workforce. The early adoption of this contradictory code, albeit in a different form, is more reminiscent of the black underclass in America than of the white working class, leaving open the question of where this contradictory code goes in the real world as these students sail forth into adulthood. This emerging contradictory couplet is tied, I suggest, to an economy that leaves precious little room for a working class as these students know it.

Gender Relations/Patriarchal Relations

A second (and linked) aspect deeply ingrained in white working-class male identity is sexism. Most articulate on this point is Willis, but others have noted this entrenched sexism as well. White working-class male identity is formed in fundamental ways against and with that formed by and about females. Mental labor (which is linked to academic success), for example, is less valued than manual labor, and it is less valued because it is coded as feminine. Willis (1977) suggests that white working-class males cross-valorize manual labor and masculinity, thus "choosing," at some level at least, the most denigrated and brutal of jobs. There is, then, an element of self-damnation in the stratification process, one "that is experienced, paradoxically, as a form of true learning, appropriation and as a kind of resistance" (p. 113). The overall affirmation of male superiority is key here, as the "lads" impose upon girlfriends an ideology of domesticity, "the patterns of homely and subcultural capacity and incapacity," (p. 149) all of which stress the restricted role of women. Not only are women deposited into separate spaces and accorded less status than men, but masculinity itself is wholly dependent upon this constructed binary.

Freeway males in the 1980s high school exhibit the same virulent sexism as young men in previous studies. This is particularly striking in the Freeway context, given the emerging identity of young women, many of whom are extremely critical of gender relations in their community. Although two of the young men in the 1980s class are somewhat critical of existing patriarchal relations, or at least the way in which they play out in terms of marriage and family, young white working-class males largely affirm a virulent form of assumed male superiority and subsequent dominance which involves the constructed identity of female not only as "other," but also as distinctly "less than," and wholly subject to male control. This, as I suggest in the next chapter, throws into sharp relief the emerging sentiments of young women.

LOIS: How about your life ten years from now? What do you think you'll be doing?
ROB: Probably be married. Couple of kids.
LOIS: Do you think your wife will work?
ROB: Hopefully she won't have to, 'cause I'll make enough money.
LOIS: Would you rather she didn't work?
ROB: Naw. [Yes, I'd rather she didn't work.]
LOIS: Women shouldn't work?
ROB: Housework.

* * *

JIM: Yes, I'd like to get married, like to get myself a nice house, with kids.
LOIS: Who is going to be taking care of those kids?
JIM: Depends how rich I am. If I'm making a good salary, I assume that the wife, if she wanted to, would stay home and tend to the kids. If there was ever a chance when she wanted to go someplace, fine, I'd watch the kids. Nothing wrong with that. Equal responsibility, because when you were consummating the marriage, it was equal responsibility.
LOIS: So, you're willing to assume it?
JIM: Up to a certain point. . . . Like if she says, "I'm going to go out and get a job, and you take care of the kids—you draw all day." [He wants to be a commercial artist.] "So, I draw; that's what's been supporting us for so many years." I mean, if she starts dictating to me . . . there has to be a good discussion about the responsibilities. . . .

When both parents work, it's been proven that the amount of education they learn, it goes down the tubes, or they get involved in drugs. Half the kids who have drug problems, both of their parents work. If they are doing terribly in school, their parents work.

* * *

LOIS: When you get married, what will your wife be doing?

LANNY: Well, before we had any kids, she'd be working; but if we had kids, she wouldn't work; she'd be staying home, taking care of the kids.

* * *

SETH: I wouldn't mind my wife working as far as secretarial work or something like that. Whatever she wanted to do and she pursued as a career. If there was children around, I'd like her to be at home, so I'd like my job to compensate for just me working and my wife being at home.

* * *

LOIS: Let's say you did get married and have children, and your wife wanted to work.

BILL: It all depends on if I had a good job. If the financial situation is bad and she had to go to work, [then] she had to go to work.

LOIS: And if you got a good job?

BILL: She'd probably be a regular woman.

LOIS: Staying at home? Why is that a good thing?

BILL: I don't know if it's a good thing, but it'd probably be the normal thing.

Without question, young white working-class men in mid-1980s Freeway envision family life in highly male-dominant and controlling terms, seeing the possibility that their wives might work outside the home, but only out of "necessity" or, more likely, before children are born. They imagine their own income as sufficient to support a family, expecting to earn "the family wage," thus enabling their wives to assume the "normal" role of taking care of home and children. Young men offer that they would "help when they could," but see children as basically the woman's responsibility, and they intend their wives to be home in a "regular" womanly fashion.

Only two of the young men interviewed in 1985 envision a future other than the above. Vern reflects upon the high divorce rate which makes marriage unattractive, and Tom talks about marriage as "a ball and chain."

Lois: What kind of person do you want to marry?

Vern: Someone who is fairly good-looking, but not too good-looking so she'd be out, with other people screwing her up. Someone who don't mind what I'm doing, let me go out with the guys. I won't mind if she goes out with the girls either. I want her to have a job so she ain't home all the time. 'Cause a woman goes bonkers if she's at home all day. Give her a job and let her get out of the house....

People tended to get married as soon as they got out of school, not as soon as, but a couple of years after. I think people nowadays don't want to get married until twenty, thirty.

Lois: And that's because of what?

Vern: They've seen too many divorces.

Among the boys, only Vern entertains divorce as an impediment to marriage; in sharp contrast, every girl in 1985 brings up the subject of divorce. In spite of Vern's apparently more open-minded attitude toward women, he nevertheless envisions himself "allowing" his wife to work and sees himself controlling her time and space. He does not, for example, mind her "going out with the girls" and wants her to "have a job so she ain't home all the time."

Tom wants no part of marriage—equating it with prison:

Tom: I don't want to get married; I don't want to have children. I want to be pretty much free. If I settle down with someone, it won't be through marriage.

Lois: Why not?

Tom: Marriage is a ball and chain. Then marital problems come up, financial problems, whatever. I don't really want to get involved in the intense kind of problems between you and a spouse.... To me it's a joke ... I look at my father and mother. They don't get along, really.

The vast majority of young white working-class men in the mid-1980s cling to a fantasy that swirls around the establishment of a home space in which they exert complete control over their wives. Significantly, they imagine a home in which they go out to work and their wives stay at home, tending to them, the house, and their children. At the center of the young men's identity, then, sits the dominant male in both the home/family sphere and the paid labor force.

This core expression of male dominance is borne out by classroom observations. Young women, although challenging the male fantasy rather fundamentally in some respects, as I suggest in Chapter 2, do not speak out against the boys in class, leaving an envisioned male-dominant future intact, at least in the public space of the school. Interestingly enough, when this vision is interrupted, it is by male teachers, virtually all of whom are from the community in which these students reside.

Social Studies, December 3, 1985

MR. KINDIG: Why should women be educated? [A lot of chatter; many males saying they shouldn't be, or perhaps that they should be for secretarial science.] Look, you [the women] are better equipped to teach the children; you are better able to communicate with your husband if you are an educated woman. Also, today not everybody gets married. The better the education, the better the opportunity for a good job for *both* men and women. Women today probably need education more, because today, in broken marriages and divorces, the women normally have the children.

DAVE: But men have to pay child support—a hundred dollars a week ...
MR. KINDIG: Hey, you talk to many women, they don't get a penny from their former husbands. What about the guy who just got laid off from the steel plant—how are you going to pay a hundred dollars a week?

Dave talked to Mr. Kindig after class and said his dad sends $120 a week for child support. Mr. Kindig says, "Great, but isn't it true that your mom has to wait for checks; sometimes some bounce; so isn't it better that she has her own job?" Dave says [rather sheepishly], "She works, too."

* * *

Social Studies, December 4, 1985

MR. KINDIG: We were talking yesterday about whether it was a waste of time to educate women, and we concluded that it wasn't. I concluded that it wasn't, and you agree if you want to get the right mark.
JIM: Who asked you?

* * *

Social Studies, December 12, 1985

[Page 103 of the text.] Mr. Samuels goes over the multiple-choice questions and asks students to answer.

MR. SAMUELS: Question: Women are basically unwilling to assume positions in the business world. Agree or disagree?
SAM: Agree.
MR. SAMUELS: Why?
SAM: Because women want to raise children and get married.
MR. SAMUELS: All women?
SAM: No, but most.
MR. SAMUELS: Anyone disagree?
[No disagreement.]

No doubt the "correct" answer is "disagree," but the teacher does not push for further discussion.

White working-class young men in the 1980s envision a future in which they inhabit the public sphere of wage labor, and women the home/private sphere. In affirming this couplet—home/private sphere = women, and public sphere = men—they set themselves up to exert control over their wives in the female-based home sphere in return for losing control in the public/economic sector through selling their labor power under conditions of industrial capitalism. Exchanging labor power for a wage packet, they similarly fantasize exchanging the wage packet for the right to dominate their wives. It is the twin parts of this fantasy which young men affirm and elaborate in the 1980s, attempting to hold on to both during times of extreme economic dislocation; dislocation that will, in fact, challenge both aspects of this arrangement. Thus the elaboration of a certain form of masculinity becomes key to industrially based working-class manhood and is the linchpin which serves to direct, in many ways, the workings of the entire class. Surely, as R. W. Connell (1995) points out, there are varying ways of being a man, but the form articulated here is, without question, *the* celebrated hegemonic version of working-class masculinity. As such, it offers the center around which all other working-class masculine forms revolve and must emerge in relation to. As we see here, Freeway young men do their part to keep this form of hegemonic masculinity alive.

Racism

The elaboration of modal working-class masculinity is also linked in this instance to deeply etched racial constructions. Freeway epitomizes the American segregated northern town, with blacks and a relatively small number of Yemenites and Puerto Ricans living largely on one side of the bridge (the one closer to the grit of the mills), and whites on the other, although there are a number of home-owning whites living in a small but contained section of the side populated predominantly by people of color. In the 1980s, virtually no families of color live in the area coded "white." The majority of African Americans live in a large public housing section immediately adjacent to the old steel plant, having been brought up in boxcars from the south during the 1920s to forestall a threatened general strike. While the roots of racial antagonism may lie in management's use of blacks to break strikes, current antagonisms are considerably more complex, elaborated at every level, expressive as well as instrumental (Ogbu, 1988, 2002). Much of the expressed racism among Freeway boys, for example, plays itself out around "access" to young women and, to some extent, drug use.

JIM: The minorities are really bad into drugs. You're talking everything. Anything you want, you get from them. A prime example, the First Ward of Freeway; about twenty years ago the First Ward was predominantly white, my grandfather used to live there. Then Italians, Polish, the Irish people, everything was fine. The houses were maintained; there was a good standard of living....

The blacks brought drugs. I'm not saying white people didn't have drugs; they had drugs, but to a certain extent. But drugs were like a social thing. But now you go down to the First Ward, it's amazing; it's a ghetto. Some of the houses are okay. They try to keep them up. Most of the homes are really, really terrible. They throw garbage on the front lawn; it's sickening. You talk to people [in the surrounding suburbs]. Anywhere you talk to people, they tend to think the majority of our school is black. They think you hang with black people, listen to black music....

A few of them [blacks] are starting to go into the Third and Fourth wards now [the white side], so they're moving around. My parents will be around there when that happens, but I'd like to be out of there.

* * *

Lois: There's no fighting and stuff here [school], is there?

Clint: Yeah, a lot between blacks and whites.

Lois: Who starts them?

Clint: Blacks.

Lois: Do blacks and whites hang out in the same place?

Clint: Some do; [the blacks] live on the other side of town. . . .

A lot of it [fights] starts with blacks messing with white girls. That's how a lot of them start. Even if they [white guys] don't know the white girl, they don't like to see. . . .

Lois: How do you feel about that yourself?

Clint: I don't like it. If I catch them [blacks] near my sister, they'll get it. I don't like to see it like that. Most of them [my friends] see it that way [the same way he does].

Lois: Do you think the girls encourage the attentions of these black guys?

Clint: Naw. I think the blacks just make themselves at home. They welcome themselves in.

Lois: How about the other way around? White guys and black girls?

Clint: There's a few that do. There's people that I know of, but no one I hang around with. I don't know many white kids that date black girls.

* * *

Bill: Like my brother, he's in ninth grade. He's in trouble all the time. Last year he got jumped in school . . . about his girlfriend. He don't like blacks. They come up to her and go, "Nice ass," and all that shit. My brother don't like that when they call her "nice ass" and stuff like that. He got suspended for saying "fucking nigger"; but it's all right for a black guy to go up to whites and say stuff like that ["nice ass"]. . . .

Sometimes the principals aren't doing their job. Like when my brother told [the assistant principal] that something is going to happen, Mr. Strong just said, "Leave it alone, just turn your head."

Like they [administrators] don't know when fights start in this school. Like there's this one guy's kid sister, a nigger [correction]—a black guy—grabbed her ass. He hit him a couple of times. Did the principal know about it? No!

Lois: What if a white guy did that [grabbed the girl's ass]?

Bill: He'd probably have punched him. But a lot of it's 'cause they're black.

Racial tension exists within the school, reflective of tensions within the community and broader society. White boys attribute much of this tension to black young men hustling white girls. This is the male version of the story; I heard no such set of comments from the young women. White males view white females as *their* property and resent black males speaking to them in, at times, offensive terms. At the same time, though, white boys say "nice ass" to white girls, and this engenders no comparable response. It is the fact that black males do it, and not that males per se do it, that is most offensive to white males. I never saw a white male go to the defense of a white female, for example, if she was being harassed by another white male. In the context of the school, at least, it is only when the "invading" male is black that apparently protectionist instincts surface, indicating a deep racism which emerges in relation to girls in particular. White boys construct white girls as "property," as a piece of the gender-based bargain linked to the economy, and resent black intrusion onto *their* property. White males who envision themselves earning the "family wage" thus express a set of rights vis-à-vis white females—rights that black males, in their opinion, have not earned and do not deserve. Not one girl in 1985 voices a complaint in this regard. This is not to argue that white females are not racist, but rather that racism functions as an offensive strategy for white working-class men as they form identities during adolescence in a way that is not the case for young women. Research suggests that white working-class women engage race as a defensive strategy when they move into motherhood, where they impose racism, discursively, as protection around children (Weis & Hall, 2000).

Observational data reveal the deeply entrenched racism among white youth. This racism is directed mainly toward blacks, although it also surfaces in relation to the children of Yemenites, whose parents emigrated to Freeway to work in the mills in the 1940s.[6] Having penetrated the "white space" of the steel mill during earlier decades, Yemenites and African Americans now constitute the primary racial "other" in the school, an "other" against which and through which white working-class young men constitute the "self."

Social Studies, November 26, 1986

SAM: Hey, Abdul, did you come from Arabia?
ABDUL: Yeah.
SAM: How did you get here?
ABDUL: I walked
SAM: No, seriously, how'd you get here?
ABDUL: Boat.

SAM: Where'd you come from?
ABDUL: Saudi Arabia.
SAM: We don't want you. Why don't you go back?
[No comment.]
TERRY: What city did you come from?
ABDUL: Yemen, if you ever heard of it.

* * *

Social Studies, December 11, 1986

ED: Do you party, Nabil?
NABIL: Yeah.
PAUL: Nabil, the only thing you know how to play is polo on camels.
[Nabil ignores.]

* * *

English, October 2, 1986

LOIS: [To Terry, who was hit by a car two days ago.] How are you?
TERRY: Look at me [sic] face. Ain't it cool? [He is all scraped up.]
LOIS: What happened?
TERRY: Some stupid camel jockey ran me over in a big white car. Arabian
    dude.

While young men construct and engage an "Arabian other" as they construct self, most racial identity work is done in relation to African Americans.

At the lunch table, February 21, 1986

[discussion with Craig Centrie, research assistant]
PETE: Why is it [your leather bag] so big?
MIKE: So he can carry lots of stuff.
CRAIG: Yes, I bought it because my passport would fit in it.
PETE: Passport! Wow—where are you from?
CRAIG: Well, I'm American now, but you need one to travel.
PETE: Can I see? [Craig pulls out his passport; everyone looks.]

MIKE: This is my first time to ever see one. What are all these stamps?

CRAIG: Those are admissions stamps so [you] can get in and out of countries.

MIKE: Look, Pete, N-I-G-E-R-I-A [pronounced Niggeria]. Yolanda [a black female] should go there. [Everyone laughs.]

PETE: [Did you see any] crocodile-eating niggers? [laughter]

* * *

In the lunchroom, March 7, 1986

Once again, at lunch, everyone complains about the food.

Vern asks about a party he heard about. Everyone knows about it, but it isn't clear where it will be. A kid walks past the table [of white boys].

CLINT: That's the motherfucker. I'll whop his ass. [The entire table says "ou-ou-ou."]

CRAIG: What happened with those tickets, Pete? [Some dance tickets had been stolen.]

PETE: Nothing, but I'm pissed off at that nigger that blamed me.

Pete forgot how loud he was speaking, and looked toward Yolanda [a black female] to see if she reacted. She hadn't heard the remark.

* * *

At the lunch Table, February 12, 1986

About two minutes later, Darcy [a black female] calls me [Craig] over.

DARCY: What's your name?

CRAIG: Craig; what's yours?

DARCY: It's Darcy. Clint told me a lie. He said your name was Joe. Why don't you come to a party at Yolanda's house tonight?

YOLANDA: Why don't you just tell him you want him to come? [Everyone laughs.]

CLINT: Well, all right, they want you!

PETE: What do you think of Yolanda?

CRAIG: She's a nice girl. What do you think?

PETE: She's a stuck-up nigger. Be sure to write that down.

* * *

At the lunch Table, February 12, 1986

Much of the time, students discuss the food. Vern talks about the Valentine's Day dance and begins discussing getting stoned before the dance.

CRAIG: Do you guys drink at the dance, too?
PETE: No, I don't know what they would do to us [everyone laughs]. There probably wouldn't be any more dances.

[Yolanda and friends walk in. Yolanda and a friend are wearing exactly the same outfit.]

CLINT: What are you two—the fucking Gold Dust Twins?
YOLANDA: Shut the fuck up, "boy"! [Everyone laughs.]

Quietly, Pete says, "Craig, they are nasty."

CRAIG: What do you mean?
PETE: You don't understand black people. They're yeach. They smell funny and they [got] hair under their arms."
Clint, Pete, Mike, and Jack all make noises to denote disgust.

White working-class young men in the mid-1980s spend a great deal of time exhibiting disgust for racial others as they simultaneously assert and act upon an embroidered protectionist stance with respect to white women. This racial distancing works against and with both black males and females in particular, although it takes a different shape and form by gender. Black males are constructed as distinctly "other" than white males, and are treated by them with anger and disdain for invading their familial, and especially sexual, property (white girls). Black females, in contradistinction, although also deposited into the largely sexual realm, are treated with simple disgust. Both, then, are seen and interacted with predominantly in the (hetero)sexual arena, albeit for different reasons and in different ways.

It is significant that white males elaborate upon sexuality largely in relation to blacks, much as Willis's lads do in relation to West Indians in England (significantly, not Pakistanis or Indians). Certainly their own identity is bound up with sexuality, but this sexuality is expressed most vehemently and clearly in relation to bordering black males and, secondarily, black and white females. Central to this are both the establishment and the subsequent patrolling of the boundaries of "appropriate" sexual behavior for whites. Under this formulation, black sexuality, both male and female, is constructed as inappropriate—unlike their own. Certainly their own sexuality is also expressed in relation to white girls, but a key point here is that the *boundaries* of acceptable sexuality are set largely in relation to blacks. The black "other," like the black other in the white American imagination and culture more generally (Morrison, 1992), becomes the repository for all that is bad, simultaneously propping up and leaving in place the "good" white (sexually responsible, clean, and so forth). Jim's earlier comments about drugs become metaphoric: "The blacks brought drugs. I'm not saying white people didn't have drugs; they had drugs, but to a certain extent." Thus the circle is complete—white males assert their goodness in the face of the constructed black "bad."

Importantly, the setting up of a black other is implicated in the staking out of the heterosexual moment at a time of intense adolescent surveillance of sexuality. In stressing the boundaries of appropriate sexual behavior in relation to women (which they do not necessarily follow, of course), as well as participating in deep critique of black heterosexuality and associated practices (invading white territory; disgust in relation to underarm hair, and so forth) they are cementing not only their own behavioral goodness in the sexual realm, but also their attraction to women and, as we saw earlier, their linked intention of setting up a male-dominant household. The construction of a black other against whom appropriate sexuality and sexually related practices can be revealed is tagged in important ways, then, to a distancing of oneself from homoerotic desires, at precisely the moment when adolescent culture is at its most vicious in terms of its surveillance of such matters. Race, social class, sexuality, and gender thus become linked in this instance to the creation of the hegemonically situated heterosexual dominant young white working-class man who intends to have his wife stay at home while he earns the family wage. The earning of a family wage in this sense, then, is once again linked to the staking out of heterosexual territory among white working-class male adolescents. Significantly, this is all played out in the United States in high racial parlance.[7] In the final moment, white working-class adolescent Freeway males leave high school with a modal identity constructed deeply in relation to the ideologically constructed identity of both black males and females, and white females.

Kaleidoscopic changes in the economy await these young men as they grow into adulthood, carrying on their backs as well as in their minds and hearts their forged adolescent youth identity which is carved (individually and collectively) along the three axes uncovered ethnographically and outlined here: (1) a contradictory code of respect toward school knowledge and culture, but one which ultimately tips toward form rather than substance; (2) virulently patriarchal constructions of home/life which position women in particular kinds of subordinate relationships vis-à-vis men; and (3) constructed notions of racial others which are intimately tied to both expressed and unexpressed notions of gender and sexuality. This constitutes a *modal* white working-class masculine cultural form, one which offers a hegemonic center around which alternative masculine forms must swirl. Such modal form moves with these young men as they grow up in a world markedly different from that of their parents and grandparents. As they plunge forward into the new world economy and its excising of the industrial proletariat, their cultural "props," most prominently "their" women, are falling by the wayside.

2

A TIME OF POSSIBILITY
Young Women at Freeway High

Marriage was invented by somebody who was lucky if they
lived to be twenty without being bit by a dinosaur.
                                            Suzanne, grade 11, 1985

Previous studies suggest that working-class white high school females
elaborate at the level of their own identity, a private/public dichotomy
that emphasizes the centrality of the private and marginalizes the
public. During adolescence, home/family life assumes a central position
for girls, and wage labor a secondary position. As numerous studies
conducted in the 1970s and 1980s have shown, working-class girls
elaborate what Angela McRobbie calls an "ideology of romance,"
constructing a gender identity that serves, ultimately, to encourage
women's second- class status in both the home and the workplace.
Studies by Linda Valli (1986) and Angela McRobbie (1978), in particular, have been important in terms of our understanding of the ways
in which these processes work upon and through the identity of young
women.[1]

This gender identity has important implications for the position of
women in both the family and the workplace in that it represents para-
meters within which struggles will take place. By defining domestic
labor as primary, women reinforce what can be called the Domestic
Code, under which home or family becomes defined as women's place,
and a public sphere of power and work as men's place. The reality, of
course, is that generations of working-class women have labored in
the public sphere, and that labor also takes place in the home, albeit

unpaid. Yet, as Karen Brodkin Sacks (1984) points out, "The Domestic Code has been a ruling set of concepts in that it did not have to do consistent battle with counterconcepts. It has also been a ruling concept in the sense that it 'explained' an unbroken agreement among capitalists, public policymakers, and later, much of organized labor, that adequate pay for women was roughly 60 percent of what was adequate for men and need be nowhere adequate to allow a woman to support a family or herself" (pp. 17–18).[2]

Although the Domestic Code was certainly subject to intense academic and practical scrutiny in 1985, it is not my intention to explore this set of challenges here. What I am concerned with is the extent to which Freeway females in 1985 elaborate an identity in high school that represents a significant departure from that found by previous investigators of this class fraction, as well as from the identity preferred by young men in the same community.[3] In point of fact, 1985 is experienced as a time of possibility by young Freeway women rather than as a space of crisis. Freeway females exhibit what I call a *critical moment of critique* of male dominance and patriarchy. This incipient critique is not, however, reflective of collective struggle around the issue of gender. Rather, these girls tend to pose individualistic/private solutions to their felt notions that old forms of male dominance both will not work for them and are, at the same time, somewhat unjust.

Work Outside the Home

The most striking point about female identity at Freeway High is that there is little evidence of a marginalized wage labor identity. These girls have made the obtaining of wage labor a *primary* rather than secondary goal. Almost without exception the girls desire to continue their education, and are clear that they intend to do so in order to gain increased control over their own lives. It is worth noting that this is reminiscent of the voices of black females in studies of romance, marriage, and the future (Weis, 1985).

Only *one* girl interviewed mentioned marriage and a family first when talking about what she wished to do after high school. The remaining students stressed jobs or "careers," with college or some form of further education specifically being discussed. Only when I actually inquired about a family did the majority of girls mention this at all—in striking contrast to boys, for whom the establishment of an envisioned male-dominant family was foremost on their mind. This reflects an interesting inversion of the past: high school boys in

Freeway now envision family life first, whereas girls focus first on their imagined position in the wage labor sector.

There is in Freeway, as in most American high schools (Rosenbaum, 1976; Oakes, 1985), a strong system of academic tracking in place. In Freeway High, approximately twenty-five out of a total of three hundred students per grade are pulled out and placed in an honors-level college prep track—which the students refer to as the "honors bubble," a track composed of courses that culminate in a series of state-level exams. In order to obtain entrance to a four-year university in the state in which Freeway is located, students must graduate with a diploma attached to this particular set of courses, and a "local" diploma is reserved for all remaining high school graduates. The proportion of students in honors-level courses in schools across the state, as in the United States more broadly, varies by the social class (and race) of students served. Affluent suburban districts, for example, might have 70 to 80 percent of their students in the mid-1980s in college prepatory-level classes, in sharp contrast with the 8 percent in such classes at working-class Freeway High.

While the male response to my questions does not break neatly into honors versus non-honors track placements, the girls' responses tend to be linked to curricular track. The first set of interviews reflects responses of girls in the "advanced" curriculum. Students in this group generally want to attend a four-year college or university and talk in terms of careers, often non-traditional ones. Girls in "regular classes" also talk about continuing their education after high school, but generally focus on the two-year college, business institute, or schools for hairdressing. Both groups stress job or "career" rather than family.

Judy, Rhonda, Jennifer, Jessica, and Liz are members of the advanced class. With the exception of Rhonda, who wants to become a medical technician, all intend to pursue careers that demand at least a four-year college degree. Some, like Jennifer, plan to go to graduate school.

JUDY: I'm thinking of [State University] for electrical engineering. I know I'm going to go into that.
LOIS: How did you pick electrical engineering?
JUDY: 'Cause my brother is an electrical engineer. . . . He works for General Electric. He has a B.A.

* * *

RHONDA: [I'll] probably go into medicine.
LOIS: Any particular area?
RHONDA: Medical technician, maybe.
LOIS: Would you consider being a nurse or doctor?
RHONDA: I considered being a nurse. But with all the strikes and them saying they're underpaid [I don't want to do it]. I read a lot about the job.

* * *

JENNIFER: [I want] to go to college, but I'm not sure where. And I want to go into psychology, I think.... I'd love to be a psychiatrist, but I don't think I'll ever make it through medical school. So I was talking with a guidance counselor and she said you could get a Ph.D. in psychology and there are a lot of good jobs that go along with that....

I think I'm forced [to go to college]. I don't think I have a choice.

* * *

JESSICA: My mother wants me to be in engineering like my brother 'cause he's so successful.... I have an interest with the behavior of marine animals. Which is kind of stupid, 'cause we don't live anywhere near an ocean, so I was thinking of going to Florida State. My parents don't want me to go to any other school but [State University], so I haven't brought this up yet. I figure we can wait a while.

* * *

LOIS: What are you going to do when you leave high school?
LIZ: College.
LOIS: Do you know which college?
LIZ: I'm thinking of [State University] in physical therapy.

Aside from Jennifer, whose father is head of the chemistry lab at a local hospital, these girls are not from professional families.[4] They are, on the contrary, daughters of industrial laborers and are now thinking of obtaining a four-year college degree and pursuing some type of career. It is noteworthy that both girls who are being encouraged by their families to go into engineering have brothers who are engineers, perhaps influencing their decisions. It might also be hypothesized that as working-class individuals obtain professional positions, they are disproportionately in areas such as engineering, which are seen as having a direct relation to hands-on laboring processes. Such jobs enable working-class persons to become educated and still do "real" work, thus bypassing, to some extent, the contradictory code of respect toward education embedded in the working class (Sennett & Cobb, 1972)—a contradictory code which, as I noted earlier, is being reworked under the current economy.[5]

Although more than 50 percent of graduating high school seniors in the 1980s go on for advanced study directly from high school, data presented here cannot be seen as *simply* reflective of overall trends regarding college attendance.[6] Scholars who use national data on college trends often make the error of combining enrollment in all four-year schools with enrollment in community colleges and other tertiary-level institutions. Although it has been suggested that 50 percent of students are now in college, we do not necessarily know *which* colleges they are in, nor do we know who goes where. In fact, analyses such as that of Jerome Karabel (1972) suggest that the elite sector is dominated overwhelmingly by students of the middle class and higher, whereas the community college sector is dominated by the working class. Michael Olivas (1979) makes a similar point with respect to students of color and their disproportionate attendance at community colleges. It is therefore noteworthy that Freeway girls in the advanced class plan to pursue careers and that these careers involve the pursuit of four-year degrees, often at relatively prestigious state institutions. When considered in light of later data on home/family identity, it becomes even clearer that these data are not simply reflective of generalized education inflation.

Statements of girls in the advanced class stand in contrast with those of girls in the "regular" classes. They, too, plan to pursue jobs, although most imagined jobs are linked with two-year colleges or business institutes and are lodged in traditionally sex-segregated fields.

LORNA: Well, I go to [a cooperative vocational education program] for food service, and I think I want to be a caterer. I don't want to be sitting down all the time. I like to be on my feet, moving. I like to cook and stuff, [but] you get to do everything, not just stay in the kitchen. . . .

    [Suburban Community College] has got a two-year course, and then, if I want to, I can transfer my credits and stuff and go to a four-year college. My mother's got a friend; she teaches food service in a college, and she was telling me about it. Like what to do and stuff.

* * *

LORETTA: [I want to go to] [State University].
LOIS: When you get out of [State University], what do you hope to do?
LORETTA: Become a lawyer, have a family, I guess, but not until I graduate from college. . . . A lot of my friends want to go to college.

* * *

SUSAN: I'll go to [the community college]. I don't want to go four years to school. I can just go two years and become a registered nurse and get a job. I volunteer at [the local hospital], so I'm hoping to have a foot in the door when it comes time for a job.

* * *

LOIS: When you leave high school, what do you want to do?
CAROL: A lot of things. I do want to go to college for fashion design. I don't know how good I'll do.
LOIS: Where do you want to go?
CAROL: I haven't thought about it. But as soon as I graduate [from high school], I want to get my state license [for hairdressing] and get a job, and then save money so that I have money when I want it. . . . I want to have my own salon, but first of all, I want to start off in somebody else's salon so I get the experience.

* * *

VALERIE: I didn't really think I was going to go to college, unless business courses. I'm going to try for a job [after high school], and if I can get a good job out of it, then I won't go to college. If it requires college training, then I'm going to go.
LOIS: What kind of job?
VALERIE: Something with word processing.

* * *

AVIS: I want to [go to] college around here. . . . They [business institute] have medical secretary; they have a lot of business stuff, and that will help out. And they could get you a job. . . .

With the exception of Loretta, all the girls in the nonadvanced curriculum wish to attend two-year colleges, business institutes, or schools for hairdressing, thinking primarily in terms of traditionally female occupations. Avis and Valerie are thinking of being secretaries; Carol wants to be a hairdresser; Lorna, a food-service worker; and Susan, a nurse. This is in contrast with girls in the advanced curriculum, where there appears to be some desire to break out of these sex-segregated occupational ghettos.

Analysis of where transcripts are sent suggests somewhat more congruence for girls than for boys in terms of expressed desires and actual school applications. Eight percent and 7 percent of 1983 and 1985 graduates, respectively, sent transcripts to the business institute, and the rating of "the best school applied to" (Carnegie Commission, 1973) for 26 percent and 17 percent of 1983 and 1985 graduates, respectively, was the community college.

However, 32 percent and 42 percent of girls in 1983 and 1985, respectively, did not apply to any institution of higher education, in spite of the primacy of a job/career emerging within their collective identity. Thus, the same contradictory tendencies with respect to school knowledge and culture emerge to some extent for girls as for boys, although many of the jobs that girls were envisioning for themselves do not necessarily require further formal education. Heading up a patriarchal family composed of one wage earner who brings in the "family wage," such as the boys imagine, demands a great deal of money—money that, for the most part, can be garnered only with extensive education. And even then, such an income is hardly assured (Newman, 1988). The fact that boys tend to adhere only to the bare form of schooling becomes, under such circumstances, that much more striking.

This does not, however, negate the fact that girls also exhibit a somewhat contradictory relationship with schooling. They, too, simultaneously accept and reject school knowledge and culture, although not to the degree boys do, and the anti-school animus deeply characteristic of working-class males does not characterize girls and women of this class fraction to the same extent. Nevertheless, girls copy homework routinely and they, like boys, engage in the form rather than the substance of schooling.

Two key points emerge here with respect to gender and this contradictory relationship with school knowledge and culture. As noted above, girls are not envisioning themselves supporting entire families, which would certainly necessitate higher education, given that well-paying male laboring jobs are largely obliterated. While such jobs are not guaranteed if advanced education is obtained, it is clearly at least a necessary condition for such positions. Second, girls do not evidence widespread resentment toward institutional authority; they have not done so in previous studies, and they do so only minimally in Freeway. The acting on resentment of institutional authority is a distinctly male purview, tied to the historic struggle between capital and labor, thus throwing into sharp relief the more positive male attitudes toward schooling expressed in Freeway than in previous studies of white working-class boys. Since girls do not express deep resentment to begin with, their own current contradictory relationship with school knowledge and culture does not represent a stunning departure from past practice.

Marriage and Family

The lack of primacy for a home/family identity among mid-1980s Freeway girls contrasts sharply with data collected in previous investigations of white working-class females. Wolpe, for example, suggests:

> By the time teenage girls reach school-leaving age, they articulate their future in terms of family responsibilities. They reject, often realistically, advice about pursuing school subjects which could open up new avenues; the jobs they anticipate are not only within their scope, but more importantly, are easily accessible to them and in fact in conformity with their future familial responsibilities. (1978, p. 326)

Girls in Linda Valli's study (1986) similarly underscore the primacy of envisioned family responsibilities among young white working-class women: raising children and possibly working part-time:

> Experiencing office work as either secondary to or synonymous with a sexual/home/family identity further marginalized these students' work identities. The culture of femininity associated with office work made it easier for them to be less attached to their work and their workplace than men, who stay in paid employment because they must live up to masculine ideology of male-as-provider. Women's identities tend to be much less intrinsically linked to wage labor than are men's.... (p. 232)

Angela McRobbie examines the intersectionality of gender and social class. In spite of the fact that the young women in McRobbie's study know that marriage and housework are far from glamorous simply by virtue of the lives of female relatives and friends, they construct fantasy futures and elaborate an "ideology of romance," creating a specifically female anti-school culture that consists of interjecting sexuality into the classroom, talking loudly about boyfriends, and wearing makeup—ironically ensuring, argues McRobbie, their *own* less valued position in both the economy and the home:

> Marriage, family life, fashion, and beauty all contribute massively to this feminine anti-school culture and, in doing so, nicely illustrate the contradictions inherent in so-called oppositional activities. Are the girls in the end not doing exactly what is required of them—and if this is the case, then could it not be convincingly argued that it is their own culture which itself is the most effective agent of social control of the girls, pushing them into compliance with that role which a whole range of institutions in capitalist society also, but less effectively, directs them towards? At the same time, they are experiencing a class relation in albeit traditionally feminine terms. (1978, p. 104)

The 1985 Freeway youth are markedly different. Although some assert that they wish to have some form of home/family identity, it is never asserted first, and generally only as a possibility "later on," when their own job or career is "settled." Some totally reject the possibility of marriage and children; others wish to wait "until I am at least thirty," which is, to teenagers, a lifetime away. Most important, they assert strongly that they must settle *themselves* first (go to school, get a job) before entering into family responsibilities; the construction of a home/family identity is secondary, rather than the reverse. Only one of the twenty-one girls interviewed elaborates a romance ideology, and this girl is criticized severely by others. I never heard informal discussion directed at the romantic nature of boys or marriage in all the time I spent at Freeway High. Significantly, unlike the girls in McRobbie's study, Freeway girls do not construct fantasy futures as a means of escaping their current condition; they are, in fact, far more practical as they carefully plot out of their existing situation.

It is important to note that few girls discuss the possibility of marriage without invoking divorce, a possibility that is brought up by advanced and nonadvanced students in equal measure. Although students tend to differ by track as to envisioned relationship to particular forms of wage labor and future schooling, they do not differ at all with respect to their assertions of the primacy of a wage labor identity. The language of wanting to be "independent" is often used in discussions related both to home/family life and to wage labor options—assertions of "independence" in response to initial probe questions revolving around what they want to do after high school; what they wish to do in five years, and in ten years. It is only when I ask the girls *specifically* whether they wish to get married and/or have a family that they invoke these possibilities as desired. I quote at length here in order to give the full flavor of the girls' 1985 perspectives. Those of the advanced students are presented first.

LOIS: Why not just get a man to support you and then you can stay home?
PENNY: 'Cause you can't fall back on that.
LOIS: Why do you say that?
PENNY: 'Cause what if I get a divorce and you have nothing to fall back on?
LOIS: Does your mother encourage you to get a job because "What if I get a divorce?" [Her father is no longer alive.]
PENNY: No.
LOIS: So, where did you get that?
PENNY: Just my own ideas. Just how things are today.

* * *

LOIS: Do you want to get married?
JESSICA: Gee, I don't know. After I see all the problems that go on now, I just don't know. All the divorce. Just how can you live with somebody for forty years? I don't know, possibly. . . . You see it [divorce] all over. I'm not living to get married.

* * *

JUDY: I want to go to college for four years, get my job, work for a few years, and then get married. . . . I like supporting myself. I don't want my husband supporting me. I like being independent.
LOIS: You're doing something very different from your mother. Why? [Mother was married at nineteen; went back to work when Judy was in grade three.]
JUDY: I think I have to. . . . What happens if I marry a husband who is not making good money? My dad works at Freeway Steel. He's switching jobs all the time [although the plant is closed, there is still piecework

going on, and workers are called back according to seniority rules at much lower pay than they formerly earned]. He used to work at the strip mill; now he's not. Now everything is gone, benefits and everything.

* * *

CARLA: Oh, I'm going to do that later [get married; have children]. I'm going to school to get everything over with. I wouldn't want to get married or have kids before that.

LOIS: Why not?

CARLA: It'd be too hard. I just want to get my schoolwork over with, get my life together, get a job.... I want to be independent. I don't want to be dependent on him [my husband] for money. Then what would I do if I got divorced fifteen years, twenty years? You know how people are and marriages. Twenty years down the line you have kids, the husband has an affair or just you have problems, you get divorced, then where is that going to leave me? I want to get my life in order first, with my career and everything.... Maybe it has something to do with the high divorce rates. Or the stories you hear about men losing their jobs and not having any job skills, and you see poverty, and I just don't want that. I want to be financially secure on my own.

While all girls in the advanced class express a desire to get their "own lives in order before marrying," all but Suzanne suggest that they will marry eventually.

LOIS: Tell me a little bit about whether you want to get married.

SUZANNE: [Interrupts me.] No. No marriage, no kids!

LOIS: Why not?

SUZANNE: I don't like that.

LOIS: Why?

SUZANNE: I don't think you can stay with somebody your whole life. It's dumb.... Like this one kid says, "Marriage was invented by somebody who was lucky if they lived to twenty without being bit by a dinosaur." It's true. It started so far back and it's, like, people didn't live long. Now people live to be eighty years old. You don't stay with one person for eighty years. It's, like, impossible.

LOIS: What makes you say that?

SUZANNE: A lot of divorce. A lot of parents who fight and stuff. I couldn't handle the yelling at somebody constantly 'cause I wanted to get out. I just don't want to be trapped.... Back when they [parents] were kids, like, girls grew up, got married, worked for a couple of years after graduation, had two or three kids, had a white picket fence, two cars. Things are different now.

LOIS: How so?

SUZANNE: Girls don't grow up just to be married. They grow up to be people, too.

LOIS: And that means they don't want these other things?

SUZANNE: Not that they don't want them. A lot of girls in school, they're like, "Hey, you're [Suzanne] crazy. I want to be married sometime, I want to have kids" [but] they all want to wait. They all want to get into a career first; wait until they're thirty. It's [marriage] only "if," though, and it's going to be late....

You've got to do it [make a good life] for yourself. I don't want to be Mrs. John Smith. I want to be able to do something.

I mean, just from what I've seen, a lot of people cheat and that. I don't want that.... You can't rely on them [men]. You just can't rely on them.... [Also] drinking a lot. It's like, I know a lot of older guys, they drink all the time.

Girls in the advanced class state forcefully that they must get themselves together before engaging home/family responsibilities. Clearly, the conditions of their *own* lives mediate their response to family and paid work. Numerous students note the high divorce rate. Penny, for example, asks, "What if I get a divorce and you have nothing to fall back on?" Jessica states, "After I see all the problems that go on now, I just don't know. All the divorce." Carla concurs: "Then what if I get divorced fifteen years, twenty years? You know how people are and marriages. Twenty years down the line you have kids, the husband has an affair or you just have problems, you get divorced, then where is that going to leave me?" The lack of male jobs is similarly articulated as a problem: "What happens if I marry a husband who is not making good money? My dad works at Freeway Steel. He used to work at the strip mill, now he's not. Now everything is gone, benefits and everything."

Students suggest that men cannot be counted on for a *variety of reasons*—high divorce rate, drinking, lack of jobs, lack of skills, affairs, and so forth; they respond to this aspect of their lived experience by establishing, at least in principle, the primacy of wage labor in their own lives, hoping to hedge their chances both within and outside of married life.

The issue of a home/family identity and the degree to which girls in the advanced curriculum embrace primarily an identity as a wage laborer is highlighted in the interchanges between and among Amy, Jennifer, and myself. Amy has decided to drop out of the advanced curriculum in order to pursue cosmetology. She does this as an assertion that, for her, a home/family identity *is* primary. Jennifer is critical of Amy's decision, as are the rest of her friends. Amy pursues cosmetology so as to work around envisioned family life. Significantly, she is the *only* girl interviewed in 1985 who takes this position.

AMY: They [my friends] don't want to get married. They just want to go out and get richer.

LOIS: The kids in the honors class?

AMY: *Everybody* [emphasis hers] I talk to . . . they just want to be free. They're all going to college [some form of continued education].

　　Everybody in my class is . . . they have a lower opinion of me [because I don't want to go on to some form of school]. . . .

　　They talk about it [marriage] as "maybe someday." But they don't really care whether they do or don't. They won't do it in the near future . . . .

　　They [outside the honors class] want to go to college, too. They say, "Why do you want to get married so young?" [Twenty, twenty-one.] They don't want to get married until they're thirty.

LOIS: Why do you think that's the case?

AMY: They don't want to be tied down.

LOIS: What does that mean? Why not?

AMY: They think that if they get married, they're going to have to be told what to do. They won't be able to do what they want to do, and they don't, like, want nobody dictating to them; nothing like that. . . .

　　Like, if my girlfriends want me to come somewhere with them and I say, "I'm coming with him [boyfriend]," they just say, "You can come with us, let him go by himself. . . . Why do you let him tell you what to do?"

Later, Amy offers:

AMY: I want to get married and have kids and I want to be at home. It's [cosmetology] a good thing to do at home so I don't have to go out and work and leave my kids with a baby-sitter or nothin'. I just don't like the whole idea.

LOIS: When are you thinking of getting married?

AMY: Three years. We figure we'll get married as soon as he finishes college.

LOIS: Is having kids something you want to do right away?

AMY: Yeah.

LOIS: And you're going to stay home with those kids?

AMY: Yeah, I guess I'm old-fashioned. . . . When I tell my friends about that, they look at me funny. Like, why would I want to do that? They want to go out and work, not get married and not have kids. They think I'm crazy or something. I'd just rather stay home, have kids, and be a beautician on the side, at home. Have a shop in my home.

LOIS: How long do you think you should stay at home?

AMY: Depends on the money situation. Things like that. If we need extra money, I could go out and work. But if we didn't, whatever I felt like doing. . . .

I'm just like her [my mother]. I want to do exactly what she did. She started working seven years ago. She's a clerk at a drugstore and she hates it 'cause she's not making much money at all. A little above minimum. Seven years and she can't get raises. They won't give her a raise and she complains. She wishes she went to college. She can't get any kind of good jobs.

Amy articulates the Domestic Code while simultaneously noting the contradictory nature of this code in the real world. Desiring to be "just like her mother," she nevertheless recognizes that her mother is currently having difficulty getting a job that pays above minimum wage or offers opportunities for advancement. It is the Domestic Code and its attendant contradictions in today's society that are being challenged at the collective identity level by working-class white females in Freeway.

Tensions over the Domestic Code are well articulated by Jennifer, who refers to Amy in her comments:

LOIS: Do most of the kids in the advanced curriculum plan to go to college?

JENNIFER: All except for one who plans to get married and have kids [said with some disgust].

LOIS: What is your perception of that one?

JENNIFER: We've all told her on many occasions, "It's crazy." She's always been in our group, and now she is taking cosmetology and she thinks she's just going to get a small job somewhere to help support when she gets married. She's all planned out. She's going to get married when he finishes college. She's been with this guy for a while. Her whole life is all planned out, and, it's like, "Okay, fine, you get married. What happens if you get a divorce?" "My God [she says], that would never happen." "It might, you know. What if he dies, then what are you going to do?" You have to support yourself some way. Even if you do get married and you're happy now, something could happen tomorrow. You could have an unhappy marriage and get divorced. You can't say "I'm gonna have a happy marriage"; it might not work. . . .

Maybe we think it's such a waste. I mean, you have the opportunity, it's such a waste. I mean, civil rights have come so far. If it were a hundred years ago, I can see saying that, when you were being a rebellious woman if you wanted to go out and get a job. I mean, now we have that opportunity; to relinquish that and say, I mean, I'm a cautious person and thinking of the future and saying, What if something *does* happen? She isn't even thinking of that.

This same beginning challenge is articulated by girls who are not in the advanced curriculum. Although preparing themselves for jobs in largely sex-segregated occupations, they challenge the Domestic Code as vociferously as the others. *None* elevate home/family responsibilities above those associated with wage labor.

LOIS: Do you see yourself getting married? Do you think you'll have children?

VALERIE: Yeah, but not right away. I'll wait until I'm about twenty-four. . . . I just feel that I want to accomplish my own thing, like getting a job and stuff.

LOIS: Why not find a guy and let him support you?

VALERIE: Feels like I have a purpose in life [if I accomplish my own thing]. Like I can do what I want.

LOIS: As opposed to?

VALERIE: Feeling like *he* [emphasis hers] has to support me, and *he* has to give me money.

* * *

CAROL: Well, I know I'm not going to get married until I'm at least thirty, and have kids when I'm around thirty-one, thirty-two.

LOIS: Why?

CAROL: 'Cause 'Cause I want to have my own freedom to experience life, everything: to travel, to go out places without having to have a baby-sitter or worry about kids. Plus with a beauty salon [her envisioned job], it would be hard to have kids to take care of and do that [the beauty salon] at the same time.

* * *

LOIS: Do you want to get married?

SUSAN: Yes.

LOIS: When do you think you'll get married?

SUSAN: I want to prove to myself if I can be on my own. I don't want no man to have to take care of me.

LOIS: Why?

SUSAN: Because my mother told me that. I don't know what the statistics are anymore, but for every marriage that lasts, every [another] marriage doesn't, so.... Women, when they go into a marriage, they have to be thinking "Can I support myself?"

* * *

LOIS: When you think about your life five years from now, what do you think you'll be doing? Do you think you'll be married?

LORNA: I'm trying to get all my education so I can support myself. Why put effort [in] and then let somebody support you? ...

I saw my friends getting pregnant so young. If you get married young, you're going to get pregnant young, and it's going to ruin the rest of your life. That's the way I see it. . . .

Five years from now I'll just be able to go out to a bar. I'll be twenty-one. And I don't want to ruin my life in just five years. 'Cause as soon as you get married, you're going to start having kids; then you're going to have to stay home and raise them and stuff. I don't want to have to do that.

LOIS: Why not?

LORNA: I like to do things. I don't want to have to sit around all the time. . . . I just don't want to stay home all the time.

LOIS: Does marriage mean you're going to have to stay home all the time?

LORNA: Well, that's what I think of. You get married, you got to stay home. You can't just go out with other people. . . . I like to go out with my friends when I want to. I like to be able to make my own decisions, and if you're married, you have to sort of ask the other person, "Can I spend the money here, can I do that?" It's, like, you got to ask permission. Well, I been asking permission from my parents all my life, you know. I don't want to just get out of high school and get married, and then have to keep asking permission for the rest of my life.

LOIS: Will you ever get married?

LORNA: I was just talking about that today. Probably when I'm thirty. Then I'll take a couple of years to have kids.

Although girls in the nonadvanced class sound like their peers in the advanced curriculum, they exhibit some tendency to elaborate more specifically the theme of "freedom" and, in contrast, restrictions imposed by marriage. While that is true for the earlier set of interviews as well, in that a number of girls stress "independence," non-advanced girls are far more strident. Lorna, for example, states: "As soon as you get married, you're going to start having kids; then you're going to *have* [my emphasis] to stay home and raise them and stuff.... You get married, you got to stay home. You can't just go out and go out with other people.... I like to make my own decisions, and if you're married, you have to sort of ask the other person, 'Can I spend the money here; can I do that?' It's like you got to ask permission." Valerie, too, notes that she doesn't want to feel that "*he* [emphasis hers] has to support me, and *he* has to give me money."

The distinction I am drawing here between advanced and nonadvanced girls should not be overstated, since both groups stress personal independence. The nonadvanced students do, however, tend to underline the possibly oppressive conditions of marriage, whereas the advanced students more often reflect upon the divorce rate and the possibility that their husbands may leave them or may not be able to obtain a good job. Lorna assumes that once a woman marries, she starts having children, suggesting that within the bounds of a working-class marriage, one does not necessarily assume even basic control over biological reproduction. This does not reflect complete adherence to strict Catholic teaching about birth control, however, since many of these young women believe in actively controlling reproduction. It is, rather, a straightforward assertion that a woman can no longer assume basic control over biological reproduction once married. Given the sentiments of boys in Freeway, this expressed fear is understandable.

It is noteworthy that white female identity, unlike white male identity, is not produced in relation to constructed black identity. This is not to say that white working-class females are not racist; they may well be. Rather, it is to suggest that the white working-class female does not emerge in self-identity terms specifically and aggressively in relation to a constructed black "other." While this may be surprising on one level, it is not so surprising if we consider the economy under which such identities are produced. Black and white males have historically been at odds in the economic sector, in that blacks were consistently barred from well-paid union laboring jobs by working-class white males, and simultaneously used as strikebreakers by white owners and managers.[7] Historically based antagonism exists and was even encouraged, given that both groups of men were, to some extent at least, available to do the same kinds of work and intentionally pitted against one another in the industrial laboring sector, particularly when blacks moved north in search of better opportunities. In addition, as John Ogbu, Toni Morrison, and others argue, it is in the "expressive" domain that blacks have been used as the repository for all that white society fears and hates, in relation to both the white self and the black "other." The combination of the expressive and instrumental domains as they play out simultaneously in relation to the identity construction of working-class white men cannot, therefore, be underestimated.

The situation for white working-class women is markedly different. There is no comparable set of jobs for which women across race competed historically, since white women were assumed to be at best inconsistently connected to the wage labor sector. Thus race-based antagonisms, as arising in this sector, were experienced only indirectly by women rather than on a day-to-day basis in a specific formative site. This accounts for the lack of primacy of race as a key point of identity formation among white working-class female adolescents. Envisioning themselves in the labor force, young white men absorb the raciality of the working-class laboring experience. Young women, it can be argued, have a very different connection with race and raciality, at least during the teenage years.

I argue here that white working-class girls' emerging identity exhibits a beginning challenge to the Domestic Code. Young Freeway women envision their lives very differently than girls in previous studies, and very differently than investigators such as Lillian Breslow Rubin (1976) and Glen Elder (1974) suggest that their mothers and grandmothers do. For them, the domestic is *not* primary; wage labor is. If patriarchy rests on a fundamental distinction between men's and women's labor, and currently on the domination of women in both the home/family sphere and the workplace, these girls exhibit the glimmerings of a critique of such arrangements. They understand, to the point of being able to articulate, the fact that too many negative consequences result if one depends on a man to the exclusion of depending on oneself, and that this means engaging in long-term wage labor.

Most significantly, these young women do not suggest the "part-time" work solution and/or flights into fantasy futures offered by girls in previous studies. Angela McRobbie, for example, chronicles most convincingly the ways in which white working-class girls offer fanciful futures as they imagine their future husband and accompanying married/domestic life—a scenario that bears no resemblance to the lackluster and drudgery-filled domestic/married life their mothers and grandmothers experience in full view of fantasy-filled daughters.

In this sense, then, 1985 white female adolescent collective identity boldly embodies a *critical moment of critique* of an underlying premise of patriarchy: that women's primary place is in the home/family sphere and that men will, in turn, "take care" of them. Hoping to fly on their own, they do not revel in the possibility of a man who swoops them off their feet and situates them in a beautiful castle which they, then, happily tend to. Moving forward, they want to "be independent," take care of themselves, and think about marriage and children only after "everything is settled." A markedly different group than their mothers, grandmothers, and even white working-class adolescent girls in recent studies, Freeway girls desire to strike out on their own, exhibiting a "glimmer of critique" with respect to women's place in the white working-class family and community.

The potential for such a critical moment needs to be considered carefully, and I pursue this in Chapter 5. Suffice it to say that while the girls' identity suggests a glimmer of critique, informed both by the women's movement (which they do not necessarily ally themselves with) and by economic changes which ensure both that women *must* work outside the home and *can* obtain jobs, such a critique does not necessarily prefigure collective action; rather, it tends to fragment, suggestive of individualistic private solutions rather than political struggle designed to change the prevailing gendered social order.[8]

In 1985 white working-class modal male and female identities are on a collision path, with boys loudly affirming male-dominant relations in the home, and girls exhibiting a challenge to these relations in key ways. Moving toward a wholly restructured world economy and the excising of the industrial proletariat, the question is, among others, what happened?

Part II

2000

3

WE MEET THE MEN AGAIN

Reconnecting with students in 2000 demanded intensive investigative work. Through the phone book, I was able to track seven of the students. Through calling them, I began to piece together the whereabouts of the class of 1987. Of the original twenty white males interviewed in 1985, I was able to locate all but two of them; four of those I located declined to be interviewed. Larry, voted "most likely to succeed," let me know, "If you had called me two years ago, I was doing well [he was selling cars in Texas]; now it's just not good for me." Larry lives with his grandmother in subsidized housing on the "white" side of town. Though he had boldly asserted in 1985 that "I want to own a home. I don't ever want to use the term 'make ends meet,' " his dreams, at least for the moment, have not materialized. Vern, a popular student at Freeway High and president of his junior class, was involved in an embezzlement scandal. He refused to be interviewed, despite my numerous calls and letters, as well as his brother's intervention on my behalf.

Most striking is the fact that I was able to locate all but two of the white male students, and all of the white women. John knows Larry, and John works with Pete's uncle down the street at the automotive shop. Sam's uncle works with Ron's sister, and Steve, Ron's brother, is now in Texas. Suzanne's mom works with Lorna's mom in the restaurant down the street, and she put me in touch with both women. I frequented the local American Legion, bars, and donut shop (which looks, in this working-class community, like a bar)—all served as sites for locating former students. Cries would ring out: "Do you know where so and so is? She's lookin' for 'em." "Yeah, he's down working with Ed at the Deltasonic"; "She teaches down by Sam, at the high school"; "Check with her mom—she's up the street working with Joe"; or "Oh, yeah, you're lookin' for Jack—he's head of maintenance at the school now."

While the focus of *Class Reunion* is working-class whites, I originally interviewed ten students of color who will be the subject of later writing (this brings the number of those interviewed in 1985 to fifty-one: one woman of mixed-race international ancestry; one Puerto Rican man; three African American men; one Puerto Rican woman; and four African American women). When reconnecting with white students in 2000, I inquired as to the whereabouts of the above-mentioned students of color: significantly, no one knew where any of the students were. While these students are not the subject of this volume, it is noteworthy that white students do not hear about them, do not see them, do not talk about them.

My point here is the virtually complete separation of the racial communities fifteen years after high school, particularly in the case of African Americans and whites. From a space of school desegregation wherein African Americans, whites, and a relatively small number of Puerto Ricans and Yemenites attend school together, students return, as adults, to almost wholly segregated lives, with African Americans, in particular, on one side of town and whites on the other. Whites in Freeway and the surrounding environs do not know where their former African American classmates are—the very classmates who provided the foil against which their own subjectivities, in the case of men, evolved. Sharing space within the high school as a result of court-ordered "integration," white students, men in particular, used the space of racial togetherness to stake out intense difference. Years later, jobs (available or not), ways of obtaining work, and racially segregated neighborhoods led to the eventual excising of African Americans from the white landscape. For whites, African Americans with whom they attended high school fifteen years earlier simply do not exist. Clearly the racial category continues to exist in the white imagination, but individuals who attended school together fifteen years earlier no longer have anything to do with each other.

The situation is markedly different with respect to Yemenites. Recall that adolescent racism swirled around "Arabians" in high school as well around as African Americans, although it did not circulate around issues related to sexuality (much like Willis's lads' "Pakis") and was not nearly as widespread or intense. Although not offering a deep racial foil in the same way as African Americans did, Yemenites were nevertheless viewed as different, less than, and a group from which the "good" white must distance himself. By 2000, an appreciable number of Yemenites live on the "white" side of town, having moved there with money bought from hard work in corner delicatessens throughout the urban metropolitan area. Now the situation is different. People of color live in areas marked as "white"—but they are not the same people white adolescents feared in 1985. Yemenites are largely hardworking immigrants who bring their families to work the American Dream, and it is they, rather than African Americans, who constitute the current object of substantial racism in Freeway. African Americans, to be sure, are still disliked, and affirmative action and quotas are hated. But these are largely abstractions to Freeway men; the Yemenites are real, "driving Lexuses" and buying homes "next door to mom." The concrete day-to-day battle over "race" in Freeway is now constructed and fought over Arabs. African Americans are on television, particularly blasting in negative fashion across the six o'clock news (McCarthy, Rodriguez, Meecham, David, Wilson-Brown, Godina, Supriya, and Buendia, 1997), in the newspaper and in films, but they are not living in the neighborhood. Yemenites are, and Freeway men hate it. As Bill states, "They think their shit don't stink, you know what I mean?" In the mid-1980s Bill asserted, "Like my brother. He's in trouble all the time. Last year he got jumped in school. About his girlfriend. He don't like blacks. They come up to her and go, 'Nice ass,' and all that shit. My brother don't like that when they call her 'nice ass' and stuff like that. He got suspended for saying 'fucking nigger,' but it's all right for a black guy to go up to whites and say stuff like that ['nice ass']."

Bill is a former toll collector with the state thruway system, having been recently dismissed for "punching out" a coworker. His adolescent hatred of the embodied other of color—then African Americans—dumps easily onto Yemenites.

Changing Economies, Changing Gender

In this chapter and the next I probe varying ways in which white working-class men remake class and masculinity in the context of massive changes in the global economy, changes that most specifically target the former industrial proletariat. Data gathered at two points in time—during the men's third year of secondary school and again at the age of thirty or thirty-one in 2000–2001—enable me to interrogate the relation of macroeconomic and social relations to individual and group identities; to excavate the social psychological relations "between" genders and races, as narrated by white working-class men; and to explore the nuanced variations among these men. Here we see identities carved in relation, in solidarity, and in opposition to other marked groups and, most importantly, to what the economy "offers up" over time. It is in the push and pull of these men, both with hegemonic high school-valued masculine forms *and* the currency of such forms in the new economy, that we can begin to understand the remaking of the white working class as well as those individuals who are able to negotiate space and position outside of this class. Significantly, for white working-class males in the United States, struggles to assume symbolic dominance in an ever-fragile economy sit perched on the unsteady fulcrum of racial and gender hierarchy.

Stretching to situate themselves within the postindustrial world, young white working-class Freeway men take their individual and collective selves as forged in relation to the three primary definitional axes that are defining characteristics of their youth identity, as discussed fully in Chapter 1: (1) an emerging contradictory code of respect toward school knowledge and culture not in evidence in key previous studies of this group; (2) a set of virulently patriarchal constructions of home/family life which positions future wives in particular kinds of subordinate relationships; and (3) constructed notions of racial "others." Through careful engagement with data collected in 2000–2001, I suggest here that it is the ways in which individual white working-class men simultaneously position themselves and are positioned vis-à-vis these three major axes that determine, to some extent at least, both where they individually land fifteen years later *and* the broader contours of the new white working class. Tracing the push and pull of hegemonic cultural form as defined in high school, we meet four men who are emblematic of the larger group. In this chapter we are reacquainted with two of these men, who, it can be argued, have crossed the border between working class and middle class. In Chapter 4 we meet men who stretch into what can be called the new "settled" working class, as well as those whom I refer to as the "new hard livers."

Here we meet, as representatives of larger formations and struggles, Jerry and Bob, both of whom were in the "honors bubble" in high school, and thus already positioned outside of, to some extent at least, dominant white working-class male culture as described in Chapter 1. Jerry, a star athlete, lived mainly inside the honors group in school; Bob, on the other hand, did not. Bob, loving heavy metal bands, wearing their T-shirts, in continued fights, and getting stoned and drunk all the time when I first met him, exhibited a set of attitudes and behaviors which placed him squarely within the hegemonic working-class masculinity elaborated during the high school years of Freeway students. Virtually all of his friends were in the non-honors classes, leaving him little time or interest for his peers in the "honors bubble." Both men ultimately, however, distanced themselves both in thought and in action from normative male white working-class youth subjectivity—Jerry is now a middle school science teacher and Bob is completing his degree in veterinary medicine at what is arguably the most prestigious vet school in the country.

JERRY: I grew up in the Second Ward, which is a lower- middle-class neighborhood. I'd say maybe where I live now, it's middle-class.... My dad was definitely proud of me; he got to expect that of me and always congratulated me, and I think I made him very proud of me. All my siblings went to college. None of them ... scored as well academically. I'm a little bit more serious than the rest of them.... Yeah, it is weird that our close immediate five to ten group of people [not including Bob] that were in that advanced group together all had a lot of similar beliefs and goals and we all wanted to go to college, wanted to succeed. And that's the minority. If you look overall at that class [Freeway High, 1987], you wouldn't find as much success, but in that group, I don't know. We were all competitive with each other, and yet still friends.

LOIS: What do you think happened to some of the rest of the kids that were not in that [advanced] class?

JERRY: I don't know. Probably just went out to work wherever they found a job, and maybe they'd have high goals for themselves, but a lot of them are still living in Freeway.

LOIS: [Fifteen years ago] we talked about your parents, what kind of work they did. You said your mom is not educated past eighth grade. How does she talk about her work? Does she work now?

JERRY: No. She's retired also [like his dad]. She actually made envelopes. She worked full-time and then there were times when she worked part-time when the kids were really young. And I remember once for a few years, when I was very young, she worked on the night shift and she stayed home with the kids during the day. Then my dad came home and she went to work at night. I remember going with my dad to go pick her up late at night. How did she talk about it? I never once heard her say, "I hate my job." I never heard her say she loved her job. She never really talked about it a whole lot.... Except when she was happy when she brought a box of envelopes home that she got at work.

LOIS: You're describing [earlier he did so] your dad as a pretty traditional

Italian man. Sometimes those men are not real happy when their wives
work outside the home. How did that play out in your household?

JERRY: I never sensed that he might feel that. We needed ... with all the
kids [five kids] we needed two incomes in the family ... I don't know, it
was pretty, like I said, traditional, what I think of back to the 1950s, how
when my mom cooked, my dad expected a meal when he came home.
You look back now at how silly it was. But that's how they grew up, and
that's how it was.

LOIS: Can you describe a typical weekday in your house [now]?

JERRY: Typical weekday, yeah. From morning, getting up and coming to
school here, extra early, always having kids here before school. Giving,
really giving of what I have as I teach. I kind of work very hard until the
school day is over. Then I'm involved with extra- curricular activities,
whether it be running the fitness program after school, or when softball
season comes, coaching the teams, which involves practice every day.
But then, coming home and cooking dinner. I like to cook dinner ... I
do it more because I like to, and so she'll [his wife] do more of the
cleanup work, which I hate to do. So, we share that responsibility. And
then, whether it be working out or just relaxing watching TV or going to
a sporting event or coming back to school to watch a sporting event,
watch the kids play. ... So, that's a typical day. ... Weekend? Sundays
are pretty typical of going to mom's at one and having a big dinner and
staying there for a couple of hours. And then coming home, doing the
laundry, grocery shopping, and planning for the next school week. But
Saturdays are the ones that are changing. Usually we'll do more fun
things. That would be going to a movie or something.

A committed student in the honors class, Jerry went on to college,
where he "had a rough time," quickly realizing how poor his prepara-
tion for college had actually been at Freeway High—not surprising, in
light of the fact that Freeway is recognizably a low-performing district,
with only 20 percent of students being deemed proficient in English
and 16 percent being deemed proficient in math (*Metro News*, 2000,
October 13, p. 1). After a brief stint in banking and finding it dull,
Jerry went back to school to become a middle school science teacher,
which he loves. Jerry represents an early departure from dominant
white working-class masculine identity. Capable and pleasant, he is
now piecing together a solidly middle-class lifestyle, outside the
Freeway boundaries. No children yet; he and his wife are concentrating
on a newly acquired puppy. Eschewing traditionally working-class
union organizing, Jerry refuses to participate in the teachers' union,

preferring to come in at 7 A.M. and leave when his work is completed, often long after 6 P.M. When I interviewed him at the school, it was 5 P.M., and the teacher next door popped in to "make sure there was no trouble," fearing an unhappy parent, given the length of time I was there. Both teachers, who appear to be fast friends, were at the school that evening until long past 8 P.M. Stating that "unions served a purpose a long time ago," Jerry notes that "there are some people here [school] that live by the union contract—'Why are you here so early?' 'Why are you staying so late?'—and that turns me off."

Jerry had several things going for him that enabled him to stake out a nonhegemonic form of white working-class masculinity as far back as middle school. Although solidly in the white manual laboring working-class (he describes his neighborhood as "lower middle-class"), his parents worked to instill a strong work ethic in their children. This, though, is not enough to explain Jerry's class repositioning. Many, but certainly not all, of the Freeway parents had a strong work ethic tied to manual labor, and many in the 1980s desired that their children go on to school (Weis, 1990), asserting strongly that schooling is their only chance to secure an economic future. Jerry's break came when his measured intelligence (whatever that may mean, it can have serious consequences) placed him in the honors classes in middle school, classes which he and a number of his friends took seriously for the next six years. By his own admission, and that of most of the honors students whom I interviewed in the mid-1980s, he associated with only this group of students, the majority of them holding together as a group formed in relation to the nonhonors students. For the men, this provided the space to elaborate a form of masculinity forged centrally around academic achievement rather than physical prowess, sexism, and racism (which I suggested earlier was the valued and modal male subjectivity at Freeway High). This does not mean that Jerry did not have in mind marrying a girl like his mother, who could take care of him. Indeed, evidence suggests that he did have such a girl in mind, whom he dated throughout high school, and both he and his former girlfriend (whom I also interviewed and reinterviewed) attest to this. But, as he grew into his twenties, he moved off this point and now participates in family life in which he does a good portion of the domestic activity: he does all of the cooking, for example, something unheard-of in his father's generation, while she "cleans up." Ironically, the honors track encouraged the formation of a different kind of working-class masculinity, one that contrasts in important respects with that outlined in Chapter 1 as hegemonic within this class fraction, although the young men were not necessarily conscious of this at that time. Nevertheless, a substantial portion of these students socialized and learned only with one another over a six-year period, beginning in grade seven, when intense academic sorting took hold for these students. Young men could thus stand squarely on the space of a somewhat different kind of masculinity, and virtually every one of them, save two, did so in the mid-1980s, although it must be remembered that this involved only ten to twelve boys out of a high school class of over three hundred.

Significantly, the honors bubble had no African American or Puerto Rican students (unlike the broader school), and only two students of color—one Yemenite male and one female of mixed-race international ancestry—in spite of the much larger representation of students of color in the school as a whole. Thus, core masculine culture in the honors track was *not* formed in relation to people of color, women who were positioned as less than in precisely the same way as occurred in the larger class cultural configuration (although there were certainly elements of desired male dominant families inside the imagination of honors track boys in the mid 1980s, they, by and large viewed the honors track girls as "smarter," "more serious," "more future oriented," than non-honors girls), *or* the contradictory code of respect outlined earlier. Rather, like the men from professional families whom R. W. Connell talks about (1993, 1995), dominant masculinity in this tiny segment of the working class was etched more significantly around academics, offering an alternative to the blasting hegemonic masculinity that permeated the 1980s white youth in Freeway as well as being ensconced in existing broader class cultural relations. Jerry's hard work, parental support, connection to athletics, winning personality, and sheer smarts allowed him to move out of the class space into which he was born. Now that he is married to a young woman from an affluent suburban family, Jerry's class background is largely invisible. As he notes in 2000, "I can give my kids [when born] more of everything now. Plus more traveling experiences, which I never really did as a kid. I can give them more luxury items ... vacations and better sporting equipment, for example, things like that."

Bob, in contrast to Jerry, was positioned differently in relation to high school hegemonic masculinity. Although an honors student by virtue of his measured intelligence, he was most certainly one of the "bad boys," listening to heavy metal music, participating only minimally in school-based knowledge, culture, and activities, and coming to school stoned as often as did many of his non-honors soul mates.

Having a pregnant girlfriend at the age of seventeen, Bob married her, and appeared to be living out a form of new working-classness that would deposit him into a highly marginal economic existence. However, as these things go, events shot changes through his life and he began his long move toward the completion of a highly valued veterinary degree. Soon to graduate from one of the most prestigious vet schools in the world, Bob embraced, over the years, a wholly new form of masculinity, one intimately connected to academics rather than the anti-school animus so characteristic of white working-class men. His high school years, although spent in the same classes as Jerry, smack of prior white working-class hegemonic masculine form. In 1985, for example, Bob states: "Mr. Strong is an asshole. He just starts acting like God or something.... He's got a negative attitude toward me and my friends maybe cuz of the way we dress.... I hate these guys."

Even so, Bob admitted in 1985 that school had some value, reflecting the contradictory code of respect toward school knowledge and culture embedded in the emerging white male working-class modal cultural form.

LOIS: Why is everyone into college these days? Your dad didn't go to college.
BOB: Money [laughter]. And something to do. [You can stop at high school] if you want to be a nobody. Like, if somebody wants to work at Burger King the rest of their life, they can do it, no problem with me, but I don't want to work at B.K. the rest of my life.... I want to be my own boss eventually.

In 2000, Bob reflects on his high school years and subsequent experiences.

BOB: I grew up.... I liked playing sports. I liked hanging out with my friends.... I didn't ... I didn't play on any of the high school teams. I just kind of hung out with my friends, playing around with them. I liked to party....

I have two boys that live in North Centreville. My mom lives, I don't know, half a mile or a mile from where I lived when I grew up. So I do get back into the area. She lives in ... actually lives in South Centreville. Just like down by Torcivia Cheese. I get back there. I don't really hang around Freeway at all. We rode around in the streets with my friends in high school making fools of ourself ... [laughs]....
LOIS: Here's a picture of you in high school. Can you describe yourself to

me at that time? What kind of person were you? What memories are evoked by this picture?

BOB: I remember being a wise-ass . . . [laughs]. . . . It doesn't evoke memories so much. I remember sitting in Joe Danville's garage. One of my biggest, stupidest memories is that . . . we had . . . we got a beer ball and we had a tap that his father had used on propane, so we were drinking beer that had rainbow propane floating out of it . . . [laughs] . . . I also remember in my senior year, that math was the only class I've ever failed.

LOIS: But yet you were in this sort of advanced section. So how did you get in there?

BOB: I don't know . . . [laughs] . . . I wouldn't have admitted it in this picture. School was important to me. I always wanted to be an intelligent person. Yeah, because I felt that some members of my family weren't. And I can tell that that held them back. And I didn't want to be held back. I don't know if it's because they weren't intelligent, or because just of the . . . the deal . . . the cards they got dealt in life, you know.

LOIS: Like who, for example?

BOB: My dad. . . . Well, he wound up actually being a negative role model for me. I wanted to be the opposite of what he was. He's had a lot of different part-time jobs. He worked for Towne's . . . [Vending] . . . Company for a while. He worked for Service Systems, which is another vending company. He was a home health care assistant for a while. Now, he's . . . my mother and him recently divorced, and now he's living off Social Security or, I don't know what he's getting. I haven't talked to him in a couple of years. . . . He quit school, which was . . . that was the biggest thing that I never wanted to do. You know, I never wanted to quit school. That's probably why I'm still in school. He quit. Halfway through his senior year he quit. Which I thought was really stupid. . . . And he never worked in a plant. Which surprised me, because if I was him, I would have worked in the [steel] plant at that time, when it was booming. I don't know why he quit. I think . . . his story was he quit to help support his family. My mom's story was he quit because he was failing and didn't want to put any effort into it.

LOIS: You called yourself a "head" [in the 1980s], and you were interested in heavy metal is what you told me. Can you talk to me about your closest friends in high school?

BOB: Tom, I would describe as my equal. I mean, you know we're in the same class, same groups, and everything. Matt and Frank, they were more into the . . . like the auto shop and vocational, which is fine.

Nothing wrong with that. As far as our time together, we listened to music a lot. Just really . . . in Freeway, you know, you sit in front of the . . . [convenience] . . . on South End, and you play your music as loud as you can until the cops come. My friend Jay O'Rory, who didn't go to Freeway, he's . . . he's a machinist tech. He's living down in Florida now. But him and I would really just walk around, I mean, just hang out. Go play video games at the corner store, smoke cigarettes, didn't have that glamorous of a life, now that I look back at it, but it was fun. . . . I haven't seen Dan or Matt or any of those guys, because I don't know where they are or what's become of them.

LOIS: Right after high school, you went into the Army. . . .

BOB: Yeah, I went in the Army . . . I started off in Fort Benning, Georgia, did my basic training and advanced training there. And then went to Fort Polk, Louisiana. And from there went to Korea for nineteen months. It was supposed to be twelve months, but that's when Desert Storm was going, so everyone got stuck wherever they were. And they decided that January 1, 1990, was going to be the date that if you left anywhere after, then you couldn't move. January 3rd I was supposed to leave Korea. I got stuck for an extra seven months. . . . I was married at the time, and that was—for a plethora of reasons, not the least of which was the fact that she [my wife] got pregnant by somebody else while I was in Korea—was going downhill. . . . There was no engagement in Korea, but for three months . . . if you do three-month tours in the DMZ [Demilitarized Zone], and that's as close to real combat as you'll ever get without firing a bullet; we were patrolling back and forth, and you can see the North Koreans right on the other side of the line. We did a lot of . . . a lot of training, a lot of direct fire—mortar, man, which is kind of like the smaller version of artillery. A lot of training, a lot of blowing things up, a lot of just learning basically how to kill people if the time came. At the time I hated it. Oh, God, I hated being there, because it was just total culture shock, and I never got used to the country or anything like that. But it was the best experience . . . and actually, if I put any one person as straightening me out . . . it would have been my platoon sergeant in Korea. Sergeant James. He was insane. But he got me straightened out. . . . He was hard-core. You know, he was the epitome of discipline, the epitome of, you know, "Be the best you can possibly be in everything you can ever do." And that's what got me . . . I think got . . . part of what got me to come here [vet school]. That's what's keeping me here, because this [vet] program is nuts . . . [laughs]. . . . That's what's keeping me afloat. You know, it's just that I know that I can do this. I know that I can get through it if I put a hundred and fifty percent of myself into it.

LOIS: So you were nineteen months in Korea, never particularly liked it, but really got yourself turned around. . . .

BOB: And actually, some of the best people I knew were in Korea. Because you made pretty tight bonds with people. . . . When I joined the Army, I joined while I was still in high school. I went into the late entry program. While I was still in high school, I was in the military. I wasn't doing anything. My name was on the line and I was going [into the military], no matter what. Basically, coming out of high school, I just thought I was going to be Rambo, you know . . . an M-16 machine gun with a belt of rounds across my chest just like Rambo. I think I thought that the whole killing idea was cool in some convoluted sense. I think it was . . . it was just the . . . the macho and the tough guy thing.

Bob moved from his working-class roots by means of a long struggle that cut through a marriage when he was seventeen, the birth of two children, a tour of duty in Korea, his wife's ectopic pregnancy by another man when he was overseas, his fantasy of killing her, the expressed recognition that his colleagues in the service are "dumb," and a long climb through undergraduate school, which he started at the age of twenty-three, to his current position as a third-year vet student. A smart young man, Bob nevertheless elaborated hegemonic white working-class masculinity when he was in high school, doing little other than listening to heavy metal music, getting drunk and stoned continuously, hiding his intelligence, and participating minimally in school knowledge and culture. Having impregnated his high school girlfriend at the age of seventeen, he married her; he later divorced her when he found out that she had become pregnant by another man while he was in Korea. Acting on his self-proclaimed Rambo-styled masculinity, Bob joined the Army, imagining himself with an "M-16 machine gun with a belt of rounds" strapped about him as he stormed through the jungle, blasting the enemy. Moving from this space through real encounters with men in the service, which proved to be far less glamorous than he had imagined, Bob began the slow climb toward his current status and an enacted masculinity formed in relation to continued academic engagement and achievement. Plunging from one university experience to another as he racks up degrees, Bob is now poised to join a vet practice in Maine. His current wife, "a super-intelligent woman" who has a master's degree in biology, is now working on a Ph.D.; he met her online discussing research, and she is far removed from the mother of his two children. His ex-wife remains in Freeway, waiting tables on a part-time basis at the local diner. Cashing in his "bad boy" hegemonically based masculine persona over a period of fifteen years, Bob breaks the class ceiling, leaving, by his own admission, his old friends behind

Working against and with the image of his father—a ne'er-do-well who had little relationship with his son—Bob never wants to "stagnate." Living in a church-owned house rented for a small sum of money to an obviously poor family, Bob's mother augmented the family income, which could never be counted on, by taking in one foster child after another. As he said in 1985, "We take in foster babies plus my father works in a warehouse. This is our thirty or thirty-first [foster baby]. I think he [my father] just stamps cigarettes and stocks boxes."

Working at Home Depot after marrying his pregnant seventeen-year-old girlfriend, earning the minimum wage, and eventually entering the service, it looked as if the trajectory of Bob's life was to be like his father's, in that he would play off of and live out deeply rooted and well articulated hegemonic working-class masculine forms as they deposit in the early twenty-first century economy. Ironically, the traditionally hypermasculine site of the Army interrupted this, offering the space within which his marriage was to be brutally severed. He was mentored by his platoon sergeant, and ultimately he found God, which he sees as a life-changing experience. Now desirous of a male–female relationship in which he takes seriously his role as protector, he claims that his wife, although highly educated and the daughter of a university faculty member, would like to bake pies, make quilts, and ultimately "open a Christian bookstore." Whether or not his wife would agree with this is open to debate, but in many ways it is unimportant in terms of the current discussion. Bob has been catapulted or has catapulted himself across whatever class border may exist for a man from his social class background. Whatever fantasies Bob may or may not have about his wife's future pie-making activity, the fact is that his wife, born into a professional family, is highly educated, possesses a research-based master's degree and is working toward a Ph.D. in the sciences, and has a wage-earning job. And, by Bob's own admission, they share on a day-to-day basis all household tasks, totally unlike his family of origin. He is, in fact, almost completely responsible for his two teenage sons when they come to visit, which is often (the entire summer and two weekends per month, in spite of the fact that he lives three hours from them). Bob has moved far from his high school enactment of working-class core white male masculinity. He, like Jerry, sits in a new space within the economy, one very different from that occupied by their parents and substantially different from that of the vast majority of their high school peers. Significantly, both men are physically distanced from Freeway; both metaphorically and actually crossed the bridge that links working-class Freeway with the wider society.

4

AND THE BEAT GOES ON
Those Men Who Stay

In the last chapter we met men who were catapulted *across* the border of the newly articulated white working class, entering, by virtue of job- and family/home-based cultural practices, class terrain notably unfamiliar to them. In this sense, they exhibit and enact a middle-class habitus, one which distinguishes them both from their family of origin and from the "hard" and "settled" livers discussed in this chapter. Of all the men reinterviewed in 2000–2001, only Jerry and Bob clearly fit the profile of the "border" crosser, and while I did not track the entire class of 1987, we can assume that the number of such men is quite small.[1] Here we meet those men who stayed—whether in Freeway itself or in a somewhat upscale but distinctly working-class white suburb outside of Freeway or a comparable city in another state. These men are far more numerous, ultimately embodying and projecting the contours of the new American white working class, a class which can be understood only through careful attention to issues which swirl around masculinity, whiteness, and the new economy. Masculinity, in particular, serves as a linchpin around which the contours of the re-configured white working class can be best understood.

Work on masculinities has become increasingly popular in the late twentieth century and into the twenty-first century (Kimmel, 1996; Jackson, 2002; Mac an Ghaill, 1994) and, as Connell notes, there has been a "great flowering of empirical research on masculinities" (2000, p. 24). Central to this work, according to Jackson, are four tenets: "1) masculine identities are historically and culturally situated, 2) multiple masculinities exist, 3) there are dominant hegemonic and subordinate forms of masculinities, and 4) masculinities are actively constructed in social settings" (pp. 39–40). As Kenway and Fitzclarence (1997) argue, "Hegemonic masculinity is the standard-bearer of what it means to be a 'real' man or boy and many males draw inspiration from its cultural library of resources" (pp. 119–120, as cited in Jackson, 2000, p. 40). Jackson further states:

> Hegemonic masculinities are located in a structure of gender/sexual power relations, and within these, boys define their identities against the Other (Epstein, 1998). Gay masculinities feature in the "Other" category as does an attachment to "the feminine" (Kenway and Fitzclarence). Evidence suggests (see for example Epstein, 1998) that undertaking academic work is perceived by young people as "feminine" and therefore, if boys want to avoid the verbal and physical "abuse" attached to being labeled as "feminine" or "queer," they must avoid academic work or at least they must appear to avoid academic work (academic achievement itself is not necessarily a problem for boys, but being seen to work is a problem). (Jackson, 2000, pp. 39–40)

The young men I worked with in the mid-1980s were no exception here, although little overtly oppositional behavior was lodged against school knowledge and culture, unlike the case in previous investigations of this population (Everhart, 1983; Willis, 1977). Nevertheless, while the young Freeway boys exhibited an emerging contradictory attitude toward schooling and school culture (in other words, they think they "need it"), they embraced only the form of such knowledge and culture rather than its substance. Young men who embraced the valued masculine form in the mid-1980s did little to no school-based work, either in school or out, just enough to "get by" or "pass." This, paralleled with deep assertions of both white and male superiority in relation to a constructed "other" (all women, Yemenites, African American males, and gay men in particular) were defining characteristics of hegemonic masculine form in this white working-class community and school. Paul Willis, whose work on the "lads" is legendary, offers the following:

> It is important to appreciate that the anti-mental animus of the counter-school culture, while highly relevant in opposing and penetrating the demands of the school, also continues to orient and help direct the attitudes of "the lads"—like a soldier's courage in the absence of war—long after the transition and across the board.

This "locking" impels them toward a certain kind of culturally mediated experiential set of meanings throughout their lives. There will certainly be future situations in which these attitudes and practices produce worthwhile "payoffs," but the danger is that the whole world might henceforth be divided into two—the mental and the manual. (2000, p. 42)

Drawing upon his well-known notion of cross-valorization, Willis notes "a further twist":

The anti-mentalism and masculinity of the lads become intertwined, fused, in their sense of themselves. A manual way of acting in the world is also a manly way; a mental way is effeminate. These two things reinforce and lock each other into, if you like, "a market masculinity" on the one hand and a "patriarchal manualism" on the other—mutually producing a locking of dispositions and sensibility, which may quite literally last a lifetime. (2000, p. 44)

Whether the "locking" of masculinity and anti-mentalism lasts a lifetime or not is, of course, an empirical question, one which is directly relevant here. While not designed explicitly as a study in masculinity per se, recent scholarship informs my work in key ways. Given kaleidoscopic changes in the global economy, changes which hit the former industrial proletariat the hardest (read, largely white men), the remaking of the class is tied in key and critical ways to issues which swirl fundamentally around masculinity, as well as the wages of whiteness and a remaking of the feminine. Like the "missing postman," a man who wanders about, continuing to deliver one last letter before being laid off, "many men can only see loss ahead of them and cannot face what feels like a loss of manhood and feminization, or, what Cohen and Ainley (2000, p. 83) call the loss of 'musculatures of the labouring body' " (Walkerdine, Lucey, & Melody, 2001). It is within this context that I saw and heard the Freeway youth with whom I worked in the 1980s, grow up.

Here, for illustrative purposes, we meet two men who stayed in Freeway or the immediately adjoining working-class suburb. Emblematic of the majority of white Freeway men of this age cohort, they work in what might be thought of as an assemblage of both "new" and traditional working-class jobs: paralegal, electrician, warehouse worker, highway tollbooth collector, foreman of the high school maintenance department, hospital technician, credit card collector, pizza supplies delivery man, worker at a muffler shop, among others. Some of these men, those who remain closest to normative white working-class masculinity as constructed in high school, fall more centrally in the "hard living" category flagged by investigators several decades ago (Howell, 1973). Others, those who tended to move off the space of hegemonically constructed white masculinity, fare better, establishing for themselves more "stable" or, to use Howell's term, "settled" lives. Significantly, it is the movement *off* the space of white working-class hegemonic masculinity—that masculinity which emerged in relation to the old industrial economy—that now encourages this stability, since more "settled" jobs tend to be those associated with schooling (read, feminine in hegemonic parlance) and those traditionally coded as feminine (such as nurse, paralegal, hospital technician). Such jobs also demand, to a great extent, a partner who earns roughly comparable money if one wishes an economically nonmarginal lifestyle under terms generally offered to children of the former industrial proletariat in the new economy.

In addition, under this scenario, child rearing requires the ongoing time and attention of both parents, since both men and women are working full-time in the paid labor force and, generally speaking, working-class families both cannot afford day care and simultaneously do not trust it, feeling that the children should be reared in the home, "not by some stranger" (Zinsser, 1991; Riley & Glass, 2002). It is arguably the case that this is reflective of the type of paid child care available in working-class communities as well as the fact that working-class women have staked out child rearing as something that is both their responsibility and that they "do well"—claiming it as their own gender-bounded creative space (Zinsser, 1991). Under the current economy, and assuming that child rearing is still largely lodged in the home (even if it is not, the same point holds for day care arrangements), such child care must be patched together and carved out of the nonpaid labor time of both parents, including who drops the children off at school, tends to younger children in the home, picks them up at grandma's, takes them to after-school hockey (a very popular luxury, particularly for male children in cold climate working-class communities), and so forth, depending on the age of the children. Stay-at-home mothers can no longer be counted upon to perform all of this unpaid labor. Thus the carefully imagined rendition of a wife's future domesticity as lodged in high school white working-class hegemonic masculinity and outlined in Chapter 1 *must* be held in check at some point and re-articulated in action if "settled" working-class lives are to be attained under the restructured economy.

This is equally true, of course, for middle-class and even upper-middle-class masculinities, as increasingly such class lifestyles demand two-income families and comparable negotiation around child care. Yet, child care in working-class families is still fundamentally and distinctly lodged in the home, making such child care arrangements necessarily and obviously tied to a specific dissolution of former gender dynamics in the family. Certainly upper-middle-class men pick their children up from nursery school and may have carefully negotiated home-based responsibilities in relation to the family (laundry, shared cooking, and so forth). In contrast, many white working-class men now take an eight-hour home-based shift during which time their partners work outside of the home and they are wholly responsible for feeding, clothing, and watching the children. Not insignificantly, male and female family members often join forces to make this all happen (a wife's brother may take a home shift, for example, caring for the children of two families while she, her sister-in-law, and her brother-in-law are out earning money; the next shift may belong to the wife or his sister).

At the heart of the remaking of the white working class lies the reconstruction of male/female relations and, most important in light of young men's high school desires, the re-articulation of appropriate and valued adult working-class masculinity. It is, though, not simply the *verbal* rearticulation of masculinity that is at issue here, since virtually all of the men interviewed *verbally* express a desired form of gender roles and relations that are wholly different from those expressed as desired in high school. No man reinterviewed in 2000–2001 suggests the gender regime he envisioned in 1985 as one that he currently values. The important question here is the extent to which these men actually *live* gendered relations that enable a "settled" new working-class lifestyle. Those who are unable to live and accomplish gender as a set of relations vastly different from those of their parents and grandparents are the new "hard livers" in a restructured world economy which hits the former industrial laboring class in particular kinds of ways (Reich, 1991, 2001). A related question is what men think of the ways in which gender must be reconfigured if "settled" lives are to be enacted, a question to which I return in Chapter 5.

Women, and even some men, tend to conceptualize this lived rearticulation of gender as a giving up (or not) of "the partying kind of life."

In other words, those who are seen as being able to "settle down," much the same way Lilian Rubin's respondents offered in her classic *Worlds of Pain* (1976) are seen as those for whom the new economy will work, paralleling Howell's original notion of "hard" versus "settled" livers. What I am suggesting is far more complex, though, than the giving up or not of the "partying life"; rather, "settled living" is now fundamentally bound to lived rearticulations of gendered forms and the ways in which such forms enable what becomes a stable and valued working-class existence. Ironically, then, gender is, once again, the fulcrum upon which forms of working-class life balance, but in wholly new ways than enacted under the old industrial economy. It is those men who are willing and able to transgress the constructed working-class gender categories and valued masculinity of their high school youth for whom the new economy can produce "settled lives." It is, in point of fact, *only* those men who engage in school, coded as compliant and feminine under terms of working-class white hegemonic masculinity (Jackson, 2002; Connell, 1989; Reay, 2002; Martino, 1999; Willis, 2000; Arnot, 2004; Mac an Ghaill, 1991, 1994; Martino & Meyenn, 2001), and enter into and maintain partnerships/marriages with individuals who earn as much money as they do, if not more, who can be other than "hard living" in this newly minted class fraction.

In this latter regard, a domestic partner need not necessarily be a lover—one of the Freeway men has formed a working domestic liaison with his sister, for example, and they live together, pooling human and economic resources to raise their children, ages three (his, to whom he is devoted and whom he sees constantly although the boy lives primarily with his former girlfriend) and nine (hers; her boyfriend left her before the child was born, and he has no contact with their daughter). My point here is that the thorough colonization of the public sphere by men, as well as men's imagined total domination of women in the home/family sphere as envisioned by Freeway working-class boys in the mid-1980s, must be thoroughly reworked if men are to be among the "settled" new white working class. The "settled/hard living" binary as pitched by Joseph Howell (1973) and others still offers great explanatory power, then. Like gender itself, however, the binary has been destabilized and must be reimagined under the new economy.

Under conditions of a place-bound industrial economy and the hard-won accompanying capital–labor accord, the male family wage could, at least in principle, support and maintain "settled" family life. If nothing else, men and women could imagine and behave in terms of the possibility of family life linked to male earning power wherein men could obtain the secret guarantees of earning the family wage: "sacrifice–reward–dignity" (Willis, 2000, p. 93). Embedded in this past is the fact that women had few options in the paid labor force, a situation which is markedly different today. Neither the available "family wage" for men nor the relative lack of paid work for women characterizes today's economy, and not a single man whom I interviewed in the early 2000s suggests that it does. Some men, however, behave as "new" or radically altered working-class men, irrespective of their private thoughts, thus transgressing gendered borders articulated in previous generations, while others do not. Those who do not, may or may not have additional deeply rooted problems, such as alcoholism, drugging, and so forth, which may or may not lie at the heart of their inability to enact a necessary new masculinity. Those who enact this reformatted masculinity may also have problems with drinking and drugs. Nevertheless, their lived and reformulated masculinity at this moment in time, irrespective of such problems, allows them to purchase a home, raise their children, earn part of a living family wage, purchase a car, buy hockey skates for their sons, and even have extra money with which they can add an outdoor deck to their home by doing the manual labor themselves, with help from their similarly positioned new white working-class buddies—buddies who have the manual skills embedded in the habitus of the old working class (carpentry, electrical wiring, house painting, and so forth).

All of this, however, is dependent upon having a partner with whom one can merge money—a partner with whom one also shares the day-to-day, minute-by-minute work of parenting following the birth of children. Without this duality of male/female public-sphere-generated income as well as work around the domestic sphere, the "settled" life with its potentially accompanying and valued (partially class-coded) material and social goods—including homes, NASCAR tickets (auto racing), fireplaces, barbecue pits, wet bars, dirt bikes, cabins for hunting, professional football and hockey tickets, and so forth—simply could not be accomplished.[2] The "settled livers"—those men who are able to stake out stability in the newly forged white working class—thus challenge, through their day-to-day lives, traditional gendered boundaries and definitions deeply etched in prior working-class hegemonic masculinity and working-class family life more generally, as well articulated by the young men in the mid-1980s when I first met them.

In line with the new economy, the particular job a man engages in will, in all likelihood, change over time—men enter the workforce as individual wage laborers, making and re-making themselves, to some extent at least, much as they did before, although the nature of the available jobs, as well as wages and benefits guaranteed by such jobs, have obviously changed. Ironically, it is now the collective formed in relation to *family* life that enables this all to "work" rather than the collective formed in relation to the work space, as was the case under the industrial economy, where male collective culture served both to offer necessary dignity *and* simultaneously to constitute a space of struggle for increased wages/benefits and a safer working environment. The work-based collective (shop-floor culture and so forth) which formerly enabled a better standard of living has thus been replaced by a necessary (and more stable, in many cases, than that of the work-place, in spite of divorces) home-based collective—one which now serves the function of bringing money into the household as both men and women negotiate the economy *as individuals* (neoliberal subjects) who must fashion themselves to "fit" its changing needs.[3] With a great twist, then, the locking of masculinity and manualism in this class fraction renders the old-style "winners" not only superfluous in the new economy but also unable to produce the family-based collective necessary to secure status within the new white working class.

This does not mean that all is well with gendered relations in the family and community, a point which I explore at great length in the next chapter. What it does mean, though, is that in the traditional white working class, hegemonically forged masculinity offers a linchpin around which individual men with whom I worked in the mid-1980s swirl as they grow into adulthood. Thus the located 1980s cultural form of masculinity, one tied in specific ways to the industrial economy, offers a point of departure as men move forward in a wholly restructured world economy. It is in the movement forward—the nature of departure and/or stability *in relation* to the original form, rather than the original form per se—that we can see a template for future lives. This set of departures/stability must, though, be theorized in relation to what the economy has to offer men and women in the late twentieth century and into the twenty-first. It is, then, the collective youth cultural form (here the hegemonic form of masculinity which many others have noted as well) and later individual movement *in relation to this form* (one forged dialectically in relation to the old industrial economy and the gender-based bargains within this old economy for the working class) that offer powerful material as we work to understand the world of the new white working class. More important, of course, this all sits underneath and in relation to massive realignment of the global economy, which touched off this entire set of negotiations to begin with, as well as tighter and more clearly articulated sorting mechanisms related to formal schooling. Given that formal schooling in this class fraction is traditionally coded as feminine, this speaks volumes about the gendered fulcrum upon which so much of the remaking of the white working class rests.

Clint and John, whom we meet in this chapter, are emblematic of the split detailed above. Unlike men such as those in the last chapter, both remained in or immediately around the Freeway environs, and it is arguably the case that both are part of the "new" white working class, a class descended from the traditional proletariat but no longer embodying its features. Clint is currently a "hard liver" and John is not. Although they were very similar in high school in terms of their attitudes toward school, school-based behavior, academic track location, daily activities, and expressed masculinity, John now lives a new masculine form, one which enables/promotes both the shared form of a family living wage and the accomplishment of child rearing. Clint, in contrast, embodies the opposite. While giving lip service to a desire for women to work outside the home (in contradiction with what he said in high school), and seeing himself as thoroughly on board with respect to new gendered locations and relations, Clint does not, in fact, live his verbally expressed new masculine form at all.

In 1985, John's father asked: "Wouldn't you rather have people waiting on you? Go to school and get an education. Learn a trade or something so [you] won't have to do that [pick up dishes] for the rest of [your] life." John's dad never finished high school; he wanted his son to go on. As John said to me at the time, "You can't be doing nothing much around here. All steel is closing. Downtown's starting to fade" (1985).

In 2000, I spent a long evening in his home, with family activity in high motion as we talked:

JOHN: I own this home. My sister-in-law actually lives upstairs. Last year, my wife worked full-time. So we needed a baby-sitter. And she [sister-in-law] was living rent-free, but she's baby-sitting for us. That's as much as you're going to pay for day care. Sam's in school, so now we don't need a baby-sitter. . . .

I'm an O.R. [operating room] tech. I work at St. Paul's Hospital in surgery. I set up cases—cases as in surgery. And assist the doctors, and then when we're done, you clean up. Yesterday I was in a craniotomy from eleven until six. And okay, it's five-thirty, I'll go to lunch now. Or like, when we do total joint, do a total knee replacement, or a total hip replacement, and there are people that have been working there for twenty years that don't know how to do those. When I started, I was ambitious, I guess. I mean, I would be bored just doing little piddley stuff all day long, you know. That's the downside of it, is that I'm always busy.

LOIS: And how about your wife? What does she do?

JOHN: My wife is an ultrasound technologist at St. Paul's also. She started working . . . actually, I found out that there was an opening, and I told her about it. She got the job. I used to work with her other sister, her eldest sister. I used to work with her. Ultrasound is part of X-ray. . . . [When I got out of high school] I joined the Air Force. I was in the Air Force for about three years, and I did this in the Air Force. . . . I was on the one hospital with the one doctor. So I went back to school at Midway [a local two-year school] to broaden my base. My brother-in-law's trying to get me into GM [General Motors]. Hopefully around Thanksgiving, I'll know what my chances are. It'll be a skilled trade, which I'll start off making seven dollars more an hour. I mean, I like what I do; I'm good at what I do: I don't get paid . . . what I'm worth. You know, especially the way I get abused every day. You know, there's six, seven people sitting around doing nothing. And I just get done with this big case, and "Okay, John, go do this now. And John, can you stay later? John, can you come in earlier?" It's not worth it. . . .

I'm really underpaid. I mean, when I help this doctor, he's going to make, you know, they earn their money from all the training and the years and years and years they had to do this stuff. I understand that. I mean, the nurse's making, you know, twenty, twenty-four dollars an hour. She's sitting on her ass. She didn't check the case. She didn't set up the case. She opens it up and sits down. She preps the patient. I understand that. And then, she does nothing until the case is over unless I tell her to give me something. She makes twenty-four dollars an hour and I'm making fourteen dollars an hour. . . . If I get into GM, I'm hoping that my wife can go part-time. I can only work so much, you know, so she went full-time. Yeah, she wants a car . . . and I got my little car out front.

LOIS: Is it fair to say it's been tough financially?

JOHN: Well, I can't say that, because I've been a lot worse off. You know, when my parents first got divorced [when he was fourteen], living with my mom, I mean, she couldn't do for me what I can do for my kids now. I started working when I was fourteen years old so I could buy my school clothes, so I could get a new pair of sneakers. These kids don't have to worry about that. We just spent three hundred dollars on Tom, on his hockey. And then it's like another hundred and fifty so he can join this league he's in now. You know, that's expensive. But, whatever.

LOIS: Can you describe a typical weekday in your house? Like, you get up in the morning. . . .

JOHN: You know, Sue gets up about six; gets in the shower. She gets up, wakes up Tom [thirteen-year-old stepson]. Tom gets in the shower. Me and Sam [son, age five] get up at seven. And Sam will watch *Pokemon* until seven-thirty. By that time, Sue's gone and Tom is gone. I make him [Tom] lunch, and they go. You know, Tom catches his bus at seven-thirty. Sue has to be at the hospital at seven-thirty. And then I'm with Sam, you know, feed him, get him dressed, brush his teeth, make him lunch, go sit out on the porch at eight o'clock, wait for the bus. Then I come back after he goes on the bus. I come back and then I'll shower, and, you know, make the beds and eat something, make myself lunch, do the dishes; basically clean up the house before I go to work. And I get home at six o'clock, you know. If there is no real dinner made, I'll just scrounge around for whatever. And Tuesdays and Thursdays, Sue's at the gym working out. She belongs to Jack [Jack's Gym]. I find something to eat. And then, you know, do what needs to be done, got to do laundry; I mean, clean up the house, give him [Sam] a bath, whatever. When it's summertime, cut the grass, go outside, screw around with the kids for a couple hours, you know. Depends on what's going on. I have to go out and do whatever.

LOIS: Were you raised in one of those homes where the dad kind of expected. . . .

JOHN: [He interrupts me] The dinner every night? Yeah, that's what it was. My mom never worked up until my dad got laid off. You know, my mom stayed home and cooked and cleaned or did the laundry. Ironed the clothes and made dinner every night; yeah.

John had some hard years; when he was in high school, he lived in a now condemned building after his parents were divorced. Soon after the divorce, his seventeen-year-old sister became pregnant and lived with them until the baby was born. Having worked at a pizzeria below his apartment throughout his teenage years, John had no illusions about what the future holds. He told me fifteen years ago that "College prep is the only thing to do. Well, around here, 'cause there's nothing else. Everything's going down south. Like any kind of good jobs, a better education's what you're gonna hafta need unless you plan to sweep the floors someplace the rest of your life. And that ain't really gonna be my style."

Most of the fifteen- or sixteen-year-old Freeway boys expressed similar notions about the value of schooling when I knew them in the mid-1980s. They did not, though, act upon this new valuation at the time; most did virtually nothing in high school except "get by" through minimal studying and copying each other's homework, engaging in the most low-level form of education but certainly not in its substance. What this did mean, though, is that for the moment the overt and boisterous opposition to school noted by previous investigators of this group was not apparent in Freeway. This split valuation of school, then, emerged sharply during high school years and was a core element of valued white working-class masculinity in the 1980s. In this sense, white working-class young men mirror what we find in many studies of African Americans, wherein schooling is valued and not valued at one and the same time (Ogbu, 1974, 2002). White working-class youth in high school at least verbally valued schooling for what they thought it could get them: they valued what they saw as its instrumentality. They did not, though, *act* on the positive end of this set of assessments, except insofar as their passivity prevented *active* disruption of the teaching-learning process. In fact, most participated in the bare form of schooling, never engaging its substance.

As a young adult, John is among the new "settled living" working class. He owns his home, and has one son and one stepson, mirroring the re-combined family form discussed by Judith Stacey (1990). He no longer lives in Freeway, but in a white working-class suburb immediately adjacent to Freeway, having bought a home four blocks from the Freeway border, a home that puts his children in a different and somewhat better set of schools. As we see, though, his stable or "settled" new working-class existence, which he values highly, is wholly dependent upon his breaking away from the hegemonically constructed white working-class masculinity of his youth. He went into the service, gained some skills, and, upon leaving the Air Force, immediately went to a two-year college for an associate's degree, engaging finally in the substance side of the form/substance split with respect to education, which neither he nor the vast majority of white working-class male youth did while they were in high school. In this sense, he crossed over what Willis calls the "anti-mental animus" embedded within white working-class masculinity, reaching over the mental/manual split as it cross-valorizes the feminine/masculine. Here it is significant that John is in what might be seen as a traditionally female field—hospital technician—although he carefully differentiates himself discursively from the female-coded nursing arena and resents the nurses for the $10 more per hour that they earn. Although skilled, he earns only $14 an hour, substantially less—in his mind, at least—than he could earn at General Motors. His settled life is now wholly dependent on his own job coupled with that of his wife (ultrasound technologist). It can be assumed that she earns approximately the same money as he does, or perhaps more, having earned an associate's degree the same year he did, from the same college.

Most noteworthy are John's responses to questions about domestic labor. Unlike his father, "who expected dinner on the table every night at 5 P.M.," John takes full responsibility for much of the household-related work, stating that his wife "works too." John gets his son ready every morning for school, makes lunch for his thirteen-year-old stepson, makes the beds, makes himself lunch, does the dishes, cleans the house before he goes to work, and often makes dinner because Sue is not yet home. Instead of expecting to be waited on after sacrificing himself through continual giving of his labor power (the secret guarantee of the family wage—sacrifice, reward, dignity), John lives domestic life as a partnership in which both adults need to participate if they are to purchase a house, maintain a home, encourage the children to play hockey, own two cars, and belong to Jack's Gym. While all this is not, of course, necessarily what his wife would say about the domestic arrangements (a great deal of research notes the double burden of women as they enter the paid labor force), it is nevertheless obvious that John moved off centrally located working-class masculine space in order for this all to be accomplished, although using traditionally masculine space in the form of the armed services to catapult himself across the Freeway border and into a new form of settled working-class life. Ironically, then, as in the case of Bob in the last chapter, traditionally hegemonic male space (armed forces) acts as a bridge to the enactment of a new masculine form—a masculine form different from the old working-class hegemonic masculinity and one which is demanded in this class fraction if a man is to be other than "hard living" in the restructured economy.

John, like other "new settled livers," has engaged in a new working-class life wherein the point of felt collective production lies *within* the family rather than outside of it. John sells his semi-skilled/mental labor power for a wage, engaging the workforce as an individual. He and his wife, who similarly engages the workforce, join forces to raise their children collectively and produce a "settled" lifestyle. John knows that his settled life is highly precarious; his lifestyle is expensive, and he senses the fragility of his current domestic arrangement. Most important, though, he had to invest, over time, in a new form of masculinity in order to make this all work. Stretching beyond talk about shared responsibilities, John engages in the day-to-day labor associated with his settled working-classness—a set of arrangements far from centrally located and valued masculinity forged under conditions of the capital–labor accord. Significantly, under this arrangement, either he or his wife, if choosing to exit the domestic unit, could topple this fragile stability—a stability won with a set of labor-related negotiations *inside* the family rather than outside of it, as was the case under the capital–labor accord.

In stark contrast to John, Clint lives largely the same life he did in high school, never straying far from the masculine space occupied and expressed as one valued for the future during his secondary school years. In 1985, he majored in "auto collision," informing me at the time that "you learn more by doing. Instead of sitting there and telling you how to do it for three hours, they'll tell you how to do it for five minutes and then let *you* do it. They don't treat you like a student. They're more free with you." In 2000, we sit in the local donut shop as Clint reflects upon his life since high school.

CLINT: My parents basically still live there [house where he grew up]. Well, I still live there, too. And back and forth between there and my girl-friend's. . . . Now I'm working on cars, doing the same thing [that I did in high school]; that's what I'm doing for a living. I'm running a Deltasonic [car wash] now. I'm on contract with them.
LOIS: I'm going to show you a picture of yourself from high school.
CLINT: Man, that was a long time ago. Guess my hair was kind of short [now it is in a pony tail]. Kept in touch with a lot of the same people I got there [written down underneath the blurb in his senior yearbook picture]. . . . I was in trouble in high school. We always had a good time. Out partying all the time. Not going to class. We were good at that. Ah, we might have gotten thrown out of the parking lot a couple of times [for smoking ciga-rettes or marijuana]. We had a lot of good times, though. Man, I haven't looked at these books in years. *Actually, we all still do the same thing when I see all these guys* [emphasis mine]. Go out and party. Especially Bruce [whom I also interviewed] and T.J. Bruce more than anybody,

though. We just go out drinking, go to a ball game, whatever. Watch a [car] race. We went to a wedding a couple of weeks ago. That was a wild one. Bruce couldn't go, though. His girlfriend was there. He couldn't go. He was watching the kid. That's an iffy situation there. . . .

I just did what I had to do to graduate. That's about it. One of them "get it done, get out of here" kind of things. Everybody just wanted to graduate, get it over and done with, and get out of here. That's the way we all ended up being. They [the school] wanted you to stay in school, though. . . . You think about it now, and maybe I shouldn't have rushed that much. And then you look back now and see all you do is get up and go to work, go home, go to sleep, get up and go to work, go home. Especially the way I work, ten hours a day. Seven-thirty to five-thirty, Monday through Friday, and seven-thirty to two on Saturday. I don't necessarily stay all those hours, but it's the hours we're open. Right now I just manage it. The last eight years I was doing it; the last two years I haven't been really doing it that much. Since I screwed up my back, I haven't done it at all. I did that back thing in April [this is November]. I blew out a disk. Lifting something. And then I went to work back in June and then I pinched a nerve like two weeks ago. I was going to take some night course just for—I was going to go into welding. . . . I don't know. It was a thought. I'm going to have to see what happens with my back. If I don't go back to work soon, it's possible I might lose this job. That's why I'm going back after I go to the doctor tomorrow. I'm gonna go back Monday just for the fact I don't want to lose my job.

LOIS: Can you describe your money situation now, compared to when you grew up?

CLINT: Right now, not very good without me working. I'm still waiting for a Comp check. I do all right. I live with my girlfriend, but like I said, it's back and forth. I don't own a house. I didn't buy a house yet. My girlfriend has an apartment. Her seventeen-year-old daughter lives with her. She's divorced. . . . I go wherever I want, whenever I want. She don't like the fact that I just bought a fifteen-thousand-dollar motorcycle. She likes the bike. It's just she thinks I should've bought a house instead. I wanted it [the bike], so I went and bought it. . . . We been fighting a lot lately, so I don't know how much longer this is going to last. Just the fact that I come and go wherever I please, do whatever I want. Nobody tells me what to do. I just do what I want, is what it comes down to. You know, like that.

The last straw will be, let's see, what is today, the second? I give it another week when I tell her I'm leaving for Atlanta to go to the race [car

race]. That'll probably be the icing on the cake. But that's one of them
things. NASCAR race. Winston Cup car race. Last race of the year in
Atlanta. Me and a couple other guys are going. We were at a friend's
house—the guy who got married. Everybody started talking about it and
the next thing I knew, my phone rang and [he said], "I already called, I
looked it up on the computer. I called tickets and we're going. You
going?" and I said, "Sure." So she don't know about it yet. She's not going
to be happy. We've been together since '92. She works at Unibase, a
uniform company. She works in the warehouse.

Unlike John, who was very similar in behavior to Clint in high
school (although John did not do "collision" courses), Clint remains
largely on high school-constructed masculine space. He spends most of
his time with the same individuals he partied with in high school and,
by his own admission, engages in largely the same activities—drinking
and smoking grass. "Out partying all the time" as a teenager, he has
not seen his life change much except for the fact that he can now
legally drink and he puts in many hours working at the local Deltasonic car wash. Sounding much like men of the old industrial working
class (Willis, 1977; Sennett & Cobb, 1972), he now regrets not putting
more time into school, suggesting that "Maybe I shouldn't have rushed
so much."

Clint rests within what I call the new working-class "hard livers"—
bouncing back and forth between his parents' house and that of his
girlfriend, not sure how long he will have a job, spending a great deal
of time in bars with his buddies from high school (whom I also interviewed and who are in the same sketchy position both in wage labor
terms and in terms of their domestic life), and just generally doing
"whatever [he] wants," not feeling accountable to anyone or anything.
Although Clint took some vocational courses in high school, most of
his high school friends did not take such courses. The important
distinction here is not whether 1985 boys were in vocational classes,
but rather, their more generalized connection to hegemonic masculine
form over time. While Clint certainly does not valorize patriarchal
gender relations in the same way he and virtually every other Freeway
young man in the mid-1980s did, and he recognizes that his sister
works at American Axle on the assembly line and "works harder than
most guys I know," contributing to a "settled" working-class lifestyle
in her own family, he has been unable and/or unwilling to move
himself into that space which would allow a "settled" working-class

lifestyle for himself. He has not gone on to school, still coding it as boring, repetitive, and docile (in other words, feminine); is still firmly planted in the anti-mental animus with regard to his own labor, thereby living a form of "patriarchal manualism"; and does not participate in a particular kind of domestic life in which resources, both human and material, are pooled. Clint, then, has stayed largely within masculine space forged and valued in high school, and his current life is circumscribed by the ways in which such space deposits in the new economy. He thus remains unable, and perhaps unwilling, to facilitate an alternative trajectory—a trajectory which demands a different lived stance vis-à-vis gender than that fantasized about and enacted in secondary school.

Significantly, the new working class can be only partially understood around particular forms of wage labor. The collective domestic unit I describe here can be accomplished whether a man (or woman) engages in traditionally manual *or* mental labor, thus undermining the patriarchal manualism of the old working class. He (or she) can be a nurse, nurse's assistant, electrician, tollbooth collector, carpenter, or what have you. No matter what the job—and I do recognize the still largely sex-segregated workforce—men and women are taken into and out of the workforce primarily *as individuals*—selling their own labor power, without the benefit of place-bound plants that enable union activity. Nevertheless, the white working-class fraction still offers a distinct habitus—one that is now produced, or accomplished, through altered family form and destabilized notions of the masculine/feminine. It is important to note that this can accommodate new family forms as well. There is nothing that says this new unit of production/consumption must be a long-term married couple, a married couple at all, or even necessarily a man and a woman, although all relationships among the Freeway cohort group are, at this moment, heterosexual. It is the new domestic unit of wage earner/child rearer as it operates in the new economy that not only destabilizes old hegemonic notions of the masculine/feminine binary but also allows this all to work. Under this formulation, an individual, whether male or female, can take his or her wage-earning self and form a new domestic unit. This obviously challenges the basis of the working-class family of prior generations.

Obviously I recognize both the sex-segregated workforce *and* the fact that women by and large earn less money than men. However, this latter point is less true than it used to be and, more important for this discussion, less true in this community, where gender-based wage levels have evened out as the new economy takes hold in a working-class community (McCall, 2001).

On Race and Racism

Both "hard" and "settled" living forms of the new white working-class fraction rest solidly on the protection of whiteness: whiteness as race, as privilege, as distinct social space, as social construction (Fine, Weis, Pruitt, & Burns, 2004). As noted at the beginning of Chapter 3, the black–white racial divide is virtually complete fifteen years after high school. Students, particularly young white men, take great pains in high school to preserve white space, with a core part of white working-class male identity revolving around not being a person of color, particularly not black.

In the year 2000 this virulent form of whiteness production and protection persists, although tending to emerge in relation to "Arabians" (Yemenites) rather than African Americans in this particular community. African Americans, after all, are in many ways not a part of their lives. Whites in their early thirties are no longer in school with African Americans, and the jobs they now obtain tend not to be those in which they work side by side with African American men. Such jobs are obtained through both investment in further schooling, in some cases, and, most important, connections embedded deep within the white working-class community, a phenomenon which persists in this class fraction, as noted by numerous investigators (Corcoran, Datcher, & Duncan, 1980; Wilson, 1996; Aronowitz, 2004; Aronowitz & DiFazio, 1994). Every man interviewed in 2000 obtained his job— or, more accurately, jobs—over the years through knowing someone. It takes time, perhaps, but these connections are alive and well, and serve to place working-class whites, both male and female, in the work world. Jan's sister, for example, is already working at St. Paul's Hospital and hears of an opening; Sam's brother works for Tom in maintenance down at the school, and they are looking for someone; Jack needs a wiring guy at the shop. This form of hiring, as well as residential neighborhood patterns (including bars that are frequented; after-school activities for children; sports activities for children) mean that white men in the year 2000 have very little contact with black Americans.

In contrast to the old Freeway-based factory space, where members of different racial and ethnic groups routinely worked together (not always convivially), although often in separate parts of the factory and earning race-linked wages, these white men in 2000 no longer work with black men.[4] They also do not live among blacks, since Freeway, like many American cities, is racially divided, with whites on one side and African Americans and Puerto Ricans on the other. Those who left Freeway, like John, who we met in this chapter, moved either to an immediately adjacent white suburb (across the Freeway border) or, in the case of one woman, to a more affluent area that is virtually all-white as well, although recently it has been attracting professional men and women of color whose children often attend one of the prestigious private schools across town. It is in the traditionally working-class areas where whites potentially live among nonwhites due to relatively lower housing costs, that one finds the most virulent and conscious forms of racial border patrolling, both psychological and physical.

Freeway is not a wealthy town; it has poor parts (where African Americans, Puerto Ricans, Yemenites, and some whites live) and parts inhabited by what I am calling the new white working class, whether settled or hard-living. Significantly, both settled and hard-living new working-class whites stake out whiteness as a way of setting up borders around what they see as *their* community. Indeed, it can be argued that their white working-class community and the specific space of the new white working class in the world economy, as distinct from that working-class which traverses borders of race, ethnicity, and gender that Julie Bettie talks about (1995), still rests *fundamentally* on the protection of whiteness. Unlike those who moved to virtually all-white working-class areas or, in the one case, a wealthier area that is also overwhelmingly white, those who remain in Freeway continue to engage in day-to-day racial border work; in other words, the setting up of physical and psychological borders related to who lives where, who associates with whom in school, who and what is valued, and so forth. Members of the middle and upper-middle classes, as well as working-class whites who live in entirely working-class white communities, feel less urgency to engage in this particular form of border work (Lombardo, 2000). Thus those who left Freeway have a different day-to-day stake in relation to protecting racial borders, given that such borders are already protected by virtue of more costly neighborhood living space and accompanying school attendance patterns.

Racial border work in 2000 Freeway plays itself out mainly in relation to Yemenites. It is the same border work that these individuals engaged in as teenagers in the mid-1980s, although the object of derision has shifted. Alongside the contradictory code of respect toward schooling and enacted relations with women, then, proximity to and type of racial border work engaged in is also linked to expressions of and movement away from 1980s-style hegemonic white working-class masculinity. This is not to say that those who stay in or leave Freeway, or those who are settled or hard-living, are more or less racist. Rather, I am suggesting that continued proximity to centrally located 1980s masculine form is linked to current position in the class structure and has a distinctly racial dimension.

Racial border battles now center primarily on the issue of "Arabians" moving onto the white side of town. It must be noted that this is one year prior to September 11, and that there was no senti-ment in the white community at the time of the reinterviews that this group did not bear political allegiance to the United States. This has shifted dramatically in this particular community, and at the time of this writing, such sentiment is in high gear. I would suggest, though, that the recent questioning of "national allegiance" easily piled onto already existing hatred of the Yemenite community, a deeply rooted dislike which I tracked in the school as far back as the mid-1980s.

The present-day protection of whiteness spans "hard" and "settled" lives: Clint, Bruce, and Ron are "hard livers"; Sam is "settled." All embody the unique characteristics of the category as outlined earlier, yet all engage similarly in the explicit protection of whiteness. We begin with Clint, whom we hear from at length:

LOIS: If you have kids, will you send them to the Freeway schools?
CLINT: No. No. If I had kids, I'd be moved by then. And they'd be in a different school district. I wouldn't send . . . there's no way. Just the way the school district's run. They're not going to change it, so that'll never happen. Just the way everything's handled. Nothing's handled the way it should be, or even any way near the way it should be. . . .

Now you look at the racial tension, and back then it was . . . now, I consider that [back then] nothing compared to what it is now. As far as the way it escalated and the way things have changed. Like I said, we used to run just from the principal; now you have policemen running around with a gun. Things changed a lot, you know. . . . There weren't as many Arabs [when I was in school] as there are now. But I know there's a lot of them around here now. It's increasing. And they're buying up everything. Businesses, houses, everything. They're buying everything. Nobody gets what they get. Free taxes for seven years, and they get all kinds of extra gifts. And then they go live in their brother's house and they move around. They play . . . they got a game. They play a game, get free taxes for so many years or whatever. They all live in one house, then they put the house in the other guy's name. They're worse now than the blacks. Just as far as . . . as far as just being a problem. Just being here. They're the worse ones right now. It's just a common thing. Well, they just bought the pool hall down the road by Johnnie's [restaurant]. Yeah. It used to be the unemployment office, then it was a furniture store, now it's a pool hall. Arabians own that. I heard rumors about the bank in Michigan and one guy goes every week. One guy goes and deposits money. I talk to a lot of people. I heard enough that I know the things they do aren't right. They get away with a lot. As far as opening businesses and that go, because they get the tax break. They come over here and they hand them seven thousand dollars or whatever to get a business. Don't pay any taxes for seven years. That's why they all open stores. They don't have to pay business taxes.

They're rude. I deal with them a lot [at Deltasonic]. I threw them out. I threw, about a month ago, I threw one out. "Don't come back." I mean, they're rude. I know people who have gone as far as bought the house next to them, and they got nobody living there—just so they [Arabs] wouldn't buy it. You know, they want everything for nothing. Ignorant. Real ignorant. That's why if I buy a house, it won't be around here. Every time you turn around, that's all you see [Arabs]. In the school it used to be there was only a few of them. There's probably forty times more than that now. They're all over now, not just in the First Ward. I haven't seen them in my mother's neighborhood yet; I know they're down this way, though.

Bruce concurs:

I don't go to any of those things where everybody winds up being together. I know there is a lot more now. Moving around. A lot of A-rabs have moved in the area. They're a lot more, but most of the places I go, they're not there. They don't go to the local bars where I go. . . . There weren't as many [when I was in school] as there are now. But I know there's a lot of them around here now. It's increasing. And they're buying up everything. Businesses, houses, everything. They're buying everything.

And Ron continues:

They're [Arabians] spread out now. And they own 7-Elevens and every-thing around here. And the, like the corner stores, they're all . . . if you go right down there, next store to the Express Market [they own it, too]. It's just going to get worse. This city is almost bankrupt now. They're everywhere. Look around. All the food stores, you know. They have a little ... the Arabian network thing where they have a whole warehouse of the food. They put all their money together. They buy it in bulk and they're not paying taxes, so they can afford that.... [The Arabian] kids don't have respect for anybody. For nobody. I mean, one time I went, you know, I'm older now, and I was at breakfast. This was late at night with a couple people and they [the kids] were just, you know, out of control. They were just causing, causing hell in the restaurant we were at. You know, don't have any respect for other human beings that aren't Arabian. That's what I feel. You know, they were calling, shouting, calling people names. If I was younger, one of them would've got a fat lip.

Rob states:

They [Arabians] used to live in the First Ward. Now they're on this side of town. Moving on up. I don't know how they did it, but when I was a kid, people were a lot friendlier. Now they don't like each other. Most of them stick to their own races. I mean, they don't wander from their own race. You can see them walking together. There is whites walking together, there is blacks walking together [he is in charge of maintenance at the high school]....

It is not a problem as long as they take care of their houses. And there are not thirty people living in a single-family home.... They have kids everywhere. Garbage everywhere. Some of the houses aren't being taken care of. People aren't used to seeing them [on the white side of town]. If they're not taking care of the house, they're not used to it. Then they have a problem with it.

Sam agrees:

Let's see, the racial groups. When I was in high school, the blacks and whites got together okay. Puerto Ricans and the blacks and the whites got together; it's just the Arabs that I would say were the troublemakers. I mean, I didn't care for them. I just didn't trust them. I really didn't trust them. There's just something about them ... just the way they acted and the way they were around the white girls and stuff. Trying to get in with them and stuff like that. Trying to pick up all the white women and stuff like that. And driving around ... we're scraping dollars together to drive an okay car and you're driving around in brand new cars and stuff like that? Because their parents, wherever the hell they got their money from, you know. . . .

[And things are worse now.] Somehow they got it divided off with the new section [in the school] as compared to the old. And I guess you can't stand in the halls like before, before classes; the bell rings, you go right to your class, you can't stand out there. They've got the police walking through all the time. They had a problem a couple of years ago. I'm not sure if it was an Arab or a black; there was an off-duty cop there and he jumped him . . . he punched him. I remember that. It was in the papers. I'm not sure how the story goes, but the guy, the kid punched a cop that started trouble over there. . . . I think a lot of things have got to do with blacks. I mean, I don't have no problems with the blacks. But, like the white kids are trying to imitate . . . trying to be black and stuff, and it's causing trouble with that. You're white, you stay white. Don't try and be somebody you're not. The way they act and stuff. And just the way they carry themselves. That's what you think. But, I mean, I see the kids nowadays, I'll sit outside on the porch, I'll see them walking and it's "F" this and "F" that, and they're smoking, like fifteen years old. I think a lot of it has to do with the parents and what they see on TV. . . .

And the Arabs, right down the next street over on Milner, five, six houses down, they're starting to buy them. They're moving around, and I know my parents don't care for them and the next-door neighbors, they don't care for them. For some reason, I think, and my parents are the same way, they're [Arabs] just sneaky. That's what I think. I don't trust them. I never have and I never will. Like the blacks, when I'm out going to the bar and something and I see blacks, I got no problem with them. I'll talk to them and stuff like that, and it's just the Arabs I don't care for.

Conclusion

I am suggesting here that the reconstituted working class in America is living a newly created form of splitting between "hard" and "settled" livers, one which rests on the fulcrum of gender definitions and relations. While there is a "superclass" of "mostly men on high salaries" (Adonis & Pollard, 1997, as cited in Walkerdine et al., 2001), the remainder of the workforce must, as Adkins (2001) notes, take on characteristics ascribed to femininity, and "both women and men are increasingly performing the aesthetics of femininity" (pp. 8, 83) in a range of jobs (cited in Walkerdine et al., 2001, p. 9). Such jobs, as I have noted throughout, are often linked to schooling and/or taken up by those who are performing "settled" lives.

Like Connell (1995), then, I am affirming different masculinities, but noting that the nature of such masculinities, whether embedded within an individual and/or a social class, can shift markedly over time. Looking at the 1985 Freeway boys and these same individuals as men in 2000–2001, we see that the ways in which they position themselves in relation to high school hegemonic masculinity has a great deal to do with where they end up fifteen years later. All the young white men meet the harsh economy they feared they would while in high school— just five or so years after the major steel plant closed in Freeway, a closing that hit the white working-class in the area hard. As Reich (1991, 2001) and others argue, the old industrial sector is gone, and with it the kinds of jobs that pit working-class males in a routine manner against the brutality of heavy industry. It is in the push and pull with adolescent axes of identity development that Freeway men stake out and are able to stake out adulthood. It is the combination of structural forces "determining," to some extent, the shape and form of the economy and culture, as well as the ways in which individual men take up positions within this set of structural pushes and pulls, that both "determines" future individual place *and* the perimeters of the class fraction itself.

This set of theoretical understandings challenges both structurally (Bowles & Gintis, 1976) and culturally (Willis, 1977) rooted theories of reproduction. Mechanistic notions of reproduction of the economy, the culture, and the individual obviously will not do here, given massive economic realignment. But neither do more culturally based theoretical understandings. What I am suggesting here is not only that collective cultures emerge dialectically in relation to structures, as Paul Willis (1977) suggests, but also that there are elements within these collectively based cultures—in this case masculinity, as well as individual negotiation of these elements over the years—that set the stage for later relations and sensibilities. It is in the *struggle* with such collectively based cultures that adult lives begin to play out in a drastically changed economy. It is only through employing a form of ethnographic longitudinality that we can begin to recognize and understand these theoretical challenges, a point which I explore more fully in the Theoretical Coda.

In this way, too, we can begin to understand the lived reconfiguration of the entire class. This is not to say that large structural determinations are not there. Surely they are, as I have noted repeatedly with respect to the changing global economy. It is equally not the case that collectively based youth cultures are irrelevant to future life possibilities and the broader shape of society. I agree with Paul Willis (1977) that we cannot assume a "continuous line of ability in the occupational/ class structures," but rather "must conceive of radical breaks represented by the interface of cultural forms" (p. 1)—cultural forms that are, to some extent at least, under the control of those who produce them. Nevertheless, it is in the ongoing and ever-changing interaction with these two major sets of forces (structural and cultural) that both individual future *and* broader social structural realignment can be best understood. In the case at hand, it is in the reinforcement of and/or pulling away from what is defined within high school peer groups as hegemonic white working-class masculine form that we begin to see how young people, in this case young men, move toward adulthood. Ultimately this enables us to trace the movement and emerging contours of the class fraction as a whole under a massively restructured global economy. Ironically, as we see here, while the old industrial order rested upon a stable gender regime, it is the unsteady fulcrum of gender (roles, definitions, and hierarchy) that lies at the very heart of reconstituted white working-class life.

5

REVISITING A "MOMENT OF CRITIQUE"
Freeway Girls All Grown Up

LIZ: Well, we were just about on welfare at one time; when the plant closed down, it was havoc for an entire year and we didn't have nothing. . . .

LOIS: Do you hope to get married? Do you hope to have children?

LIZ: After college and everything's settled . . . I know where I'm going to live. I know what I'm going to be doing; my job is secure; the whole thing. Nothing's open. Everything's going to be secure.

LIZ, 1985

Young women, unlike their male counterparts in working-class Freeway, took a stab at reworking gender while still in high school. Unwilling to accept the lives of their mothers and grandmothers as their own, Freeway High white girls strut forward, exhibiting an inchoate sense of "girl power" while attempting to remake the class/gender intersection more to their liking, engaging in the "remaking of girls and women as the neoliberal subject; a subject of self-invention and transformation who is capable of surviving within the new social, economic and political system" (Walkerdine, Lucey, & Melody, 2001, p. 3). For Freeway youth this meant a female-based income, one earned in the public wage labor sector; a perhaps ill-defined sense of independence ("the freedom dream"); and a life which could conceivably move forward comfortably even if they experienced the divorce then so commonplace in their community—a phenomenon that virtually every young woman commented upon in the mid-1980s.[1]

Energized by the possibility of a life markedly different from that of their mothers and grandmothers, young women plunged forward, generating a female version of life in a working-class community under the new economy. For they were not to be their mothers. Given the shift in the world economy, corporate America was seeking female labor in a wide variety of service positions at the same time that their men could no longer earn the "family wage." In this context, young working-class white women continued their education, not ensnared by its hegemonic working-class masculine coding as negative, in spite of the fact that they bounced through the contradictory code of respect in relation to school knowledge and culture while in high school. Since it is psychologically easier to land on the substance side of this contradiction if one is female, these young women exploited the opportunity to go on to school. While the men in their lives experienced increased unemployment and what they continue to see as underemployment—the economic sector with which they were linked having been virtually excised—women experienced the moment of possibility in economic terms that they desired. Like the postman's wife (from the BBC serial) who "comes to life after her husband's disappearance," reinventing herself with great panache as an interior decorator (Walkerdine et al., 2001, p. 20), Freeway women faced the prospect of self-transformation with great anticipation

Of those interviewed in 1985, 48 percent had completed their B.A. as of 2001, compared with only 29 percent of men. Every single woman interviewed in 1985 and reinterviewed in 2001 pursued some form of higher education, whether four-year university, community college, or nursing school. The men have a far less noteworthy record in the education arena, with 50 percent attending some form of postsecondary institution and less than half completing their intended program. Both the men and the women are from similar family circumstances: 79 percent of men come from families that owned their own homes while they were growing up (the symbol of working-class stability), and 76 percent of the women come from such homes. Seventy-one percent of those women interviewed are now married—compared with 36 percent of the men; 64 percent of the men are in what can be defined as committed relationships (including those married), in which they are living with their partners. None of the women are in relationships where they are living with partners but are not married. All the women but one currently work in the wage labor sector, with jobs including respiratory therapist, teacher, registered nurse, licensed practical nurse, chemical engineer, catering manager, paralegal, radiologic technician, waitress (simultaneously a full-time college student in a teacher education program), social worker, manager of a department in a bank, and health plan representative.

Freeway women have, in fact, moved into postsecondary education and accompanying skilled positions with great gusto. They are uniformly married to men who have either new or traditional working-class jobs—police officer; (nonunion) machinist; state trooper; (nonunion) truck driver; bar owner/delivery man; foreman in a construction company; head of maintenance crew at the local high school; car salesman; desk job at a car parts dealer; home improvement worker. In some cases the jobs held by their men demand great skill, but not necessarily skill obtained through formal schooling. In other cases, necessary skills are minimal. In only one case is a woman married to an individual who has a professional position—he is a financial adviser and she is a teacher. With their menfolk, then, these women established "settled" new working-class lives, such lives being wholly dependent on their earnings as much as on their husband's.[2]

As I suggest in Chapter 2, the young women's emerging identity exhibited a beginning challenge to the Domestic Code, what I called a "critical moment of critique" (Weis, 1990) around issues of gender relations and patriarchy. Young white working-class women envisioned their lives very differently from girls in previous studies and very differently than investigators such as Lillian Breslow Rubin (1976) and Glen Elder (1974) suggest that their mothers and grandmothers did. For the young Freeway women, wage labor trumped the domestic in terms of imagined/desired future. If patriarchy rests on a fundamental distinction between men's and women's labor and men's accompanying domination of women in both the home/family sphere and the workplace, these girls exhibited the glimmerings of a critique of that. They understood that too many negative consequences result if one depends on men to the exclusion of depending on oneself, and this meant engaging in long-term wage labor. Significantly, they did not suggest the part-time work solution and/or flights into romantic fantasy futures (McRobbie, 1978) offered by girls in key previous studies. In this sense, then, their identity embodied a critical moment of critique of an underlying premise of patriarchy: that women's primary place is in the home/family sphere and that men will, in turn, take care of them. In so doing, they challenged the validity of the male "family wage," a challenge which matched the opening up of economic opportunities for women. Rather than affirm existing patriarchal arrangements, then (which *must* be held out as a distinct possibility), young Freeway women psychologically blasted through them.

Here I offer portraits of three young women in 1985, all grown up by 2000. Judy, a former homecoming queen whose working-class life seemed so perfect when I interviewed her in 1985, reveals how the brutality of her patriarchically bound existence as a teenager rendered her life pure hell. All smiles, kindness, and exuberant beauty, a fine student in the context of Freeway High, which prepared students only minimally for college entrance (*Metro News,* 2000, October 13, p. A-1), Judy lets us in on her secret—only too happy to do so in order to help the next generation of young women, her niece included, whom she fears is entrapped in the same vicious dynamic. Suzanne, angry at her drunken father who offloaded all his pain on a human triage scenario including herself, her mother, and all black Americans, was, it turns out, wholly out of control in the 1980s. She had, back then, few friends and a sarcastic mouth, set in sharp contrast to Judy's, yet she also had her secrets. Suzanne had a boyfriend who was thirteen years older than she was and a father who flew into drunken rages at all hours of the day and night. Carla, too, lived with an actively drinking alcoholic father, and ultimately found herself with a boyfriend who beat her mercilessly. Carla stumbled into physical violence at a slightly later point in her life than Suzanne or Judy, although she knew of many physically violent relationships while in high school.

All three women were from working-class families filled with sharp secrets, and all lived lives of pain, with two projecting a "good girl" image and the third exuding "bad girl" venomous anger. All wanted out of life as they knew it; none saw the ostensibly gentle hand of male support as possible and/or desired. All three wanted their own job, space, and time. What I was not privy to when they were teenagers (although I knew them fairly well) was the deeply rooted male brutality that laced their lives, particularly in the cases of Suzanne and Judy. In retrospect, it was the pain linked to physical and emotional violence which they wished to escape; an envisioned job was seen as a way out. The three women's stories illustrate the pain and brutality which festered barely beneath the surface of this class fraction—and, in retro-spect, it is this pain which spearheaded the critical moment of critique regarding gender relations and the Domestic Code. While both the opening up of the economy to women and the larger middle-class women's movement offered important contexts for young white working-class women's actions and sentiments in the mid-1980s, it was the seen and felt brutality that triggered the critique. Although they were teenagers, and therefore largely unable to articulate the linkages at the time, it is clear from an adult point of view (mine as well as theirs) that physical brutality embedded in this class fraction is much of what they wished to escape. As such, their stories are emblematic of what such a moment of critique can become—what a movement of women at the end of the century, whether understood this way or not, can build toward as the American white working class remakes itself against the kaleidoscopic backdrop of changes in the U.S./world economy.[3]

Judy

JUDY: We had a lot of ups and downs—the steel plant was closing. A lot of ups and downs, just with the steel plant and my dad being out of work and that type of thing. And my mom went to work when I was eight, just for that reason. And she felt guilty about it forever, and still probably does. But otherwise I think we were pretty normal. We lived in a very small apartment, though.

This is my dream home [laughs] ... yeah, this is truly, yes, this is. Actually, my husband grew up in a nicer house than I did [in a first ring suburb], but we grew up in a little apartment that was three bedrooms and one bathroom and it was very small [for five of them].

LOIS: When you were in high school, you did talk to me about your dad being laid off. Do you reflect back on that at all?

JUDY: At times, yeah. Especially now, with having kids [one three years old and one two months old]. I think back ... like I said, I remember the first time my mom really talked about going back to work and how guilty she felt leaving me when I was eight. And like now ... when I think back about how my grandmother used to come, or my grandfather would come down [they lived upstairs] if I was sick, because my mom had to go to work, and take care of me, and my mom wouldn't have done it if my dad wasn't laid off at the time. Because actually it was more when I was in junior high school when a lot of it was going on.

LOIS: What did your mom do when she went to work?

JUDY: She's actually still doing it. She works ... it's almost like an accountant, but she doesn't have an accounting degree. And it's called Jacobbi's now. It used to be called Augustine Electric. So she worked there. Still does. Now I'm happy for her 'cause she does it. It's definitely her pride and joy. She does very well at it and she loves it. Loves the freedom of money finally....

When my dad was laid off, and then go back, and he would get unemployment, I think it bothered him a lot. But my dad's not the type that would go out and get another job. Not that he *couldn't* do it. I don't know. He just . . . he didn't. Because there was like, the steel plant was all he did and all he knew. And that's, I mean, I can never see him even like going to Home Depot to work, because I don't think he has enough self-confidence. I don't know if that's what it is . . . even now, with being retired. The steel plant opened back up, but under a different name, for a little while. And they called him, and he went back for a few months and then stopped. He was getting paid garbage money and he was standing in oil and it just wasn't his thing. He didn't go back after that. So . . . he was in his late fifties when the steel plant closed finally [completely], and he retired. He was . . . pretty much collected unemployment, and I mean, I think he just had hoped that it would always be there and it would be fine. . . . My dad used to do, like, little projects around the house . . . the house we lived in was four apartments. It was actually my dad's dad's house. And when he passed away, my dad and his brother got the house, so they split it . . . and my dad would do little things around the house. Type of fixer-up things. Not decorative or major projects, but just putter around. As far as like, laundry, cooking . . . [laughs] . . . he didn't do any of that, really. Yeah, he was just home a lot. That was it. I mean, there was definitely some tough problems there. I mean, with my dad and my mom. And so for a while it was very rough. And I think it all stems . . . from that. Plus my dad was injured in the steel plant. He had a finger cut off. So that had a big psychological effect on my father. I mean, I didn't like to go back [to think about it] when I was growing up and like, now, like I said, I've been thinking about it. And I think that [his injury] played a big part of it, and he probably should have done something to even get out of there [the steel plant], but he didn't. It's just, like I said, that's all he knew. And if it was up to him, I think he'd still live there [in Freeway—in the same house]. . . . Yeah, he just wanted to stay in his little world.

LOIS: Can you describe for me where you live now?

JUDY: Oh, it's tremendously different [laughs]. This is like my own little piece of heaven here, actually. I just wanted property, 'cause, well, in Freeway the house next to us, you could stick your arm out the window and it was right there. You heard everything. Everybody heard everything. And I just wanted space. So now we own thirteen acres . . . and the house is, to me . . . it was huge compared to where I grew up.

Almost from rags to riches would be the way in which Judy describes her life—a life that began in a run-down section of Freeway and meandered to a beautiful home on Salk Island. She, a two-year-college graduate and radiologic technician in a local hospital, and her husband, a construction worker, have pieced together a materially comfortable life twenty miles from Freeway, one which rests largely for him, and partially for her, on the skills and contacts embedded within the white working-class community (Wilson, 1996; Aronowitz & DiFazio, 1994). Her husband's job as a construction worker represents the culmination of a set of skills obtained as a youth, and he now works for a family friend. Judy works at General Hospital, a job she learned of from her sister-in-law, who also works there. It is these skills and contacts—in Bourdieu's terms, class-coded forms of social capital and working-class habitus—that not only helped Judy and Ron obtain jobs, but also enabled them to build their home (the contractor, for example, is a family friend, and her husband and his friends did much of the work themselves), a scenario shared by many of the "settled livers" in 2000.

Judy and Ron's present settled lifestyle is as dependent on Judy's job as on her husband's, for it is the two-income family and the collective production of domesticity that enables the necessary cobbling together of resources, both human and material. The young Freeway women's teenage desire to "be independent," "get a job," "not live off a man," and "live my own life" has encouraged these women to eagerly seek postsecondary education (Fine & Weis, 1998) as well as work in a wage labor capacity. As Judy said in 1985, "I want to go to college for four years, get my job, work for a few years, and then get married. I like supporting myself. I don't want my husband supporting me. I like being independent." Ironically, it is the very desire to escape brutality and *dependence* on a male breadwinner that has enabled/encouraged *settled familial dependence* on two incomes. In fact, women are as much dependent on this form of domestic arrangement (two-income family/collective rearing of children) as are men, if they wish to accomplish "settled lives."

Young working-class white women's push for "independence" *has* served to alter gender relations in the family, at least to some extent. In this sense, then, these women have lived out the "moment of critique" around patriarchy and wage labor articulated in high school. They are not wholly economically dependent on a man. Rather, men and women are economically dependent on one another if a comfortable family lifestyle is to be attained.

On another level, however, the youthful moment of critique has not necessarily interrupted male brutality in women's lives, even though it is the brutality which in large part propelled this set of changes to begin with—a brutality which sweeps through the white working class with a great intensity (Fine & Weis, 1998). Although the new economic and social context enabled white working-class women at least to imagine exiting lives laced with home-based violence, Judy, like many others, harbored a dark secret, one which she took great pains to conceal.

JUDY: My [older] brother is an electrical engineer. He actually did go away to school, just for a couple of years. Ended up coming back and finished up at State College. And he got a job and was doing really well, and my sister, the same thing. *And I wanted that....* And then I think going around to ... like, in our senior year, when you had the chances to see colleges, or like, college representatives would come, and sometimes these girls would come in and they're all dressed up and I'm like, "That's what I want. I wanna be like that. I wanna have a career and be independent and just be like that." *Do* something instead of being a stay-at-home mom. Or ... I'm not saying there's anything wrong with that, either [being a stay-at-home mom], but I just wanted, I wanted that ... I guess, the self-esteem and self-confidence in myself. I didn't wanna depend on anybody. And the not depending on anybody thing I think comes from [everything] with my dad and how my mom and dad were, and I just didn't wanna be like that. I didn't wanna live a life like that.

LOIS: How were they? You've talked about that twice now....

JUDY: They had their rough times. My dad at times was abusive to my mom. More physically than mentally. Mentally he was fine. I think it was ... now thinking back on it ... I think it was just problems he had from the steel plant and all that. But ... sorry [she is crying]. Yeah, and it was bad [crying] ... that's why I said I just wanted bigger and better. My family and my kids ... and I have a wonderful husband.

LOIS: You're so lucky.

JUDY: I am. He's wonderful. He knows all about it, so ... I wouldn't even think that [the abuse] would ever even happen here. I know it wouldn't, and I love that comfort, knowing that it wouldn't.... I think like ... get me outta here [Freeway] and I'll forget all about those horrible times. That's how my mom deals with it, because when we talk ... or my dad was getting a little funny actually a month ago. That's why this is ... [laughs] ... a little upsetting. It was getting a little on edge again, and I was, I was getting nervous again about it, and I brought it up to my mom. And she'll almost act like it didn't happen. Or she'll say, like, "It wasn't that bad." And then, like I have these vivid memories and I'm like, "What do you mean it wasn't that bad? How can you say it wasn't that bad when we spent nights locked in the bathroom 'cause it was the only door in the house that locked?" type of thing, you know?

LOIS: Was he drinking?

JUDY: No. You almost wish it did [explain it], 'cause you had a reason, you know? Or it's easier to get help that way. His was definitely . . . I mean, I don't know if he ever had a nervous breakdown. Now I think that's probably what happened at some point in time. And I think he probably needed help but never did anything about it. And my mom hid it from everybody. I don't think anybody knew. I mean, she would just call in sick to work . . . she had black eyes. I remember her laying on the couch with the black eyes and stuff, and she would just call in sick to work, and nobody would know. . . .

That was like a big part of my childhood, 'cause I remember it always being there. I don't remember a point when it wasn't. Yeah . . . I wanted out of there [Freeway] for that reason, I'm sure.

LOIS: Did anybody try to tell him to get help?

JUDY: He's not open to that . . . I mean . . . and it happened when we were older. I called the cops twice. And there was a whole embarrassing thing, 'cause of course, the front pages of the local newspaper, and they would put the Sheriff's Reports in there. And it said, "Domestic, 25 Seneca" in there. And I remember somebody came in school the next day and said, "What happened at your house?" And I made up this whole story about these people living upstairs had this fight. And I was like, "This is terrible." I was embarrassed. I acted like it didn't happen. Maybe it was in my thinking [that] I didn't *want* it to happen. And now when I think, thinking about it, me and my sister and brother have turned out pretty good [laughs], considering how bad it was.

Judy and her family fell victim to the abusive elements festering within white working-class male culture. While she sees her current marriage as more than she could ever have hoped for, her escape from Freeway, and simultaneously from Carl, her low-key Freeway High School boyfriend, led her down a treacherous path, one laced with abuse. After running into Mike, who also was from Freeway, in college, she saw him as a way of "getting out of the Carl situation" and moving along the road to new experiences. Judy and Mike dated for three years after having met at a local softball game; she was still smarting from the pain.

JUDY: I guess when it first started happening, yeah, it's just like that little push, little shove, and I didn't . . . I guess I just didn't think of it, and I didn't think that it was gonna go anywhere. And then as it got worse, I think I was more like, "I can't believe this is happening." You know, it's not real, or it's gonna stop. And I was ignoring it, probably how my mom just, like, ignored things [the abuse] and didn't do anything. I just let it go. And I could say that I was in love with him. Definitely. I mean, if he wasn't like that, we'd probably still be together. . . .

He was unbelievably jealous. Unbelievably. I mean, I couldn't even look at somebody the wrong way sometimes, and he would start. He was just very obsessive type of thing. And then I got to the point where people started finding out. My mother started questioning and, you know, I'd have bruises. He did stuff in front of all my friends. We went to Chowder Point and it was really bad there. And that actually distanced most of my friends because most of them were just like, "Judy, you need to get out of it," and "Judy, why are you still going out with him? If you go out with him, we're not gonna bother with you guys anymore, 'cause we don't wanna deal with it." And that's kinda what happened. And I did. I stayed with him, and there was definitely a few years there that I was not as close with everybody because of it. . . . My parents were upset . . . my brother saw something . . . when he [Mike] hit me . . . and he [brother] got really upset and called Mike's parents. And I knew it was, it was just out of control. He [Mike] was out of control. But at one point he was going for counseling. I actually had him talked into that, and he was doing it, so I'm thinking to myself . . . "I can do this, I can change him, it'll get better." And I think that was stemming from my father, thinking, you know, "I can help this, I know. It can get better." And I wound up getting to the point where I had to get restraining orders and stuff. Actually, I had to get two restraining orders. Yeah, I got one and then, of course, I wound up going back to him. But then, when I started going to County Community College, we separated for like nine months. I ran into him at a bar and he's like, "Judy, I wanna talk to you." We started talking. He seemed genuine and sincere, and then we started dating, but something wasn't right there, and then he started again. And then he actually attacked me . . . right in front of all these people, and scratched my car and all this stuff. And that was when I was like, "I've had it." I already had enough self-confidence, and I think my self-esteem was back, so that I was like, "No, I don't need this. I'm not gonna put up with this." And I got another restraining order at that point, and that was when we severed our ties. And I did. I mean, he lived four houses away from me growing up, and then I wound up moving to that apartment [her parents' apartment in Freeway], and I was in college and I ran into him a few times there . . . I mean, we talked a couple of times and then a couple of times in the middle of the night he'd come to my apartment. And then I just wanted nothing to do with him. And I was happy to say that at that point, because at one point I was like, I would have probably . . . done anything for him.

LOIS: And if you had a niece who was in this situation, what would you tell her to do?

JUDY: I have two. We're approaching this point. I guess [I'd tell them] always be self-confident. To really look for help, and hopefully they'd have a friend or someone that they could talk to that would always be there and stand by them. And not leave them to be . . . like [thinking] this is all you have, you know? To let them know that there is more out there. To be so much more self-confident themselves that they don't need that; they don't need anybody. Honestly, I would love to talk to girls in these situations because I've been there, and I know how hard it is, and I know how hard it is to get out. *And just do it!* I mean, it was really bad there for a while. My mom hit a point where she came to me and said, "Please, Judy, I don't know what to do to stop it, but I just don't wanna be seeing you in your grave."

Two restraining orders later (one was useful; the other was not), Judy exited this situation. Terrified to go to a battered women's shelter because her one phone call to Safe Haven led to a connection with someone she knew from Freeway on the other end of the line, Judy took years to extricate herself from abusive relationships. Having spent her entire childhood and teenage years hiding the abuse in her family, and later, as a young adult, fleeing those who might know her and label the abuse for what it was, this mid-1980s homecoming queen harbored her secrets well. Crying as she took the blood red roses at her high school dance, Judy, a young woman determined to "support herself" and "be on her own," like virtually all of the young women I interviewed in 1985, lurched from the violence of her home to violence embedded within young love. Now a radiologic technician whose income enabled the construction of her dream house, Judy walked a path strewn with sharp rocks. Part of a collective expression of "a moment of critique" among white female working-class youth in the mid-1980s, she continued forward toward her dream but, like most of the working-class white women I worked with when they were teenagers, she was unable to escape fully the physical brutality associated with men in her life. Most significantly, though, she is no longer in an abusive relationship. Taking charge of herself in the economy ultimately encouraged her to "be so much more self-confident."

Knowing how hard it is to feel oneself worthy of more than abuse at the hands of a man, she tells young people to "Just do it!" Looking around her kitchen filled with wonderfully happy cut-and-paste glittery pumpkins produced by her family, she reflects on her struggles and triumph.

Suzanne

Suzanne exhibits a different pattern than Judy; she has no children and is not married. Informing me in 1985 that "Marriage was invented by somebody who was lucky if they lived to be twenty without being bit by a dinosaur," she retains her feisty sarcasm fifteen years later. But Suzanne also has a story to tell. Currently a seventh grade math teacher in a city middle school, she, like Judy, lived her dream of "not being trapped." As she said in high school, "Back when they [parents] were kids, like ... girls grew up, got married, worked for a couple of years after graduation, had two or three kids, had a white picket fence, two cars. Things are different now.... You've got to do it [make a good life] for yourself. I don't want to be Mrs. John Smith. I want to be able to do something." Besides, she told me in 1985, "You can't rely on them [men]—it's like, I know a lot of older guys, they drink all the time."

SUZANNE: Dad spent most of my growing-up years either at work—he's a city firefighter and also worked at Macey Boiler Works—or at a bar for 70 to 80 percent of my growing-up time. Mom went back to work when I was about eleven or twelve years old. When she went back to work, it was very part-time [she is a waitress]. There's a lot of family conflict because of Dad being so unavailable. Mom found comfort elsewhere. I ended up getting involved with somebody much older than me in high school ... I met Joe [long pause] probably eighth grade summer, going into freshman year. I met him when I was thirteen. We became involved, sexually involved, [when I was] sixteen, but he was much older than I was. He was about seven years older than I was at the time. He was twenty-one when we met. We ended up being together pretty much on, most of the time, for about eight years. Yeah, it was very long-term. Did not end well. It was very ugly....

As I look back on it, quite honestly, parts of the relationship were extremely destructive. Parts of it were very instructive, in that I learned a lot, especially [about] sex. He was the first one that I was ever with. He was very active, and had no problems teaching me everything he knew, for better or worse. And, of course, you know, of course you're learning something and you take a certain pride in learning how to do something well. And I look back, though, it was destructive, in that in a way he developed into a father figure for me. I would look to him for guidance when I really should have had a father to look to for guidance. We would get into extremely heated arguments. I mean, oh! It was a very passionate relationship on all levels, not sexually passionate . . . if we fought, we fought all-out! I mean, we threw everything that we could at each other. He was good at throwing things back at me, and I was never as good at throwing things back at him. . . . He would remember something I had done six months, a year, two years earlier, and throw it back in my face. . . . You know, now I have the wisdom of knowing better, and I can say that it [the entire relationship] was blamed on my father and his drinking because I couldn't run to him [for support]. First of all, I didn't have a male adult in my life to learn how adult men treated adult women. My father's the kind that would come home and yell and scream. You know, he's gonna sell the house, kill the dog . . . you know . . . usually it was only after he had been drinking. Mom has typical dependencies for spouses of alcohol abusers. You know, the whole co-addictions. She's addicted to nerve pills to retain her sanity. And, of course, if he took something out on her, she would take it out on me. If he took something out on me, I took it out on her. If they took something out on me, I took it out on Joe. So there was the whole interaction of things going on. And the further away from high school that Joe and I got, the more brutal our arguments about things would become. It eventually got to the point where he would scream at me, "You have nothing to say! Don't even say anything; you have nothing to say about this!" And eventually it became true. I had nothing to say.

Like Judy, Suzanne centers on her father as the source of current and past problems, a centering that rests squarely on abuse associated with alcoholism. Her relationship with her father, or more accurately the lack thereof, colors her relationship with all men, and she attributes her destructive involvement with Joe to this source.

It is certainly true that individuals from a variety of social classes, both men and women, abuse alcohol. It is also true that such abuse saturates a family, causing untold damage to all family members— partners as well as children. What is striking about the Freeway data in this regard is its very *layered typicality*; whether with respect to physical violence or to obvious alcoholism. A very high proportion of the white women I knew in 1985 narrate, as adults, a set of family encounters with alcohol and/or domestic violence that spans generations. This mirrors what Demi Kurz (1995) uncovered as well as what Michelle Fine and I discuss in *The Unknown City* (1998), where an overwhelming majority (92 percent) of the white working-class women we interviewed across two cities report childhood abuse (physical or sexual) and/or adult domestic abuse, aimed at themselves or a sister, at the hands of a father, a mother's boyfriend, or the woman's husband or her boyfriend. As Finkelhor (1983) notes, family abuse is an abuse of power "where a more powerful person takes advantage of a less powerful one" (p. 18). Additionally, research is clear that such acts are "carried out by abusers to compensate for their perceived lack of or loss of power" (p. 19), an analysis increasingly fitting the situation of white working-class men. Contrary to the Norman Rockwell images of a family sitting down to eat dinner, these women's lives drown in various forms of abuse, leaving them too emotionally drained in many instances to deal with the festering anger of the men who continue to surround them.

SUZANNE: Dad and I are better off not talking about anything controversial whatsoever. Dad's not capable of having an intelligent conversation; he just doesn't have the resources.

LOIS: You told me that when you were in high school. Has anything changed?

SUZANNE: No, nothing! It's funny that I was that articulate in high school! Yeah, he's just not capable of having an intelligent conversation with someone.

LOIS: Did anyone ever try to get him into a program? Or rehab?

SUZANNE: Oh, God, no! You're just asking for trouble. I can remember having an argument with my father, this was the first time I ever moved out of this house. It was in the springtime of '94, because it was right around Valentine's Day and it had gotten to the point . . . I had gone into a rather severe depression that semester [in college]. This was after the first time I dropped out of college. Because this was '94, just before I graduated . . . the second time I went back. And in the spring of '94, around Valentine's Day, things in this house were horrendous. I was not functioning at all. And I had to function somewhat because I just had to get out of the house. This is not a house that you can just stop functioning in, because as soon as you stop functioning, it gets very ugly. I moved out of this house. I moved in with a girlfriend out in Centreville, and I'm pounding out of my room with my things and screaming at my father . . . because my father was home, drunk as usual. Mom was at work, and I looked at him and I said, "What do you care about? All you do is sit on a bar stool and watch the world go by. You don't care what happens in here!" And he turned to me and looked at me, and he said, "I've earned my right to drink." I thought, "You know, fine. You've earned your right to drink. You've earned the right to not have a family, because you don't have one." And, you know, from that day on, I realized there's no point in ever trying to get him to stop. I don't want him to stop. I wish to God he'd drink himself into his grave, quite frankly. Or at least move away from here and not come back, because he's more damaging than he is anything else. I can't say that I wish him dead. My mother can. I can't. . . .

LOIS: Your mom ever say anything to you about not getting married because of her own situation?

SUZANNE: Never. Well, she didn't have to say, "Don't marry a man that drinks." No, she would prefer that I was married, because she is under the impression that I cannot take care of myself, you know, with the debt that I have and the disasters that seem to happen [a series of bad relationships; loss of a job]. She just doesn't think I can take care of myself. And she thinks I need someone to do that for me, which I don't agree with.

Whether Suzanne "needs someone to take care of her" or not is not at issue here. What is important is that Suzanne has lived out her teenage dream—she is "independent," earns her own money, is not married, and has no children. In her 1985 words, she is not "Mrs. John Smith" standing behind a "white picket fence." She told me then that "you've got to do it [make a good life] for yourself ... you can't rely on them [men]."

On the downside, Suzanne was in a highly abusive relationship for many years with a man seven years her senior, a relationship that began, nonsexually, when she was thirteen. She hates her father, who continues to drink, verbally abusing her and her mother, as well as all black Americans, when drunk. She attributes her own destructive relationship with Joe to her lack of a father. Within the last two years Suzanne had suffered two nervous breakdowns, lost one teaching job, and experienced endless bad encounters with men. At one point last summer, she could not get up from the couch for a full week—she just lay there, crying.

Suzanne did not emerge unscathed from her family dynamics, continuing to suffer under the men of her class. I asked her at one point where she meets men, since her interactions with them constitute so much of her story. She responded that she goes to bars. "Which bars?"

I said. "Oh, you know," she responded, "the ones that people like me go to—the guys are rough, not very educated, and like to have fun. I don't go to bars that educated guys go to." "Why?" I asked. "I don't feel comfortable there," she responded. "I need to be with people who are from places like Freeway." Suzanne is a seventh grade math teacher in a city school. Her social class of origin, her surrounding habitus, travels with her.

Suzanne's story clarifies and at the same time throws into sharp relief the contradictions embedded within the high school girls' desired "freedom" and "independence from men." While pursuing "independence," Suzanne becomes a math teacher, but one who carries the baggage of her youth with her, including that associated with her father and her older lover. Stretching to grow into adulthood, she runs into one abusive situation after another, having nowhere to "meet men" but places within which she "feels comfortable"—places where the "guys are rough," not very educated, and "like to have a good time." Her heterosexuality and relative youth drive her to seek out men; her social class of origin suggests that she will "choose" to meet them in certain places, profoundly illustrating the effects of Bourdieu's structuring habitus (in this case, white working-class) and field of action. Since she is by herself, and has numerous school loans and substantial credit card debt, Suzanne is also in serious financial trouble—trouble that prevents her from paying whatever fee is owed so that she can complete her master's degree, which would appreciably raise her salary. Her mother is rightfully concerned about this situation, and suggests that Suzanne cannot take care of herself—a sentiment which Suzanne resents, although admitting that she had a "nervous breakdown" last summer.

Suzanne's apparent "freedom," then, is illusory: she carries a particular form of her class habitus in her soul and on her back as she moves into adulthood, suggesting, in this case, a continual tangle of bad relationships with men. The fact that she has no partner also means that she has little money, since the "settled" life of which I speak tends to demand two incomes. Although Suzanne is a teacher and arguably a member of the middle class in occupational terms, she is nevertheless firmly entrenched, through her day-to-day practices, in her class of origin, spending virtually all of her time with individuals she knew from Freeway or those who are from comparable working-class communities and remain similarly positioned in class terms. It is, then, at some level her "choice" to remain part of her collective of origin while pushing at the boundaries of gendered possibilities. In this sense, although living a single version of working-class femininity in the year 2000, she is like her Freeway peers: all the women interviewed except one are partnered with men of their class of origin. While not in a steady relationship, Suzanne spends all of her social time with men and women like herself.

Carla

CARLA: [Thinking back to her mom.] If I think back, she wanted more for me than she had. She worked maybe for six months and she got married and a year later I came along, and she was just a stay-at-home mom. But nobody's mom worked back then. But to this day she hasn't gone back to work. I think, so I didn't have to depend on anybody else, I went to college [she is now a sixth grade teacher in Freeway, where, by district rules, she must reside]. And, if I wanted to go my own way in the world, I could. I wouldn't have to depend on a man.

LOIS: Did she ever say that to you?

CARLA: I think it was kind of unspoken. You know, do you want nice things in life? Do you want a nice house and all that? Well, then you have to go to college. I don't know if she saw the future coming when two people had to work or what . . . I don't know what my mentality was back then, because I had a boyfriend that I was with off and on and off and on. Oh, God, I was probably about fourteen years old. And it was understood that we were going to get married someday, and he was going to take care of me. And I don't know that I foresaw that I was going to work [laughs] for the rest of my life, but you know, I mean, in today's society you really don't have a choice. Unless you marry a doctor. I did not [laughs]. And even then, you know, life is really expensive. And if you want these wonderful things here [looking around her new home, which her father, husband, and she built], you gotta work.

Carla was in the nonadvanced curriculum in high school and was also somewhat less connected than the vast majority of young women to the idea of an independent future, having had a boyfriend since she was fourteen and being swayed by his understanding of what the world would be like for them. Her mother pushed hard to have Carla attend Comprehensive College and become a teacher. Carla did not marry her high school boyfriend and, in fact, married only just last year, when she was twenty-nine. Ironically, she married close to thirty, which is what the majority of Freeway girls said they would do as teenagers. Like Suzanne, she lived with an alcoholic father.

CARLA: I don't think I really knew my father till I built this house, and spending so much time with him, and yeah ... I know when they married, he had a drinking problem, and I think she more or less railroaded him and told him: "If you are going to stay with us, get off the booze, or get out!" And I remember a lot of nights, just the fighting and stuff. He was always very quiet after that. . . . It was hell when he drank. I remember sitting at the kitchen table one day. My mother had made, I remember ... roast beef and mashed potatoes, and she was on the phone. My brother's crying. He was in his high chair, he's crying because he was hungry. My father had stormed out of the house because they'd gotten into another fight 'cause he came home late, or he was out drinking. And she's on the phone to my grandmother, crying and crying and crying. And I'm sitting there crying, going ... and, "You want me to eat roast beef?" And, you know, "Is Daddy coming home?" And that year he didn't come back. And it was Christmas morning and he came over in the morning to see me open gifts and left again. And I don't know, was that because he wanted to leave or because she made him leave? I don't know. I was only ten. I call it the Christmas That Almost Wasn't. I mean, all the presents were there under the tree, just like they always are. But Dad wasn't there.

LOIS: Did you ever ask him about this, or ask your mom?

CARLA: No, I didn't ask him. And she would reconstruct the story to her liking. So I don't bother. Because my mom and I didn't get along for a long time, either. Because she was so domineering and always trying to, you know, shepherd me along, and I didn't want to be shepherded. I wanted to do my own thing. . . . We fought viciously. I swore the minute I turned eighteen, pfft!, I was going. . . . I just wish she wouldn't have been so strict, and maybe we would have been closer and we wouldn't have fought so much. Because I really feel that we missed out on a lot.

The picture that emerges is of a father who drank too much and stayed out late, and a mother who was trying to hold it all together: keep the house in order, raise the children, and, for the sake of the family, control her alcoholic husband. In the midst of her father's drinking and her mother's continual stabs at controlling the situation, Carla became involved with a very abusive man.

CARLA: My mother despised him. He was not allowed at the house; he wasn't allowed to call the house and visit me. But it wasn't a good relationship. And like right after it ended, we [Mom and I] got closer and closer. Now we talk three times a day on the phone and she lives ten minutes away [laughs].

LOIS: What is it that she didn't like about this guy?

CARLA: She didn't know. She looked at him and just saw something she didn't like. Go ahead and ask, "Was she right?" Of course she was right. She just looked at him and she says, "He's got a mean look to him." I says, "You can't tell by looking at somebody what they're like." And sure enough, he was really mean. I saw him for four years. He never finished high school; I didn't tell her that [Carla had just completed four years of college]. He was working at Don Pablo's when I met him, but he got into construction shortly after that and was doing concrete, and that's what he's still doing. . . .

He was just physically abusive. He was very violent. And like, pretty much when he was drinking. And he was definitely an alcoholic because, you know, I would leave at night and [he would say], "Oh, yeah, I'm tired and going to bed." And it came to the point where I would drive by his house the next morning or on my way to work and see, "Well, his car's not the way it was when I left. It's pointed the other direction. I know he went to the bar last night." So, you know, I knew it [alcoholism] was there, but I was going to fix it. I was gonna make him a better person.

LOIS: Yeah. Did you make it better?

CARLA: No . . . I left. It must have been about '96, '97 [four years later], because I had met Jim, who's my husband now. Things with Bill got really bad. I mean, there was one instance, he was slamming my head off of the arm of a couch, I mean there's wood there; it's hard, and it was . . . it comes to a point he's either going to kill me or I'm going to kill him. My response initially would be to leave, but he wouldn't allow it; he wouldn't let me out of the door. [It went on] probably two and a half years. Yeah, my mom knew about it. You could only hide so many black eyes. I'm sure my whole attitude changed. I don't think I was a very pleasant person. She saw the marks; she saw the bruises; and she would lay into me. She would lay into me so bad. He was never allowed in the house, ever. From the moment she set eyes on him, she just knew. She said from the minute she set eyes on him, she knew that there was just something that wasn't right about him. But to hear him tell the story, there wasn't a problem. [He said] "I never laid a hand on you in my life."

LOIS: So Bill never recognized it, even when you confronted him?

CARLA: Well, "Oh, I'm so sorry." And blah, blah, blah. "I didn't mean to, I won't do it again." And, "Okay, I'm going to fix it, I'm gonna. . . . " Right after we broke up, they put him in the hospital. He threatened to commit suicide. I didn't go back to him. He called me at three o'clock in the morning and said if I didn't go back with him, he was gonna kill himself. And I got to the point I said, "You know what? If that's what you feel you need to do, then go ahead and do it." Because how many phone calls at three o'clock in the morning can you take? I lived with my seventy-five-year-old grandmother; I don't want this kind of disruption in her house, you know? So, if that's what you need to do, then you go ahead and kill yourself. And his mother put him in a hospital. I don't know exactly what kind of hospital, or if it was a detox. I don't know what it was. But I know he is still drinking. Whatever it was, it didn't work. . . . Before that, though, Bill and I had gotten in a fight over something. I don't remember what. And I drove up to his apartment, and I just wanted him to get out of my car. I just wanted to go home. We had been drinking. And he broke the windshield on my car. He broke my glasses. We went upstairs to talk; he was so upset that we had to talk. We went and talked and he beat the hell out of me that night. His roommate heard it and never came out—never helped, never did nothing.

The hand of the male was not gentle for Carla—it was hard and cruel as she was growing up, and vicious under her ex-boyfriend, whom she stayed with for four years. The bruises, black eyes, angry phone calls at three o'clock in the morning—all encircled her life with Bill. Her mother just knew—there was something mean about him. She was right. One drunken night he called her up, after slamming her daughter's head against the wall, threatening, "You better say goodbye to your daughter, because this is the last time you're ever gonna hear from her."

Carla, like Judy, extricated herself from this horrific situation after years of abuse, vowing never to let herself be abused again. Like Judy and Suzanne, she lived out the "freedom dream," attended Comprehensive College, and ultimately became a teacher. Hoping to avoid having to "depend on a man," she obtained a B.A. Unfortunately, her education could not act as a hedge against her abusive boyfriend, a boyfriend who did not complete high school although she had completed college at the time she was seeing him. Her own class habitus, like that of Suzanne and Judy, led her to seek out certain kinds of men, men who embody a shared social class of origin, with all that might imply in the late twentieth century with respect to lived-out differences between men and women of the former industrial proletariat (in this case, their level of education). Carla was lucky: she lived through an episode that might have resulted in her death. To her credit, she, like Judy, escaped her abusive relationship.

Piecing her life together, Carla married Jim, also from a working-class background—a part-time physical education teacher. Having spent the last two years building their dream home with the day-to-day help of her father, who designed the entire structure, Carla and her husband reflect the porous nature of today's social class categories. Both she and her husband are teachers living in a solidly working-class community alongside members of what I am calling the new "settled" white working class. Indeed, it is her father (whom she now loves and depends upon, despite their history) with the labor, skills, and contacts embedded in their working-class habitus and associated forms of social and cultural capital, coupled with money earned from her job and secondarily from her husband's, that enable their current lifestyle. Carla and Jim live in a beautiful home replete with wet bar and outdoor deck, a home built with their own hands in concert with the hands of the larger class cultural community. It is the bleeding of the old industrial proletariat into middle-class jobs, by a select number of children of the former industrial proletariat, that produces the most affluent lifestyle within this particular group. Significantly, in the case of Carla and Jim, such affluence is wholly dependent upon the white working-class habitus as carried on their back in addition to their current location in a relatively low-cost working-class community; a community within which Carla feels totally comfortable because she grew up there. As Carla says: "My mom lives here, my dad, my sister, my friends, they all live here." Carla and her husband would be unable to accomplish this particular iteration of affluence if the skills and know-how of the old industrial proletariat did not accompany them. Again, though, Carla carries with her not only the skills and contacts of men such as her father, who enable this material accomplishment, but also the physical abuse which lies just below the surface of this class fraction.

Judy, Suzanne, and Carla—a radiologic technician, a middle school teacher, and an elementary school teacher, respectively—lived out the 1985 Freeway girl's dream. Each has a postsecondary degree, and all have jobs that at least enable them to support themselves should they be on their own; none is wholly "dependent on a man." Juxtaposing the deeply etched youthful desire for "independence" against their current full-time and relatively stable positions in the labor force, the question arises: What came of the moment of critique packed within the modal female culture as it emerged during the high school years? In other words, where does it deposit, and why? All live out to some extent the fantasy of not being dependent on a man, yet all three women simultaneously experienced episodes of vicious abuse. Certainly not all of the Freeway girls experienced such violence after high school, but *most* have, to the point where those who have not lived through violent episodes are the exception rather than the rule, signifying the very normativity of the experience. While Freeway men may live distanced from their high school desire to set up patriarchal families in which they labor outside the home/family sphere and women reside within it and tend to it, the all too common physical brutality speaks to an underlying male desire to control and dominate their women. For women, the lived-out moment of critique has not wholly been able to challenge all that goes on in the private sphere. The new collective unit, upon which working-class men and women are now totally dependent if a "stable" life is to be accomplished, is still punctuated by raw physical male power, much as the working collective of old was punctuated by raw bursts of violent capitalist power, supported by the state. Both the site of collectivity *and* essential punctuating moves of physical power as a disruption to the site have radically changed under the new economy, yet both a necessary space of collectivity and disruption to such space through brute force remain.

Past and Present

Based on a 1956 survey, Elizabeth Douvan and Joseph Adelson (1966) concluded that girls are less clear about their future work than boys, and that adolescent females focus on marriage and motherhood as a life plan rather than on the world of work. Education and work are seen as providing access to marriage and motherhood rather than as goals in and of themselves. More recent studies by Linda Valli (1986) and Angela McRobbie (1978) reach largely similar conclusions.

When I conducted the Freeway ethnography in 1985, it was striking that adolescent girls differed so markedly in terms of gender consciousness from those in previous studies. Female youth did not emphasize the private sphere of home and family; instead, they stressed their participation in the public sphere, boldly and almost uniformly asserting that they would consider the private only after being established in a job/career.

Taking these data into account, I suggested that these working-class white females exhibited some potential for feminist critique—that their identity signified a moment of critique that could, at some point, be linked to a feminist position of collectivity and struggle. This was conceptually akin, although from a feminist perspective, to Paul Willis's (1977) notion of "penetration," a term he coined in *Learning to Labour* and reaffirmed in *The Ethnographic Imagination* (2000). Penetration, as he defined it, refers to "impulses within a cultural form towards the penetration of the conditions of existence of its members and their positions within the social whole but in a way which is not centrist, essentialist or individualist" (1977, p. 119). Paralleling Willis's theorized notions of limitation and partial penetration, Freeway High did not provide a context in which young women were able to explore their positions *as* women. In fact, the mid-1980s school served to promote the assumed dominance of white men rather directly, fracturing in many ways (although, as I argued, contradictory impulses regarding gender operated within the school as well; Carnoy & Levin, 1985) the very beginnings of what was arguably an emerging form of feminist consciousness in the white working class (Weis, 1990).

Dorothy Smith (1987) and others suggest that the working-class family is characterized by marked subordination of women to men. Working-class women lived out a discipline that almost totally subordinated their lives to the needs and desires of males, reflective of an implicit contract between husband and wife under which she provided household and personal services demanded by him, in return for which he provided for her and her children whatever he deemed appropriate. Under these terms,

> The household is organized in relation to his needs and wishes; mealtimes when he wants his meals; he eats with the children or alone, as he chooses; sex is when he wants it; the children are to be kept quiet when he does not want to hear them.
>
> The wife knows at the back of her mind that he could take his wage-earning capacity and make a similar "contract" with another woman. As wages have increased, the breadwinner's spending money has enlarged to include leisure activities which are his, rather than hers—a larger car, a motorcycle, a boat. Even a camper often proves more for him than for her, since for her it is simply a transfer from convienence to less convenient conditions of the same domestic labor she performs at home. (Smith, 1987, pp. 46–47)

Numerous scholars similarly attest to the conditions of white working-class women's lives (Rubin, 1976), focusing on the "family wage" under the industrial economy as being a controlling factor. Martha May (1987) suggests that the family wage as ideology became and remained important because it appeared advantageous to all participants, holding out the possibility of an adequate income wherein an adult worker could support his family and enable his children to attend school. To achieve this goal, the family wage ideology both employed and maintained existing gender distinctions in work roles. For employers, the ideology held out the possibility of lower wages for some workers (mainly women) and, under conditions of a place-bound economy, a stable workforce whereby industry could amass long-term profits.

The fact that women earned relatively little in the workforce also thrust wage-earning women back on families as a primary means of emotional and physical support. Although many working-class women historically were in the wage labor force before marriage, and recent scholarship suggests the role of women in the labor movement struggle (O'Farrell and Kornbluh, 1996; Jensen and Davidson, 1984; Milkman, 1985; Kessler-Harris, 1982), the wage work experiences of women in this class fraction failed to alter fundamentally their dependence on the family, since nearly all jobs available to them offered less security and status than did the role of wife and mother.

> For the working class women, then, life outside the family was apt to be economically precarious and very lonely. It was not a life of freedom and autonomy. This was so because the great majority of unskilled women earned less than subsistence wages. They needed the economic protection of family, and without it they lacked the resources to experiment with new styles in life. Yet the price of family economic protection was, as we have seen, a surrender of considerable personal autonomy. Life outside the family, moreover, was difficult for women because extrafamiliar institutions did not offer them the emotional security, the social status, the easy personal identity of family membership. Ultimately the family provided the only world in which working class women were secure and fully acceptable. (Tentler, 1979, p. 135)

Within this context Freeway youth became intensely interesting. Given the demise of the industrial economy which had enabled the family wage to be at least an envisioned possibility (not necessarily a reality) for some segments of working-class America, and the fact that unskilled, semiskilled, or even skilled (in working-class terms) male workers were unable to locate jobs that paid anywhere near what industrial laboring jobs paid, the male-based family wage was no longer viable. In addition, as Smith (1987) and Apple (1986) remind us, the economy changed such that the demand for certain types of women's labor increased, as corporate capitalism required clerical, service, and sales workers at low cost. The implicit "contract" that restricted the employment of married women, thus reinforcing their role in a domestic economy controlled by their husbands, was cancelled, because women were called upon to participate in the paid labor force at an ever expanding rate, earning relatively more money than ever before. This relativity must be understood in two senses: women earned more money than they did during any earlier time period, and, perhaps more important, women now earned relatively more money in relation to their men *both* because female wages are higher (in standardized dollars) than ever before *and* because male wages are less available and are lower (in standardized dollars) than ever before. The fundamental shift in the world economy, coupled with inflation and rising consumer wants and needs (changes in what becomes defined as "necessary"), also means that more and more women *must* enter the paid work force in order to fulfill traditional home-based responsibilities.

All of this coexisted with a felt desire on the part of the young working-class white women with whom I worked in the 1980s for some form of "freedom"—the ability to make their own decisions and not live wholly in terms of male demands. It is the demand for female labor, coupled with the decline of available good-paying jobs for their men, that has eroded the particular form that patriarchy took in the white working-class family. A largely bourgeois women's movement simultaneously rendered the signs and symbols of "freedom" available to these young women, although most denied that they were connected to any kind of feminist consciousness (Eisenstein, 1984).

In 1985, Freeway girls offered the glimmerings of critique of women's place in both the home/family sphere and that of wage labor, challenging the notion that their primary role was to take care of their husband's children, in return for which his wage would support them. Additionally, they pierced the notion that they must account to men— that they must listen as men tell them what to do, where to go, when to have children, and what to buy. In a sense, then, the 1985 Freeway female teenagers chipped away at the ideology of thoroughly separate spheres for women and men and the accompanying notion that they must occupy a subordinate role.

It is arguably the case that the 1985 Freeway girls' identity must be understood in terms of a radically changed economy as well as in relation to altered understandings of women as a sexual class, even though the resurgence of the women's movement was spearheaded and largely colonized by the middle and upper-middle-classes. Such struggles filtered down to these girls, however, and their beginning critique of women's place must be seen as linked to these broader struggles in key ways. The language of "independence," for example, was tied discursively to a middle-class women's movement and picked up by working-class girls whether they identified with this movement or not.

The question arises, though, what have the Freeway women, now in their thirties, been able to do with this moment of critique. Although their personal lives differ—Judy is married, with two young children; Carla is recently married and has no children; and Suzanne is, in her own words, bouncing "from one bad relationship to another"—what possibilities are opened up by such critique as the years fly by? All three women pursued higher education and landed semiprofessional and/or middle-range professional jobs. Like all the 1980s Freeway girls except one, they lived out their stated desire to obtain economic independence—not to be *wholly* dependent on a man, living only to set up his household and raise his children.

What they have not been able to do, however, is escape the violence associated with the ways in which patriarchy played out and continues to play out in this particular class fraction. It is this element of class association and embeddedness—this habitus, if you will—that the daughters of the industrial proletariat have not been able to escape. Indeed, it is possible that such abuse is on the rise as working-class men move away from older patriarchal notions in some parts of their lives, yet retain violent elements meted out in the domestic realm. Given that longitudinal physical abuse data are hard to read, since any rise in such abuse may signal greater frequency of abuse or simply more extensive reporting of such abuse, it is difficult to establish whether or not abuse in working-class communities is on the upswing as a result of changes in the economy and family structure. In a frightening turn of events, though, it is conceivable that the physical cruelty of white working-class men (whether more extensive or not) becomes their last defensive resort—their last solidly and visible patriarchal stand in a world which has stripped them of alternative forms of power. Under this scenario, the power left them, as a group, is their physicality, and an appreciable number employ it (whether consciously or not) to stake out a form of continued dominance vis-à-vis women and children in the home.

This underscores points made by Angela McRobbie (1978) and, more recently, Madeleine Arnot (2004). As Arnot notes, what McRobbie found most striking was how "unambiguously degrading to women is the language of aggressive masculinity through which [Willis's] lads kick against the oppressive structures they inhabit" (p. 38, as cited in Arnot, 2004). *Learning to Labour*, which can be read as a classic piece on white working-class masculinity, is peppered with references of utmost brutality against women, suggesting that "the violence of the imagery, the cruelty of the lads' sexual double standard, the images of sexual power and domination become the lads' last defensive resort" (Arnot, 2004, p. 28). Given kaleidescopic changes in the world economy which render economically based male power in the white working class less and less likely, it is arguably the case that raw physical power increasingly becomes the last defensive resort (Finkelhor, 1983), building on existing sensibilities regarding women in this class fraction (Reay, 2002; Nayak, 2001), an aspect of living deeply ingrained in white working-class habitus. Under this habitus, men who exert aggressive masculinity so as to "kick against" oppressive structures become true products of their class. Certainly many white working-class husbands and fathers do not fall victim to this brute physicality as expression of desired and yet stripped dominance and superiority. Yet data suggest that enough of the women have experienced such raw physical abuse so as to render violence against women typical, and worthy of continued attention.

Critique, then, such as that expressed by the young Freeway women, while not necessarily "fizzling out," as some of our earlier short-term studies suggest (Weis & Fine, 1997), takes different shape and form by gender, and moves forward in the real world in markedly different ways. Paul Willis's insightful set of understandings around the theoretical constructions associated with penetration, partial penetration, and limitation, useful as they are, play over time. What I am suggesting here is not only that they play differently over time for men and women, but also that a "moment of critique" such as I stumbled upon in the mid-1980s is multifaceted, and long-term follow-up studies allow us to unravel the "sticking power" of varying elements of such critique in concrete political, economic, and discursive settings.

While both white working-class men and women are the product of their habitus (defined in very complicated terms by Bourdieu as a "structured structure" at the same time it is a "structuring structure," thereby allowing for human agency), the fact that some men can and do distance themselves from aspects of hegemonic masculinity and that some women move away from violent relationships must be factored into the analysis. It is not the case, then, that the habitus of the working-class family in the early 2000s is necessarily the same as it was under the industrial economy. Carla and Judy, for example, have moved far from what they knew as youth, and, in select ways, so has Suzanne. All are critical of the ways in which social relations played out in the working-class family of their youth, and all evolved specifically in relation to what they did not like. In this sense, it is critical that none of the young women whom I worked with in the mid-1980s engaged in the construction of fantasy futures around marriage and motherhood. This represents a marked departure from the solutions preferred by McRobbie's women—women who found safe haven in "fantasy romance."

The habitus of origin, then, can be re-worked by those who inhabit it, encouraging a possibly more positive long-term intellectual spin on white working-class women's lives than might otherwise be the case. Since the habitus exists dialectically in relation to Bourdieu's concept of *field* ("a set of objective historical relations between positions anchored in certain forms of power for capital"; Wacquant, 1992, p. 16), we can perhaps expect white working-class habitus, specifically as connected to violence against women, to change in relation to the new economy. While not necessarily characteristic of the class fraction as a whole, the moves of Judy and Carla, and to a lesser extent of Suzanne, reflect the fact that not only are gendered relations around paid work and home-based labor changing in relation to what existed in the mid- 1980s, but also that some women are refusing assertions of dominance through fists, insisting instead upon an alternative set of gendered dynamics around the inevitability and related acceptability of domestic violence. While men may be landing on a space of physical dominance as a last patriarchal stand in the face of structural assault and gendered realignment, some women are fighting back.

The Freeway girls "all grown up" in 2000–2001 reveal that their mid-1980s moment of critique enabled some semblance of control over work and family life but did not enable them, as a group, to escape the raw physical abuse of their class. Not withstanding occupational segregation, the white working class has moved into the twenty-first century with women literally working side by side men in the home/family and public spheres, both to bring in income and to raise the next generation. They are thus creating, with men, a new collective that both women and men are dependent upon, in that it enables the accomplishment of a still potentially stable and relatively affluent white working-class fraction as compared with other fractions of this broader class. Just below the surface of this newly minted collective, however, rests the potential physical dominance of the white working-class man, a dominance intensified perhaps by a deep and targeted sense among these men that their masculinities are under siege in the new global economy, yet a form of dominance simultaneously contested by at least some of their women. The apparent seamlessness with which this new white working-class fraction is accomplished, then, is, upon closer scrutiny, subject to question. As I suggest in the next chapter, it is white working-class women's *defensive* moves around race that bring the social class fraction into realignment in spite of the potentially destabilizing disruptions of gender.

6

PICKING UP THE PIECES
AND MOVING FORWARD

Like when I got out of high school, I went to nursing school for two years. I finished that. I have my nurse's license, because I was, like, halfway through, and I put all this time and energy in. It was very difficult to finish. You couldn't tell I had a problem; most people thought I just had a bad back. Because I couldn't walk up the stairs well. But I really couldn't get a job as a nurse. Muscular dystrophy is a progressive disease, and you lose a lot. Like, I equate it with dying, sort of. Like you're always losing something. Like first, I couldn't get down a curb; that's gone. Then, I couldn't like cross the street. Like walking—every year it's something else. But so, it was very difficult to finish nursing school.

But I was, like, *I am not a quitter*. I was, like, *we're going to finish this.* . . . And then, I took a year of business course, so I could get a job, and I worked as a secretary for a year. And I looked around, and I said. . . . "This cannot be me in fifty years, sitting here like these ladies." Nothing against them, but it wasn't me. So I quit my job. And I didn't know what I was going to do, as far as school. But I decided on social work, because social work is a way of helping people, and I liked helping people.

So it took me four years to do two years of work. I only went part-time. And I lived on campus. And it was very hard because I was, like, in my middle twenties, living with eighteen- and nineteen-year-olds. And I'm starting to get weaker, so my mother's got to do mostly everything. It was hard having to have my mommy come up and change my bed. It got so bad, the last year I commuted. The last semester I had to have Mommy come to the library and help me, because I couldn't, like, you know, do it myself. And it got to the point where I can only write for a little time. Because what happens is my hand fatigues. *But I was going to finish . . . because my one goal in life was to have my bachelor's degree before I died.*

[Susan graduated with a B.S. in social work in 1992. She works full-time as a social worker for an organization devoted to independent living.]

As we saw in the last chapter, the abuse in this class fraction is pervasive. What most distinguishes the lives of the grown-up Freeway girls, however, is not the abuse but their tenacity. Most stunning in the follow-up data is the degree to which white working-class women, now in their early thirties, keep moving forward in spite of the drinking, physical abuse, loss of jobs, men who have run out on them, and dreams that may be stalled. Susan symbolizes Freeway women. Although suffering from a debilitating disease, she keeps moving forward: ultimately earning her two-year nursing degree, and, when she could no longer do nursing, a bachelor's degree in social work. Unable to walk at the time of our meeting in 2000, and dependent on a $6000 electric wheelchair that she calls her "car," Susan catches paratransit at 5:30 A.M. five days a week and returns home at 6 P.M. Concerned that she can barely hold her head up as the disease further claims her body, she nonetheless strides forward with dignity.

In contrast, we remember Larry, who was voted "most likely to succeed." Larry met a few bumps in the road, and lives with his grandmother in Freeway public housing. Although Bob, who we met earlier as a third-year veterinary student, followed a tortured path toward his current position, no other Freeway man has a story comparable to that of Bob or Susan. Men, by their early thirties have either moved forward from high school along a more or less continuous path to middle-class or stable working-class positions, or live, for the most part, the life they led when they were sixteen.

I am not suggesting that all is necessarily well with the women. They have many years ahead of them and may, once again, be knocked off their chosen path, for whatever reason. Yet, what distinguishes these women is their tenacity—their willingness to move on from whatever unfortunate situation they find themselves in, rather than languish. Each of the women reinterviewed in 2000–2001, whether a stellar or even adequate student in high school, has made small and consistent moves during significant portions of her life toward something better. Slowing, perhaps, and tripping up at times, they nevertheless continue to move forward. We first meet Lorna and Chris, neither of whom was in the honors curriculum.

Lorna—2000

Like one day I said to my mom, "I remember when we were little ... very little ... and we had marshmallow sandwiches. Like we had peanut butter and jelly . . . on marshmallows." And my mom started crying. She said, "That's because I didn't have any money to buy bread."

Divorced from an alcoholic husband, Lorna now lives with a man whom she is devoted to, and is back at college, earning her bachelor's degree in elementary education. Reflecting on the brothers of her best friend (whom I also interviewed), she reveals that the men of her community have not done well.

It's just disappointing to think, like, we all grew up together. And we all had, like, these high hopes. And every one of her [Loretta's] brothers could have gone on scholarships for basketball or football or something. And not one of them went to college for it, and every one of them ruined their scholarship in one way or another. It's just everybody [the men]; they drink and party too much. Loretta's brothers are unemployed now. But like the one brother is not allowed in Sam's [her boyfriend's] bar anymore because he got in a fight in there and he really hurt somebody bad. He picked up a stool and he charged at somebody. So now he's kicked out of the bar for fighting. You know, some of these people, you see them, they haven't changed [since high school]; they still wear the chains on their belts, and the black leather jackets, and the comb in the back pocket.

Contrasting her past fifteen years with those of her ex-husband, she furthers her point:

I always worked two jobs. Sometimes I worked three jobs. Like right now, I go to school [full-time] and I work two jobs. And about our marriage . . . he would rather be out drinking with his buddies, and I was working two jobs. And, you know, I was working nonstop and I can't afford to take a day off of work. You know, there's too many things I want [she and her husband bought a house]. He was just content to take money out of the bank and go off with his buddies. He was always rebuilding; he had an old car . . . and he was always rebuilding his car and putting a hundred dollars, two hundred dollars a week into that damn car. And he was content, you know, just cutting up his knuckles [working on the car] and letting me work. I mean, that was fine for him. And that ultimately, you know, breaks up a marriage. I mean, he would stay over at his buddy's house and they'd be in the garage until three in the morning, drinking beer, working on the car. And then he would come in and he would just sit on the couch, and then he would conk out, and then he wasn't even coming home. And then it got to the point where he went through like eight jobs in a year. And we weren't paying our bills. And you know, it was very stressful. And I was the one who was working. I mean, like a couple of times he would do stupid things, even like get up and leave like he was going to work and go sit in the parking lot until I left for work, and then come home and go back to bed.

Lorna found Al-Anon, a program for families and friends of alcoholics which she heard about from her mother. Working the program, she garnered the courage to exit her marriage and put the pieces of her life together. While training a new waitress in one of her three jobs, Lorna discovered that this young woman was in a teacher education program, and she encouraged Lorna to go back to school: " 'Are you some kind of kindergarten teacher or something?' And I just said, 'No, but that's funny that you said that, because I love kids.' " And she responds: " 'You really should be a teacher; you're good at it. You know, you have patience; you like to talk to people.' "

Lorna's story is replete with individuals who help her out—people whom she believes were put in her path for a reason, like the young woman who convinced her to become a teacher. Her parents, too, always stood by her; her dad wanting her finally to terminate her marriage: "And then it got to the point where my divorce wasn't final yet, because I still owed my lawyer money. And my dad called me up on the phone one day, and he goes, 'Lorna, this is your father [laughs]. I just have to ask you something. When is this divorce going to be final?' I'm like, 'I don't know. I just have to pay him [the lawyer].' He goes, 'How much do you owe him?' I'm like, 'Like six hundred dollars. It really shouldn't take me....' He goes, 'Consider it done.' So he paid for the rest of my divorce ... just like that; he wanted it over. He wanted the stress out of my life. And then I called my mom up one day and I go, 'Mom, my lawyer called me. My divorce was final yesterday.' And she said, 'Good for you.' And I had to go to work that night, and I got to work, and my parents sent me flowers at work that night [laughs]."

Lorna will finish college and become an elementary school teacher. In high school she described the grit on the windows—"grit from the steel mill operating at full-steam. Now there is no more grit, but there are also no ready-made jobs" (1985). At the same time she let me know that "I'm trying to get all my education so I can support myself. Why put effort in and then let somebody support you?" (1985). A waitress for many years, at times working three jobs simultaneously, Lorna married an actively drinking alcoholic. Now divorced and still waitressing, she is constantly in motion. When attempting to locate her, I talked to Lorna's father: "You'll have a hard time finding her ... she works so hard and is back at college full-time. We are so proud of her." Although busy, Lorna had no trouble making time for me. Sitting at her carefully appointed kitchen table, eating home-baked bread and having a cup of coffee, we talk for hours.

Chris

Some of the women have had their own share of problems with drinking and drugs. Chris had a smart and funny mouth in high school, and was always in trouble. Often drunk or stoned, she just wanted out—out of Freeway and out of the life Freeway had to offer her. Her father, who dropped out of school at the end of sixth grade, urged her to continue her education. Like the other Freeway girls, she wanted to be independent: in 1985 she stated, "I don't want to be dependent on somebody else.... My sister's friend, she just went to high school and didn't do anything after that. She got pregnant and got married, and now she's having a lot of problems. And if anything happens, what is she to end up with? And I don't want to be like that. Her husband's an alcoholic, and I don't want to end up like that. I wanted to work ever since I was little."

Although Chris now works as a licensed practical nurse, she went through rough times:

My dad is a recovering alcoholic. Yeah, and I was his problem child. Me, I just struggled with the whole family. My senior year [in high school] I was ridiculous. Yeah, I moved in with a boyfriend. Lived on the streets for a while in [the adjoining major city]. I went to community college for alcohol counselor and criminal justice. I went for a year and a half, and I just dropped out, because then I think me and this guy broke up. And I starting boozing and carrying on.... Matter of fact, I went to [high] school graduation with a black eye, because I got in a huge fight on my graduation. I got punched in the eye. Yeah, Janet punched me in the eye. And my father made me go. I didn't even know what I was doing. That was hysterical....

I moved in with this guy my senior year. We lived with each other for four years. We got engaged and he started doing drugs. And he was acting goofy, so we broke up. Then I moved into the trailer courts with a friend of mine. And my father got sick with cancer. And I pretty much stayed away. Look ... I'm sorry I missed him. I said "I'm sorry" [she is crying]. I don't know if he heard me. It was hard to go back. I tell everybody, it's the hardest thing I ever had to do was go in that room and tell him how sorry I was. . . .

And I met my ex-husband the same year, on my birthday. And we dated a year. And I got pregnant with my nine-year-old. And I moved in with him. Larry was a year old when we got married. My mother always told me it wasn't going to work. I'd say after three years, we were getting a divorce. Yeah, he was [fourteen years] older than me. He wanted me . . . at the time I met him . . . that's what I needed, the security . . . he could take care of me. You know, he put me through school . . . nursing school. And then I was at the point where I wanted to still go out; he was older. And we got divorced because toward the end, when I was still married to him, I was going out and seeing other people. And I'd not come home. I wouldn't come home. He said, "You've got to go ask me for permission to go out." And I told him, "I don't." When he'd say "Come home," I'd be pissed. So I never came home. So when we got divorced, he got a very good lawyer, and he got custody of Larry. My mother was very upset. Like there was no one there to help me, so I did it on my own. I walked out with the shirt on my back.

Chris lurched from one relationship to another, living, over the years, out of her car in the adjoining large city; at the Freeway trailer park; and eventually in a house just over the Freeway border in a solidly white working-class suburb with her second husband. Between Chris and her current husband, they have five children: her oldest (age nine, who now spends considerable time with them), his three (ages seven, five, and two), and their baby (nine months). Experiencing severe health problems, the youngest of her husband's three children spent three months in the hospital after the child's mother died of lupus (shortly after giving birth to him). Her current husband put it to her bluntly:

"Chris, I have children. And, you know, I love you, but if you're going to continue to be this way, we can't continue the relationship." Right then I knew that either I clean up my act or else I'm going to lose everything. Like I had already lost enough, you would think I'd learn. So, I cleaned up my act. It's all in the mind. It's all willpower. I mean, I do believe it's [alcohol] addicting, but I felt I wasn't drinking because I was addicted. I was drinking because I was unhappy with my life. So I figured *here is a chance to make myself happy. Don't blow it.* So I chose to get my shit together. Now I don't drink. No one is to say that maybe I won't start drinking again, when I'm unhappy. But I don't know that. My son Larry had a hockey game. And he was playing in the arena. And I got loaded. He just turned seven. And he came in and said, "Mom, what is wrong with you? Are you on drugs?" I was embarrassed. And I swore right then I'd never do that to my kids again. So for two years, I've been sober.

Chris has a checkered past, with drinking and drugging floating at the very center. For two years, shortly after high school, she sold drugs and slept in crack houses, living out of her car and robbing homes for cash. She moved in with her aunt after her father died (when she was twenty-one) and began, in her words, the long road to recovery. Whether Chris is recovered is not totally clear. She is not in any kind of recovery program, believing it is "all in the mind," and, by her own admission, could start drinking at any time, although she has been sober for two years. While struggling with her own drinking and associated problems, she nevertheless managed to complete a nursing degree and now holds a full-time job as a nurse. She is, in addition, raising five children, including a nine-month-old and a very ill two-year-old whom I watched her minister to in her home. She and her husband, Terry, who repairs furnaces and air-conditioning units at $30 an hour, have established a nice home just over the Freeway border. Raising their five children, she manages to move forward, pulling herself, perhaps temporarily, in combination with her husband, into the "settled" working class. Chris's home is spacious and stuffed with many extras—outdoor barbecue pit; expansive, up-to-date kitchen; gazebo; and sunken family room with wide-screen television. The children get "anything they want," states Chris, to compensate for her own lean background. There is always food in the house, "more than necessary," and she and her children "shop for pleasure." "These kids," she informs me, "don't want for nothing. That's why I work, to give these kids whatever they want." Contrasting this with her own childhood, when she remembers "going to school with no lunches because we had no food in the house" after her father was laid off from Freeway Steel, Chris is "really proud" of herself.

I do not claim to know, with any certainty, what life holds for Chris. As I have suggested throughout this volume, individuals are producing themselves, as well as a social class fraction; and the nature of individual movement in relation to the old industrial proletariat and this new class fraction can, and perhaps will, shift over time, a shift captured as high school students move toward adulthood. In this sense, then, the individual subject is never stable, but fluid, as he/she moves within constructed class/cultural configurations in relation to the new global economy at the same time that such individuals (as part of a collective set of processes) shape this economy. Chris has extricated herself (perhaps temporarily) from an intense life of bars and drugs. Her male high school friends, whom I also reinterviewed in 2000, are not so lucky. Their life, as Clint states in a previous chapter, is pretty much the same as it was in high school, except that they have to go to work. Chris, in contrast, is building toward a different kind of future. The fact that she stuck with school, and even plans to obtain further nursing education, speaks to the ways in which women are using the educational system to enable a more settled lifestyle. In the final analysis, Chris, in spite of the drinking, drugs, and practices associated with that lifestyle, has, like Lorna, managed to keep moving forward.

Former Freeway girls continue to insist that their life will be different from that of their mothers and grandmothers. As Lorna stated in 1985, "I don't want to get married. Five years from now I'll just be able to go into a bar. I'll be twenty-one. And I don't want to ruin my life in just five years. Cuz as soon as you get married, you're going to start having kids and then you're going to have to stay home and raise them and stuff. I don't want to have to do that.... I like to be able to make my own decisions, and if you're married, you have to sort of ask the other person, 'Can I spend the money here; can I do that?' It's like you got to ask permission. Well, I've been asking permission from my parents all my life, you know. I don't want to just get out of high school and get married and then have to keep asking permission for the rest of my life.... I'm trying to get all the education I can, so I can support myself."

Meandering down a rough path, Lorna, like virtually all the Freeway women whom I re-interviewed, is accomplishing her goal. At the age of thirty-two, she will be an elementary school teacher, far surpassing the education/occupational status of either of her parents.

Those Most Successful

As in 1985, when the articulated distinction lay between those females in the honors track and those in "regular classes," the lives of the most successful women in 2000 do not differ substantially from those who are not as successful. For the most part, women's lives have moved in a similar direction, although some have pursued more higher-level schooling than others, and/or married men with more or less high-paying and stable jobs. In contrast, the 1985 men grew up to be a more variegated group in terms of their life course, with two or possibly three men arguably landing in the middle class and the rest split between "hard" and "settled" livers. Each of the women reinterviewed who was in the honors class in 1985 had obtained a bachelor's degree by 2000. The most successful in career terms come from this segment of the population—chemical engineer, three teachers, registered nurse, and manager of a department in a bank—although a number of women who were in the "regular" classes in the mid-1980s are quite successful as well: catering sales manager, teacher, one about to become a teacher, and social worker. The women, in general, obtained a fairly high level of education compared to men from similar backgrounds.

Most interesting is the way in which a small group of women held together in order to complete college. Three of the women (with an additional two whom I did not interview in 1985) were close friends in the honors track in high school and commuted together to the local university. Here we meet Jennifer, the only young lady to tie explicitly to any form of feminism in high school. As she stated in 1985 when discussing her friend who wanted to leave the honors track and go into cosmetology so as to pursue a traditional gendered path: "I mean, you [women] have the opportunity. I mean, civil rights have come so far. If it were a hundred years ago, I can see saying that, when you were being a rebellious woman if you wanted to go out and get a job."

Now a successful chemical engineer who is married to a police lieutenant and has a six-year old son, she reflects in 2000 upon how she accomplished her goals.

JENNIFER: I mean, Freeway was a very poor place. The schools did not equip us for college by any stretch of the imagination. And it was amazing to go [to college and] see how more well- prepared everyone else was. And it's, you know, this fighter, I don't know, this underdog mentality [we had]. And there were just a handful of us [at State University]. Rhonda, Stacey, and I drove together every day at first. We kind of separated a bit because we were in such different curriculums. But in our first semester I remember Rhonda and Stacey came to my house, my parent's house, and I was trying to tutor them in chemistry, the night before the exam in college, because it was so hard. In the end we didn't drive together because our schedules were so different. But in the beginning, we drove together every day. There was never any question that I wouldn't [finish college]. It was going to happen. I was going to do it. And it was hard, it really was. *I may have been intimidated, but, you know, I never thought of quitting.*

LOIS: Freeway went through a hard time. I know your parents were OK [her father did not work in the steel plant], but a lot of people's parents weren't. And yet, at least you and your group of friends [mainly women from the advanced class] seem to have landed with nice guys and put your lives together in what look like nice ways. Can you talk about how you think that happened?

JENNIFER: Well, I don't think that you realize you're in a tough situation when you're in it. And things were hard, I think, but everyone still had their families, and you know, church. And it was a hard time, but it passed. I only know, of all my friends from high school, only one of her parents, only one friend's parents, divorced. But families weren't falling apart left and right, and I think the stability got everybody through it. And maybe the crisis of having no money made everybody work twice as hard to make sure that they would have an education so this wouldn't happen. That you wouldn't rely on something. You know, the steel plant was almost a gift to the city, for everyone, that was around a long time. You know, it wasn't skilled labor, it was just a job. So I think maybe everyone who was in that situation decided that they weren't going to let that happen to them, and they were gonna get a skill.

Jennifer and her high school friends have remained in close touch; they drove to university together, stood up in one another's weddings, and now meet for ice cream whenever important news must be shared. Rhonda, a registered nurse with a ten-month-old daughter, is part of this group. A focal point of the group in high school, Rhonda is credited by a number of the women for keeping them on the "right path." She, in turn, credits the others:

We are all still friends. There was, like, six of us that, we speak each week and well [ask one another], "Did you talk to this one?" We meet for lunch and go out. We were all in each other's weddings, and I wouldn't give them up for anything. We were all there for each other, you know, through college, and ... I say my friends made me who I am. Such a wonderful group of friends. It would have been easy to go the other way, go with whomever, doing whatever. Everyone knew what they wanted, and we all had to go to college and, you know, work. And we all got married and had kids. When I was a teenager, I could have gone the other way. If they [my friends] were smokers, I bet I would be a smoker.

Just, you know, I tried it a little as teenager, and they were all, "Oh, you know, it's not a good thing to do." And, you know, I'm sure there could have been dropping out of college. College was tough: I worked during college. I worked full-time, went to school. . . . they were there to support. I could have dropped out and worked wherever and, you know, gotten in trouble. I really credit their support. My parents weren't college-educated. They didn't know about what ropes you had to go through for college, and we had to help each other. None of our parents really were college-educated. And then I was able to help other people's children whose parents weren't educated, you know. And I would help them with financial aid forms. . . .

You know, we all got married around the same time, I'd say. I kind of had an understanding—go to college, get my degree. If we're still together [my boyfriend, now husband], get married twenty-five or so, then, you know, have kids. We waited a little bit for that [she now has a ten-month-old daughter at the age of thirty-one].

Throughout, Rhonda's parents, like virtually all Freeway parents in the mid-1980s, stressed education, and the young Freeway women hung together to get it:

I don't think I was raised to be a housewife and a mother. You think with the four kids, and they [her parents] wanted more for us. Like when my sisters kind of started faltering in school and college, it was very . . ." You can't, you need the education, you guys." You know, my mom wanted more for us. You know, "You should have a job; you should have an education." She had the rough times with the plant closing, and four kids and food. My mom got married at sixteen. She was pregnant—a high school boyfriend. The girls keep these things secret at the time, and she was at the end of the school year. She was a junior, but she got back for the senior year. Sixteen when she got pregnant, and she was married and had the baby at seventeen. She didn't finish high school. My father went to college, he'll tell you, for six weeks, failed terribly, went to the steel plant and made good money. Life was grand; they were on their own, and you always got something to fall back on. We lived by the plant, and growing up as a kid, you could see all the colors in the sky at night when they were dumping [chemicals] in the water. And that wasn't there any more [when it closed], you know, there was no smoke coming out. We didn't sit down and have family conversations, but you know, with my brother being the oldest and the only boy, so it wasn't pushed on us, "Let's sit down and help you find a college." It was kind of "You gonna go to college?" And my brother was in the advanced placement classes, too. So that was just the way the school pushed you. You know, you're gonna go to college. That's what we're grooming you for.

Rhonda, like Jennifer, completed her schooling in the advanced section. They were part of a small group who formed strong friendships, many of which lasted into their thirties. Coming from working-class families, families that did not know how to negotiate the college process, the young women relied on one another to gain access to college and subsequently to negotiate college life. Even now, they go for ice cream—"Every great announcement, wedding or birth, all the births are announced at the Pig 'n' Whistle. Every time we go there now, it's 'Who's pregnant?' That's where we go. And you'll hear us squeal because someone just made an announcement. Or we'll go there just to go. That's like a gathering place. There are six or seven of us."

Over the years, the most personally successful of all the Freeway girls worked the female collectivity in order to "stay on track": to keep away from cigarettes and to complete college, and in some cases to obtain jobs. Whereas the Freeway men worked what remains of the job-related collectivity largely in order to obtain jobs as maintenance workers, electricians, Deltasonic car wash workers, and the like, the women used this same collective form to obtain jobs that tend to require more education. Judy, for example, whom we met in the last chapter, landed her job as a radiologic technologist through her sister, who worked at the same hospital. Most important, the female collective functioned, for this group at least, to keep the women in school, thereby contributing to the relatively high female success rate. Where Freeway high school boys maintained the work-based collective insofar as they could and used it to obtain wage labor positions as the women did, they also worked it to watch sports and/or to party. In no instance did Freeway boys use the collective in the pursuit of higher education. If men pursue post-secondary education, and some obviously do, it is consumed and accomplished *individually* rather than as part of an articulated collective, reflective of points raised in previous chapters. Significantly, the mid-1980s male collective tends to block social mobility, whereas the emerging female collective encourages it. It is the *individual* male who moves in relation to modal 1980s cultural form who can become either "settled" working class or middle-class. It is women riding and working with 1980s *collective* cultural form as outlined here who can achieve this same status.

While Freeway girls in 1985 imagined individual solutions linked to their desire to be independent, they are not, over time, quite so individualistic as they had anticipated. For women, the collective bonds are continually woven and remain strong. Men use the remaining work-based collective in the form of contacts to gain a foothold in the economy (get a job at Fred's shop, for example) and enhance and repair one another's houses and cars, but not a single man worked a gender-based collectivity related to schooling. This represents a distinct gender difference, one which enables/encourages women to move forward in the new economy in a way that the men, en masse at least, do not. It is the movement with and against youth-based cultural form for both men and women, then, that enables/encourages the accomplishment of a newly articulated and critically important white working-class collective—the family. It is, in fact, this new collective site, even more than the *particular* work-based site (reflecting the loss of "jobs for life"), that defines white working-class positionality in the new class structure.

On Race and Racism: A Point of Gender Convergence

As we have seen throughout this volume, the white working-class male self in the Northeast is highly dependent upon the construction of a black "other"—one who holds an assigned unpleasant set of social characteristics against which the "good" white male self can be drawn. Michelle Fine and I point to this phenomenon in *The Unknown City* (Fine & Weis, 1998), a study that focuses more broadly on young adult white, African American, and Latino men and women in the urban Northeast. Most important, no similar process is uncovered for girls or women, in that there is no evidence to suggest that white working-class women's identities are forged offensively and *fundamentally* in relation to the co-construction of an "other" of color—an other against whom they judge themselves to be superior in all respects. Although studies exist which explore the issue of racism among white women (Amadiume, 1987; Spelman, 1988; Hine, 1989; Ware, 1992; Golden & Shreve, 1995; Gilmore, 1996; McIntyre, 1997), there are few sociological analyses that focus on the distinct ways in which white women take up the preservation of racial borders (Frankenberg, 1993), which—at least in the case of white working-class women—appears to materialize at a later point in life than is the case for their male counterparts. What is most striking is that few scholars take as central *how* white females elaborate these tendencies as they construct identity over time.

In Chapters 3 and 4, I explored what happens to young white working-class men as they grow into adulthood, suggesting that the core hegemonic white working-class male identity offers a center around which individual white men move as they are propelled and propel themselves into their thirties. It is individual white male movement in relation to this core, as uncovered in my original work as well as that of others, that "determines," to some extent at least, a man's future position in the economy and community. As I argued in Chapter 1, a virulent racism is deeply embedded in this hegemonic construction and, as we saw in Chapter 4, men carry this racism with them into adulthood, where they continue to spend considerable time constructing and defending racial borders, both psychological and, more important as they get older, physical, in terms of desired living space. Moving from targeting solely African Americans in this particular community, they spend much time as adults denigrating Yemenites for "invading" formerly white community space. Freeway men differ from their teenage selves, however, in that racial and gendered self-identity is no longer forged specifically and perhaps even primarily inside the sexual realm—that is to say, no longer carved in relation to a constructed black sexual "other."

In contrast, white working-class female identity is *not forged fundamentally* in relation to that of a constructed black "other," and evidence suggests that white working-class women at times contest the construction of black males so prevalent among their menfolk (Weis, 2001). Ethnographic interview material reveals that white working-class women attempt, at times, to rewrite wholly negative race scripts perpetrated by the working-class white men in their lives, actively interrupting such racist constructions through direct intervention with children or intentional undermining of racist messages handed down by their fathers.

While this may be true, the Freeway girls "all grown up" engage in discussions of racial border patrolling as consistently as do their men, in contrast to key differences noted during their adolescence. It is arguably the case, then, that white working-class women's racial discourse emerges at a later age, in critique related to concerns about neighborhood and children. Like their men, Freeway women in their thirties desire largely white living space, space that enables them, whether consciously or not, to assert continued status in American society in spite of the restructured economy. Without question, white working-class community life has changed—both men and women work in the public sector, at times earning comparable or close to comparable wages (McCall, 2001). Men more often participate in schooling (read "feminine" in hegemonic terms) and engage in traditionally coded feminine work, both in the public and in the private sphere, a set of changes that enable the accomplishment of comfortable white working-class life at the turn of the century. Without this movement, members of the white working class could not stake out a unique position for the class fraction, a position which is linked in fundamental ways to their whiteness. Maintaining white space symbolizes the very maintenance of white working-class status in relation to others of color in the new economy, enabling working-class whites both to assert the right to *control* space, whereas others have no such right (they live where they are forced to live by virtue of money and so forth), and simultaneously to assert racial separateness and white superiority.

Speaking analytically, it becomes, then, very important at this moment for *women as well as men* to assert loudly the legitimacy of white living space. It is, at this historic moment, a key point of gender convergence—convergence at a time when gender relations could be, and indeed are, easily troubled. White living space stands for a relatively high standard of living, one accomplished and asserted in spite of massive changes in the economy, yet one now bought with the labor of both men and women, a point which further differentiates this group from a bordering underclass of color, where long-term partnership rates are much lower. Thus men and women work together, both figuratively and literally, to maintain a white working-class neighborhood space, one where racial borders are constantly patrolled, ultimately carving a distinctly white working-class fraction out of the broader working class, a broader working class which arguably now blankets men and women of a variety of racial and ethnic backgrounds (Bettie, 1995, 2003).

Michelle Fine and I (1998) uncover this same racial border patrolling among those interviewed for *The Unknown City,* although most white interviewees were less "settled" than those in *Class Reunion* and lived in racial borderlands—space occupied by persons of various races and ethnicities.[1] Freeway (as well as surrounding working-class suburbs) is, in contrast, still a largely segregated town, wherein whites engage in a fairly successful form of racial border work designed to "keep nonwhites out." Significantly, women who live in Freeway now sound much like their men, which was not the case in high school; those who no longer live in Freeway echo these sentiments, similarly acting to protect space still occupied, in many cases, by their parents, sisters, brothers, nieces, and so forth. In spite of stunning differences in high school identity work around the issue of race, then, white working-class men and women end up sounding remarkably similar by their early thirties, although, as noted earlier, women are still somewhat more likely to recognize individual exceptions to constructed racial stereotypes. In the final analysis, though, women, like men, engage in discourse around border patrolling strategies wherein they distance themselves, as a white working-class fraction, from the racial "other." In this community, this takes on both a psychological and a physical component. In racial borderlands, these processes, although psychologically the same, would inevitably play out somewhat differently. Sandy, Chris, Carol, and Carla speak below, focusing at length on "Arabians."

SANDY: There's beginning to be a lot of Arabians. They seem to be taking over the whole United States. They're taking over everywhere, if you ask me. Anywhere you go—just things they do. About a month ago, we had kids in our backyard. It was a Friday night, like eleven-thirty at night, and I heard voices. So I went and got my husband, and, matter of fact, my brother had his new truck right in the driveway, and it was two Arabian boys. "Oh, he's drunk. We're taking him home." They were maybe nineteen, twenty years old. And they're going across the street and they were by the guy across the street's back garage door, so my brother and my husband got in the truck and they tried to find them after that. They [the boys] ended up going, and then a couple of days later I found a learner's permit and court papers that we thought they dropped. Well, then a few days later my son was in the window and he said, "Somebody's in the back yard." I walk out there, and there they are again. Right in the yard, rummaging through the bushes and everything, looking for something. And I went and asked them, "What are you looking for?" "I threw something in your bushes the other day." "Well, what did you throw?" "My permit." I said, "Why did you do that?" "Don't worry, it's none of your business." You know, they think everything is theirs. You go into a store and they have a good sale, and you get them [Arabians] in there and they'll fill their carts up and then they sell it at their stores. I've seen it. And there is a lot of trouble with them in school now, too. In fact, my mother tells me they're giving the monitors a lot of trouble. [Her mother is a lunch monitor at Freeway High School; she has done this job since Sandy was in elementary school.] They're just lazy. You know, people used to say that about black people, but they [Arabians] are. They are . . .

lazy. You know, we've got a black couple down the street, we haven't had any trouble. They don't bother us. It just seems like the Arabians are taking over. Arabians are now living on this side of town. On the corner, on the other street . . . they're all over now. I mean, it just seems a lot of people say it. That they're taking over, you know. Just like they took over in the First Ward. It was always the blacks and the Arabians and the Puerto Ricans. But it seems that they take away from the blacks, too. You know, they're moving in and doing their thing and they're shoving them off too. [Here] they bought houses left and right. They're owning houses all over.

Sandy makes it clear that the "Arabians" threaten white space, using the examples of the young men transgressing the boundaries of her backyard and the fact that property is being purchased by "Arabians" in *her* area. That they "took over the First Ward" suggests to her that they could "take over" the white side of Freeway as well. Here Sandy sounds exactly like the white men, although she certainly didn't sound this way when I knew her in high school. In Sandy's case, there is no question but that the 2000 backyard physical border transgression would not be so noticed if the young men were not Yemenites.

Chris focuses specifically on the site of the high school, where her sister now teaches:

It's horrendous. And there are all the blacks and the Arabians. It's totally out of control. I mean, everybody goes to school with knives, and I mean, we didn't do that shit. You fist-fight. I went in there [the high school] one day, and there's like fifteen hundred Arabians standing. I'm like, "Don't you kick them out? You've got cops in your school; you've got them all standing here. They're standing in the hallway—like kick them out of the building. Why do they all congregate?" . . . There's too many, you know, racial relationships. It's a mess. The black students are all dating white girls . . . dating black guys . . . yeech! I don't know. I really don't know [what is going on today].

Carol, a catering sales manager in a town in New Jersey, still has strong family ties to Freeway. Describing racial relationships when she was in high school, she states they were "Good. Very good. I often got in trouble because I would hang out where I wasn't supposed to. Like the First Ward. My father didn't like us back there at night. We were either watching basketball because a lot of them were, they were basketball players. Or on weekends maybe going to a party [laughs]. But he [father] never punished us for it—I just got his opinion."

Carol differs from other Freeway teenage girls [and boys] of the 1980s in that she and her friends, including her sister, who is one year older, occasionally partied "over the bridge," a reference to the "nonwhite" part of town, where she clearly did not belong. Others, such as Suzanne, assert that white kids went there only to get weed— "When I was in high school, the only reason kids from the Third or Fourth Ward would have gone into the First Ward was to buy weed. Which, quite frankly, a lot of them did.... A lot of kids in my class smoked [weed]—we're the honors kids."

But Carol asserts that "apparently now [2001], it's really bad."

I did hear that, like, where we lived, it's all the Arabs and stuff now. I'm shocked at, like, how that area is now. I guess people wanna sell their houses and get out of Freeway. And if somebody's gonna buy it, they don't care who they're selling it to. My grandmother talks about it, "My whole block is all Arabs now." You know, what it is, it's change [that they don't like]. It's not the same town that it was. The back the bridge, the First Ward, was the blacks and the Arabs, and the Second, Third, and Fourth wards were white. And I would have to say that's it. And they're afraid it's gonna ruin the value of their homes. And to be honest with you, it probably has.

Kathy, now a teacher in a city fifty miles from Freeway, where her sister, mother, and other relatives still live, is even more explicit with respect to the protection of white space, although, unlike the others, she refers to African Americans as well as Arabians:

I don't say this to be prejudiced or anything, but there was something about the black population being *contained* [my emphasis] in the First Ward. I don't think it [the black population] affected the city as a whole. If they wanted to run their area down, or they wanted graffiti, or they wanted things the way they were, that was their choice. Most people from the Second Ward on, you had a very strong Polish community, and people tended to sweep their sidewalks so that you could fry an egg and eat it, it was so clean. And I think what happened, and this is my understanding—again from my viewpoint in coming home [to Freeway]—it's been that the black population has moved out into the Second and Third wards. And also you have a high Arab population that's moved in. And from what I have heard, they come in, they pay cash for a house—I believe the government gives them a seven-year tax exemption—they buy the property, they get a tax exemption where they don't have to pay taxes for seven years at all. So what they'll do is they come in and buy a house, and they'll buy like the corner store. They'll keep it for five or seven years, then they'll turn it over or sell it to a family member. Then they [the other family members] get their tax exemption for seven years. And they'll move twenty people in. They have no living room. They kind of line the beds up and then they just move their people in.

Freeway women in their early thirties engage in exactly the same kind of discursive trashing/racial border patrolling as do their men, although such border patrol work is a fundamental part of men's identity in a way that is not true for women, who tend to come to this form of expressed and enacted racism *defensively* at the point of purchasing homes and raising children. Suzanne offers:

I don't see a lot of mixing and acceptance and such. If you look around in this neighborhood, this is fifteen years, almost, after high school; we have had one minority family in this neighborhood. They have been here a very long time. If you go into the Third Ward, you'll find all whites. Second Ward is this side of the bridge; the First Ward is the other side. First and Second ward is where you'll find your other racial groups. The First Ward has become very heavily Arabic. A lot of the minorities, a lot of minority kids that were African American are, some are still in the First Ward. A lot moved into the Second Ward. Freeway is one of the old bastions of how things used to be. The nice neighborhoods were where the white kids were. The uglier neighborhoods were where the black kids were. The Arabics tried to come in wherever they could find room, and most of them were immigrants, didn't have a lot of money, so they headed up in the poorer areas, which were usually traditionally First Ward. As the African American families started to get a little bit more money, they started to move into where there used to be whites and blacks. And the white families that were there don't like it. They don't want them in there, so they move to the suburbs and further out.

Whether Yemenites are "everywhere," as well as the extent to which African Americans are "contained" within the First Ward is, to some extent a matter of opinion, partially dependent upon one's definition of "everywhere," as well as notions of what constitutes acceptable and appropriate "white space." The point is that former Freeway High School white working-class women in 2000 engage in exactly the same form of discursive racial border patrolling as do their men, in spite of the fact that white female identity was not, as we learned from the high school data, formed fundamentally in relation to African Americans or any other designated group of color. As these women grow older and establish households, however, they join their men, expressing a stake in the maintenance of "white" community space. Herein lies the convergence: by their early thirties, white working-class women engage in a form of psychological and physical border patrolling in much the same way as the men do.

In many ways white working-class men and women are not incorrect in their assessment of the "wages of whiteness" in relation to housing value. Melvin Oliver and Thomas Shapiro (1995) in their brilliant book on black versus white wealth in America argue that federal housing, tax, and transportation policies have effectively reinforced residential segregation. Though having eased in the 1960s, these policies left a legacy of residential segregation. Douglas Massey and Nancy Denton (1993), for example, report that 78 percent of blacks in northern cities and 67 percent of blacks in southern cities would have to move to new neighborhoods if housing were to be desegregated completely (p. 136).

Oliver and Shapiro (1995) are far-ranging in their analysis, looking carefully at institutional and policy factors which generate wealth inequality between blacks and whites, including housing-related factors such as differential mortgage loan rejection rates and interest rate differentials, wherein blacks pay more than whites. What is most critical for the present discussion, however, is the value which has accrued to properties in white neighborhoods versus those in black neighborhoods. Not only did federal government action finance and encourage suburbanization and residential segregation after World War II, but taxation, transportation, and housing policies promoted suburban growth. Such discriminatory policies, argue Oliver and Shapiro, "locked blacks out of the greatest mass-based opportunities for home ownership and wealth accumulation in American history" (p. 147).

The accumulated impact of this set of discriminatory policies contributed to the phenomenon related to the value of properties today. As Massey and Denton (1993) argue:

> In general, homes of similar design, size, and appearance cost more in white communities than in black or integrated communities. Their value also rises more quickly and steeply in white communities. In theory, then, whites pay a premium to live in homogeneous neighborhoods, but their property appreciates at an enhanced rate. While

this may mean that blacks find relative housing "bargains" in segregated communities, their property does not appreciate as much. We have already seen that blacks do not have the same access to mortgages as whites and that those approved for home mortgages pay high interest rates. (p. 147)

It is the *combination* of relatively higher interest rates, the greater rejection of mortgages for blacks versus whites, and the relative appreciation in property value which is critical here. Most important to the present discussion is the well-documented fact that *property values in white neighborhoods appreciate to a far greater extent, no matter what the original cost of the property, than those in black neighborhoods.* By way of example, looking at housing appreciation for those who bought homes between 1967 and 1977 (roughly the time period when Freeway parents would have purchased their homes), Oliver and Shapiro (1995) demonstrate that "whites who bought less expensive homes, with median home mortgages of less than $28,000, benefited from a $60,000 gain in home equity versus $28,700 for blacks in the same purchase bracket. And whites enjoyed a 325 percent increase in housing appreciation while the increase for blacks amounted to 175 percent" (p. 147). Within the same category of less expensive homes during the time period 1978–1988, white values appreciated 122 percent, in comparison to 79 percent for blacks (p. 148).

Although Freeway men and women exhibit racist attitudes in terms of whom they wish to have live around them, engaging in a form of psychological as well as physical distancing—and this certainly is not to be condoned—the preservation of white neighborhood space may, unfortunately, make economic sense, although the long-term consequences of the presence of varying groups of nonwhite neighborhood residents in relation to issues of housing value are not yet known.[2] It is, nevertheless, whiteness that privileges the former industrial proletariat as they carve a new white working-class fraction out of the shards of the restructured economy. In a historically and institutionally, as well as psychologically, racist society such as that of the United States, whiteness is privileged both representationally and economically. The more the new white working-class fraction asserts its "whiteness" and the legitimacy of "white space"—at least if the past predicts the future in this regard—the greater the chance of white property values appreciating, or at least remaining stable. This would encourage the uneven growth in equity that characterized past generations of white versus nonwhite homeowners, contributing to further race-based chasms in terms of the economy and its benefits. As the reconstituted white working class underlines its whiteness, we can expect the continued wages of whiteness to work in their favor, permeating, as in the past, job allocation, housing values, schooling, and general cultural representations.

White working-class men in 2000 draw upon their collective youth identity so as to continue to patrol racial borders and assert their own superiority in relation to all those who are not white. Most significantly in terms of class trajectory, at the moment of adulthood (anticipated home ownership and children), white working-class women join them, simultaneously asserting their desire for white space *and* the superiority of whiteness. It is the wages of whiteness in a racially divided and racist society that enable these men and women to construct and hold on to a new white working-class fraction in spite of the potentially destabilizing effects presented by the rearticulation of gender roles and relations within this class fraction, as well as by the fundamental challenge of the restructured world economy. Cashing in deeply and expansively lived gender superiority—although not seamlessly, as the evidence on domestic violence in Chapter 5 suggests—men nevertheless continue to insist upon racial superiority and separateness. It is at this moment that white working-class women uniformly join them. Class thus *reconverges* around race, papering over gender divisions and conflicts, as white working-class men and women, whether settled or hard living, float into the twenty-first century far more confidently than we would have ever predicted on the basis of economic calculations of the 1980s (Bennett & Harrison, 1982; Levin & Rumberger, 1987).[3]

Armed with their whiteness, men and women hold together to preserve privilege in an economy that has stripped them of the life they knew, a life which the women, at least, are happy to give up (in sharp contrast with the men). Without missing a beat, yet buoyed by a middle-class women's movement with which they generally do not identify even a little bit, white working-class women assert the right to have an independent foothold in a reconstitued white working class— a move that men may viscerally reject but are, in the final analysis, wholly dependent upon for their own continued class position. Using this independent foothold which women now demand and consistently work toward, and which is enabled and even encouraged by new capitalist forms, white working-class women join their men to assert the legitimacy and even the necessity of white family space, thus preserving the wages of whiteness, a move that enables this class fraction to continue to differentiate itself from an increasingly impoverished urban underclass of color as well as the now more racially/ethnically diverse broader working class. Collectively asserting whiteness, white working-class men and women, for the moment at least, converge as they work to position themselves for the decades to come.

7

BEYOND THE SHADOW OF THE MILLS
Men, Women, Whiteness, and the New Economy

Noteworthy ethnographic work has been conducted which both elicits working-class culture and identity (Lamont, 2000; Kefalas, 2003; Halle, 1984; Bensman & Lynch, 1987; Rubin, 1976; Elder, 1974) and describes and theorizes the production of this identity in relation to schools (Willis, 1977; Everhart, 1983; London, 1978; Valli, 1986; Anyon, 1981; Gaskell, 1992; Finn, 1999). Such discussion of the working class, and of social class in general, however, has been tempered, if not altogether ignored, since the 1980s, as scholarship targeted more specifically to issues of race and/or gender, as well as broader issues of representation, has taken hold. Such scholarship, while critically important, has often delved into issues of race, gender, and/or representations irrespective of a distinct social class referent, much as earlier scholarship on social class ignored gender and race—a point which critical race theorists (McCarthy, 1990, 1993; Kelley, 1994; Marable, 1997), theorists of "whiteness" production (Giroux, 1997; McLaren, 1994; Kincheloe, Steinberg, Rodriguez, and Chennault, 1998; Fine, Weis, Powell and Wong, 1997, Fine, Weis, Pruitt, and Burns, 2004), and feminist theorists across race and ethnicity have commented upon at length (Crenshaw, 1989; Lather, 1991; Spelman, 1988; Mullings, 1997; Roman and Christian-Smith, 1988).

Paralleling the alleged eclipse of the working class in prime-time television then, academics simultaneously participated in the production of our collective ignorance around issues of social class. With the clear turn in the global economy, one accompanied by deep intensification of social inequalities (Levin and Rumberger, 1987; Katz, 2001; Reich, 1991, 2001), the need for serious class-based analyses could not be more pressing. Although Sennett & Cobb (1972), Hogan (1982, 1985), Davis (1986), Apple (1982), McRobbie (1978), Anyon (1981), Bernstein (1990), Walker (1988), Arnot (2002), Gaskell (1992), Halle (1984), and others have done truly outstanding work that informs us about the white working class and the class structure in general, both in the United States and in Britain, Canada, and Australia, much of this scholarship was produced in the 1970s and 1980s (or, in the case of Hogan and Davis, is historical in nature), including that contained in more recently released volumes (for example, Gaskell, 1992; Bernstein, 1990; and Arnot, 2002).[1] Although powerful, then, given the "moment" of scholarly production, such work cannot take the restructured world economy fully into account. Cognizant of both the growing importance of class- based analysis in the current economic and social context, and the distinct paucity of such analysis inside this context, I embarked upon *Class Reunion*.

Ideological Transformations

The new American white working-class fraction sits inside a worldwide press toward neoliberalism. As Michael Apple (2001) argues, "If we were to point to one specific defining political/economic paradigm of the age in which we live, it would be neoliberalism. This term may be less visible in the United States, but it is definitely known throughout the rest of the world" (p. 17). For Robert McChesney (1999):

> Neoliberal initiatives are characterized as free market policies that encourage private enterprise and consumer choice, reward personal responsibility and entrepreneurial initiative, and undermine the dead hand of the incompetent, bureaucratic and parasitic government, that can never do good even if well intended, which it rarely is. (p. 7, as quoted in Apple, 2001, p. 17)

McChesney continues: "Instead of communities, [neoliberalism] produces shopping malls. The net result is an atomized society of disengaged individuals who feel demoralized and socially powerless" (p. 11, as quoted in Apple, 2001, p. 18).

In light of these assertions, it is important to consider the extent to which the new white working-class fraction in the United States embodies these tendencies.[2] Freeway girls, fueled by a sense of power attached to an almost entirely unacknowledged (middle-class) women's movement, began, in the mid-1980s, to reshape themselves as the consummate neoliberal subject—a subject of self-invention and transformation, one who is capable of surviving and perhaps even thriving in the new world order. As noted throughout this book, the ever evolving capitalist economy simultaneously enabled and encouraged this move on the part of white working-class women. Given their "real" economic and class location, however, it is not possible for the majority of women of the former industrial proletariat to create themselves as autonomous producers (and consumers) and manage to be much other than poor.

Under the assumption of largely heterosexual coupling, women hooked up with men of similar class background, men with whom they could feel "comfortable" because they were "like them," and men who, by virtue of gender trajectories explored in this book, were less apt than working-class women to have made widespread moves toward becoming the self-invented subject under the new global economy. Such liaisons were both desired *and at the same time necessary* if both white working-class women and men were to accomplish what I call a newly articulated form of "settled" working-class life. While women were perhaps desirous of creating themselves as fully neoliberal subjects while in high school, this was, in reality, virtually impossible to enact, given both their "real" class location and their lived association with particular kinds of men, men with whom they shared a class habitus of origin. This habitus, as we see throughout this book, has kept Freeway women almost entirely connected to men of a specific class background: men who go to certain bars, come from certain kinds of families and communities, possess skills and contacts deeply woven into the fabric of masculine working-class culture, and intersect with formal school knowledge in particular class-coded and gender-linked kinds of ways. Thus class inevitably reemerges, although in reconfigured form, serving to defeat, in part at least, the push toward "declassing" embedded in neoliberalism.

To be sure, the family is a unit of consumption, and the idea of the consumer is crucial here. Men and women of the new white working-class fraction in the early twenty-first century are happy with their lives largely because they can purchase valued consumer goods and forms of entertainment and services—dirt bikes, large-screen televisions, houses in working-class white communities, hockey tickets, trips to NASCAR races, and the like. But this is accomplished in ways that do not take dead aim at social class in quite the way proponents of neoliberalism might like; men and women of the former industrial proletariat have been "rearranged" in class terms due to the massive shift in the global economy, but they have also "rearranged" themselves so as to preserve a white working-class fraction—one which is distinct in key ways from what is arguably a larger working class now composed of men and women across race and ethnic groups of color. While neoliberalism may demand unattached individuals—those who can move easily from place to place in the economy and consume as a result of their continual participation in this economy—thereby encouraging a cadre of "de-raced, de-classed and de-gendered" individuals (Apple, 2001, p. 39), it is arguably the case that members of the former industrial proletariat are fighting back—insisting, on some level at least, on *being classed*, and certainly *raced* in spite of the fact that they increasingly enter and remain attached to the economy as *individuals*. While the ideological transformation around the neoliberal project "redefines citizenship" and "democracy," it has, Michael Apple trenchantly argues, as one of its effects the "de-classing, de-racing and de-gendering of people. That is, to define everyone as a consumer, and democracy as individual consumer choice is a radically individuating project with a radically individuating set of identities attached to it" (Apple, 2004, p. 188). While not necessarily calling themselves working-class (members of the American working class have exhibited a love/hate relationship with this signifier for decades), members of the former white industrial proletariat nevertheless carve out a distinct class fraction—one which rests upon uncomfortable gender realignment for the men, and the simultaneous deep patrolling of race borders by both men and women. The press of neoliberalism in this specific class fraction, then, reaches only so deep, as the class fraction continues to constitute itself around key categories of class, race, and gender, thus contradicting at the *lived* level the full imperatives and implications of neoliberalism.

Whiteness, Gender, and the Economy

In this regard, it may appear at times that I analyze women's positionality too deeply in terms of men's. As an ethnographer, I am driven by where data lead me, although obviously I retain primary position as analyst. The women in this volume see their own lives as inextricably bound with those of their men in spite of the fact that, as evidence on domestic violence reveals, the relationship between men and women of this class fraction is brutal at times. As the men and women of the former industrial proletariat forge a new class fraction, they do so fully in relation to one another, in spite of the desire for "independence from men" expressed by Freeway teenage girls. This no doubt has a psychological component, one lived out within the strictures of heterosexuality, but it is also purely economic. Neither the men nor the women could live the life they desire (one which almost uniformly includes children) if by themselves, as clarified by the "hard living" men we met in Chapter 4. It takes two incomes to accomplish what I call the new "settled" working class. Freeway girls did not, therefore, compromise their dreams of "freedom" so much as enter into necessary domestic arrangements that would allow them to support both themselves and their children in concert with their men.

As I have argued throughout, women's gendered trajectory is increasingly linked to the economy, and men's gendered trajectory is increasingly tied to what is happening within the family. Men are de-moored from prior economic space—a mooring that granted them certain rights in the home/family sphere in prior generations—at the same time that women are surging into the very sector that encourages so much of men's psychological distress. It is the crossing of home/family/wage-earning borders by *both* men and women that underlies this new class fraction, whether they like it or not. Most stunningly, as we see in Chapter 6, women keep moving forward as many of their men collapse around them. Fueled by a deeply rooted sense of possibility evident as far back as high school—a sense of possibility born of the struggles of the women's movement as well as the opening up of the economic sector to women—women now experience, at some level at least, the "freedom" they desired, encouraging them perhaps to carry the burdens of their gender/class on their shoulders. Given male collapse so evident across these women's lives, it is also possible they sense that if *they* don't hold it all together, no one will. As African American women have done for centuries (Mullings, 1997; hooks, 1990; Fine and Zane, 1989), white working-class women continue to engage the struggle for a better life, carrying their children as they go. Quietly, perhaps, or at least quietly for the moment, both their movement and their strength pave the way for the next generation.

The importance that race, racism, and raciality play in the making of the new white working-class fraction demands further attention, as does the unique role of the Yemenite community in Freeway. As noted above, neoliberalism presses toward the deraced, declassed, degendered subject—subjects who are capable of "understanding themselves as autonomous agents, producers of their present and their future, inventors of the people that they are or may become (Giddens, 1991, as cited in Walkerdine, Lucey, & Melody, 2001, p. 2). Such individuals are unmoored from community, and operate as autonomous agents responsible for their own lives. Quoting Walkerdine et al.: "If we think about the end of jobs for life and the production of a culture of uncertainty, [the notion of] self-invention through a discourse of limitless choice provides a way to manage the government of potentially unruly and disaffected subjects," a project that "requires acceptance of a certain kind of psychological discourse as a true description of oneself … so if one is out of work, one has to transform oneself into the right kind of employable subject" (2001, pp. 2–3).

In the case of the white working-class fraction in the postindustrial United States, neoliberal subjects are only partially created, suggesting only a partial "win" for the demands of neoliberalism at the lived cultural level and accompanying deep recesses of the mind. Alongside the "fixing" of a distinct social class fraction, although one tied inevitably to the practices of consumption and an increasingly individuated workforce, the former industrial proletariat in the United States simultaneously and doggedly engages in the "fixing" of racial identities—their own as well as that of the constructed nonwhite "other"—in this case, African Americans and Yemenites. Such "fixing," paradoxically, occurs at the same time that racial identity is being destabilized at other levels (Dolby, 2001; McCarthy, Crichlow, Dimitriadis, and Dolby, 2004). McCarthy (2003), for example, signals the end of the "auratic status" of race, arguing:

> [T]he notion of racial identity as residing in "origins," "ancestry," "linguistic" or "cultural unity" has been shattered, overwhelmed by the immense processes of hybridity, disjuncture, and re-narration taking place in what Arjun Appadurai (1996) calls the new techno, media, and ideoscapes now disseminated in ever-widening areas and spheres of contemporary life. Migration, electronic mediation, biometric and information technologies have separated culture from place. And, difference has become an abstract value that can be dirempted from specific groups and settings and combined and recombined in ways that allow, for example, clothing designer magnates like Tommy Hilfiger to appropriate elements of hip hop culture, to recombine semiotically these elements into new forms of clothing fashion, and then sell these new designs back into the inner city itself. These stylized elements of black culture are further marketed, with overwhelming success, to a white consumer audience. Racial identity, then, is conceptualized as a contextual performance "produced within specific historical and institutional sites,

within specific discursive formations and practices, and by specific enunciative strategies. (Hall, 1996, p. 4; as cited in McCarthy, 2003)

Catherine Cornbleth (2003) picks up on this moment of destabilization in racial/ethnic identities among American high school students. Based on extensive ethnographic interviews, she argues that young people now deconstruct racial identities rather than "fix" them as did earlier generations. As I suggest here, though, if we focus on high school students as they enter adulthood, it becomes clear that the white working-class project in the United States involves the *continual stabilization* of race at the same time that race becomes unmoored, or destabilized by larger social forces (including larger political forces such as those examined by Mica Pollack (2004), who probes discourse around racial "counting" in the state sector, particularly schools).[3]

The neoliberal subject position (without the language, of course), as pursued strongly by the young Freeway women in the mid-1980s, is, then, only partially enacted. For the former white industrial proletariat, whiteness privileges at the same time that it "fixes" race at a time of simultaneous *destabilization* of race and class in particular. With great respect for the writing of McCarthy, Crichlow, Dimitriadis, and Dolby (2004), as well as that of Cornbleth (2003), the ways in which whiteness is celebrated and simultaneously fixes "others" of color over time should not be underestimated. Racial categories are being destabilized by "hybridity," renarration, disjuncture, and so forth in ever widening arenas of contemporary life, but part of the project of the white working class as they stake out a new form of white working-classness in this new economy and culture is that they partially defeat, at their own cultural and psychological level, the intrusion of such renarration around race. As race is de-stabilized in a wide set of arenas, the new white working-class fraction fights hard to *restabilize* it.[4]

Significantly, white working-class women join their men in this "fixing" at precisely the moment of motherhood/stability, although they did not exemplify racial fixing as teenagers, in sharp contrast to Freeway boys. Their continued forging ahead under new economic and social conditions is thus shot through with pulls associated with both their race and their class, thereby preventing, in odd ways, the full production of the very neoliberal subject that their gendered trajectory revealed as far back as high school.

The particular role of Yemenites in this community also must be considered. I conducted the follow-up interviews prior to September

11, 2001, a moment that, at least in the popular discourse and imagination of Americans, changed the world forever (Giddens, 2003).
Yemenites have lived in Freeway since the mid-1940s, when they came
to work in the steel industry, and white working-class raciality has
been forged in relation to this group since their arrival. However, there
have been key changes with respect to the Yemenite community. To
begin with, in the mid-1980s, when I conducted the original research,
the work of the young white men encircled gender, heterosexuality,
and race, but did not rest fundamentally upon the construction of an
"Arab" other. Rather, as noted in Chapter 1, the work of white-
ness/class/heterosexuality and gender was done largely in relation to
black Americans, where black Americans, particularly black men, were
set up as the unacceptable sexual "other," enabling white young men
both to assert their own heterosexuality at a time of intense surveillance of sexuality and, at the same time, establish and reveal their
protectionist stance in relation to white women. In addition, by using
black men as a foil, they were able to articulate the limits of acceptable heterosexual behavior at the boundary of race—in other words,
the behavior of black American men (and women to some extent) was
seen to be over the boundary of what was acceptable, whereas their
own behavior was deftly established as normative, thus underscoring
the normativity of "whiteness" in a wide variety of areas (Fine, Weis,
Pruitt, & Burns, 2004). The defiant heterosexual moment was, in this
particular group, thus inscribed with and against race, particularly in
relation to black Americans. Although there were certainly instances
of overt racism involving Yemenites (including the fact that they were
referred to as "Arabians" or, even worse, "A-rabs"), this instance of
raciality did not reach as deeply into the white adolescent psyche or
into the crevices of sexuality. Later, however, as these white men and
women "grew up," Yemenites in this community took on particular
significance, as whiteness continued to be asserted and inscribed as
good in a grown-up world of valued family and community living
space.

At the time of the 2000–2001 interviews, a notable number of
Yemenites lived on the "white" side of town—living among those I
interviewed. It is fair to say that whiteness is now inscribed on a day-
to-day basis in relation to Yemenites, but the key point here is that it
is *whiteness* that continues to be inscribed and valued at the same time
that Yemenites (Arabs) become thoroughly inscribed as *racially
different*. The racial project around the Yemenites thus becomes a way
of "stretching" the existing United States racial dichotomy—a

dichotomy that rests largely along a black–white continuum (Seller & Weis, 1997; Omi & Winant, 1994), a point that is well articulated in literature in relation to the experiences and practices of Latinos on the mainland (Rodriguez, 1990, 1992, 1994), where such binary construction is fiercely contested.

As white working-class men and women continue to fix race—their own as well as that of others—they expand the racial "other" in significant ways, making it possible to center on whiteness without necessarily having to engage a constructed black other. This represents a significant turn of events in United States racial history, paralleled perhaps by the racial project surrounding the internment of Japanese Americans during World War II, when whiteness was, again, forged in relation to a group other than African Americans. As we see here, though, at least in this particular community, the former industrial proletariat instantiates its own whiteness and at the same time marks the boundaries of this whiteness in relation to a relatively new group.[5]

That this group is linked to current international politics is obviously important, and enables the white working-class fraction as well as others to situate their own whiteness and goodness in relation to a negatively defined discursive (*racial*) other in the context of a broader set of emerging world politics. It must be remembered, though, that this was unfolding in this particular community long before any of these people knew who Osama bin Laden was, and that this specific set of racial dynamics is attached to a larger project around the more general elaboration of whiteness in the new white working-class fraction.

In addition, it is arguably the case that since Yemenites exhibit highly circumscribed gender roles and relations on a day-to-day basis, this actually helps white working-class men swallow their own reconfigured and devalued position in the economy and family. The highly visible patriarchal family embedded in the Yemenite community perhaps enables such men to see themselves in a more positive light. They are now the "good guys"—the ones who push strollers, meet the school bus, and tend to myriad family responsibilities their fathers and grandfathers would never have touched—unlike their Arab neighbors, who "pack a lot of relatives into the house," insist that their women be covered, and "drive around in Lexuses" while their women tend to all home-based duties. The fact that media images can be sent instantaneously from the Middle East to the United States, thus reinforcing the already observed deep (and unfamiliar to even the most patriarchal male American eye) oppression of women undoubtedly helps working-class white men retain some dignity in spite of their own rearranged masculinity. The Muslim "other," then, plays an important role both in the stabilization of whiteness and in the grudging acceptance of a new gendered order in a virulently patriarchal class fraction of the not-too-distant past.[6] As Jerry said in 2000: "My dad would never have done any of this stuff.... For him, dinner was on the table at five and the kids were kept quiet."

The pouring of women into educational institutions post high school is a cross-race/class and even cross-national phenomenon (Arnot, David, and Weiner, 1999) and is reflected in data reported here. As Nancy Lopez (2003) notes:

> In 1996, there were 8.4 million women enrolled in U.S. colleges, compared with 6.7 million men, even though there were slightly more college-age men than women in the population at the time. Women also had higher college completion rates than men: 26 percent to 29 percent respectively. Not only did women outnumber men in institutions of higher learning, they also earned better grades and outperformed men on reading and writing tests. Women also comprised the vast majority of students in honors classes. It is predicted that as early as the year 2007, the gender gap will reach 2.3 million, with 9.2 million women enrolled in U.S. colleges compared with 6.9 million men. (p. 2)

Women in the class fraction explored here well reflect these trends, as young Freeway women looked toward possibilities in high school even as their male counterparts held tightly to retrograde cultural forms. It was indeed striking that the sixteen-year-old girls whom I interviewed in the mid-1980s all informed me that they didn't want to be dependent on a man—that they wanted to make it on their own first—that men "tell you what to do; where to go," and that they wanted no part of it. The reality of their own lives obviously encouraged them to move in this direction, having seen their mothers and grandmothers both beaten physically by the men in their lives and bereft of options as the steel industry collapsed around them. They watched their fathers drink, "sit around and do nothing," and their homes fall to pieces or be lost altogether as money dried up. Quite simply, young women did not want this life, saw a way out, and went for it. The women's movement was terribly important in this respect, in that it offered a discourse of possibility for women as well as actual school and work-related options tied to this discourse—options keyed, of course, to the needs of a rapidly changing capitalist economy in a global context. Although largely rejecting ties to the feminist movement, white working-class women plunged forward—holding, at the same time, the class project together.

Women's enactment of new economic roles could not, though, stave off the vestiges of male-based class violence, nor could it prevent the double burden of being a woman in the home/family and economic spheres, a burden shared by women across social classes. Nevertheless, Freeway women compare their lives with those of their mothers and come up feeling strong, much as immigrants of color in the United States compare themselves with "those left behind," thereby becoming better able to swallow the barbs of racism than "castelike" minorities such as African Americans (Ogbu & Simons, 1998; Ogbu, 2002). For the moment, at least, white working-class women surge ahead and feel relatively good about themselves. Across race, women are carrying the world on their shoulders as so many of their men collapse around them, but women of the white working class are not yet complaining. It is the combination of early messages regarding possibility linked to an economy that has enabled women to stake a claim that accounts for this phenomenon in this specific class fraction. Had this not occurred, in all likelihood far more of the children of the former white industrial proletariat would be poor, and the discrete class fraction explored here would perhaps not have materialized.

What I do not know is what will happen from here. In the latter quarter of the twentieth century, the white working class engaged in the process of remaking itself in light of a restructured global economy. Reconstituting itself on a daily basis, the white working-class fraction is effectively staging its own "class reunion"—a class reunion which, given the fundamentally altered world economy and the particular place of the former industrial proletariat inside this new economy, embodies deep restructuring along gender lines. As men and women of the new American white working class collectively assert whiteness, the class fraction solidifies, offsetting the potentially destabilizing effects of deep gender tensions and realignment. How long the class "project" will hold is open to question, thus inviting further research.

THEORETICAL CODA

Class Reunion challenges our body of what has become known as "resistance" literature.[1] In response to overly deterministic frameworks such as that of Bowles and Gintis (1976) and of Althusser (1971), numerous scholars have focused on the ways in which students, as classed, raced, and gendered beings, act back on meanings and practices distributed through schools. The impetus for such studies stems largely from what was thought to be an incorrect assumption that one could easily "read" culture off existing social structure. Thus a broadly conceived "culturalist" genre emerged, a genre which served to challenge earlier structuralist interpretations and, at the same time, to open up space for positive change within school. If working-class kids are not necessarily destined for working-class jobs, as structuralists earlier asserted, then there is potentially a great deal that can be done inside educational institutions to alter outcomes (Finn, 1999).

The first and most lasting theoretical challenge to structuralist interpretations, as they shed light on the workings of educational institutions and students inside these institutions, was Paul Willis's *Learning to Labour* (1977). Focusing on the effects of social class, Willis presents an ethnographic account of a group of working-class boys at an all-male comprehensive school in an industrial area of England. Rather than internalize messages distributed through schools, the "lads" self-consciously reject school-based meanings and spend their time "working the system" in order to gain some control over obligatorily spent time: they use school time to "have a laff." The "ear 'oles," in contrast, simply sit and listen, complying with educational authority and the notions of qualifications and credentials. Breaking new ground as to the ways in which the semiautonomous level of culture serves, paradoxically, to reproduce existing social structure and a group's "place" within this structure, Willis's volume set the stage for studies of social identity production for the next twenty-five years (Dolby & Dimitriadis, 2004).

Reflecting this deep paradigmatic shift, we now have excellent studies of cultural (re)production in schools which span issues of social class, race, and gender. Notable examples here include, but are not limited to, the work of John Ogbu (1988), Jean Anyon (1981, 1997), Patrick Solomon (1992), Linda McNeil (1986, 2000), Kathryn Borman (1991), Wendy Luttrell (1997), Michelle Fine (1991), Philip Wexler (1987), Signithia Fordham (1996), Annette Lareau (1989), Craig Centrie (2004), Robert Everhart (1983), Stacey Lee (1996), Doug Foley (1990), Anglela Valenzuela (1999), Amira Proweller (1998), and others who have probed the connections between and among culture, schooling, and the economy, offering, at the same time, practical suggestions for how schools can be reconfigured so as to offer maximum opportunities for all.

While such researchers have chronicled and theorized "resistance," few have taken up the *consequences* of such "resistance" over time. Where, for example, does "resistance" sit as youth grow older? What is possible and not possible as collective and/or individual moments of resistance are lived out? While this genre of study offers a great deal with respect to what we know about students and schools, serving ultimately to invert our understandings as to the absolute power of educational institutions and their ability to "name" others, such studies are inevitably conducted "in the moment," leaving us unable to theorize the meaning of "resistance" as it works through time in a rapidly changing context. While I am certainly not critical of such studies, since it is exceedingly difficult to engage the kind of longitudinal method exemplified by *Class Reunion*, such longitudinality enables us to engage the consequences of youth cultural form, *whether produced largely through structure or agency or some combination of both* (which is my preference). This methodological "turn" allows us to probe where snapshot data "hit" as students grow older, as well as to speculate how and why they "hit" as they do.

In this regard, Greg Dimitriadis (2003) follows the life course of two African American young men, offering a deep and sustained look over a six-year period as two adolescents grow into young manhood/adulthood. Reading off their early years, one might posit that Tony was destined for a particular form of urban-based male failure, whereas Rufus was destined for some form of "success." Dimitriadis's work over the six-year period implodes both the "good boy"/"bad boy" distinction and any predictions based upon this simplistic set of categories, thus serving to introduce longitudinality as a way of marking consequence.

This twist in method enables us to track carefully the ways in which youth forms grow over time. Most important, as we see in *Class Reunion*, such forms both take shape *and are lived out* inside a very particular local, national, and international context, and it is this context that provides the stage for the lived-out articulation of youth identities. Additionally, as *Class Reunion* makes clear, the context itself is in flux—quite simply, it is not stable. Neither, necessarily, are our young people. While Paul Willis may valorize the oppositional identity of his lads in the 1970s, speculating as to possibilities that revolve around working-class, white-male-based resistance in England, the world economy has shifted dramatically around his "lads," rendering the meaning and possibility of actions linked to such youth resistance rather different from what Willis or anyone could have predicted. A form of ethnographic longitudinality such as articulated in *Class Reunion* enables us to track *both* changes in individuals/groups as they traverse the years toward adulthood and the broader context within which this all plays.

Several examples from *Class Reunion* immediately come to mind here: Jerry, who most certainly would have been seen as an "ear 'ole" by both Willis and Willis's "lads"—thereby ultimately useless in terms of suppressing the demands for intensification of production on the shop floor as well as lacking any revolutionary potential—is now a middle school teacher and married to a woman from an affluent suburb. The context in which his "ear 'oleness" played out was such that he was able to capitalize upon his high school identity and attend college inside a massively expanding tertiary-level system in the United States. Bob, on the other hand, would have been a "lad" (although, as I argue in Chapter 1, this "laddishness" does not take the same shape and form as that chronicled by Willis; see also note 1, Chapter 1)—but he re-shaped himself inside an American educational system that, once again, allowed for such change. Bob crawled out from barely graduating high school to his recent graduation from one of the most prestigious veterinary schools in the world. A "lad" in high school, he dropped this persona over time, and, aided by his "whiteness" inside racially stratified America, became someone else. Had he remained a "lad," he would probably still be working at Home Depot (where he went directly out of high school, just before entering the service), selling wood or paint—or possibly at Target, where he would be selling electrical wiring. My point here is that there was no shop-floor culture to which he was destined to be attached—no space in which his counterculture and its attendant "penetrations" could limit, in any way at all, the workings of capitalism. To be sure, Bob changed, but so did the context around him.

Clint, also a high school "lad" (although again, this takes a specifically American form in the context of deindustrialization), never became anyone else. Rather than growing up to be part of any kind of romantic collective that capitalizes upon and engages oppositional behavior within the walls of the factory, thereby limiting the power of capital as it intrudes into working-class productivity/life as well as offering dignity for those at the "bottom" of the class structure, Clint is now just low-paid, bouncing between his mother's home and that of a girlfriend who is about to erase him from her life. Playing with motorcycles and snowmobiles, he is the consummate consumer, one with no politics to speak of other than the deep assertion of his own "whiteness." At the age of thirty, his bad back, the product of a particular kind of heavy lifting in an economy that offers limited collective (and, in the United States, virtually no health insurance) around such labor, will undoubtedly end his career in the automotive shop. Since Clint is not part of any kind of romantic collective at all, the American version of teenage "laddishness" deposited nowhere except inside his own economically marginal position as a member of the "hard living" new white working-class fraction. Not only can he not dominate his woman in the home/family sector, as he fantasized while in high school, but no woman who has developed herself as a solid wage earner—thereby being able to aid in the piecing together of "settled" working-class family life—will, by his own admission, have anything to do with him. The consequences for Clint of the American version of his anti-authority, romantically induced, drunken, loutish teenage behavior are, in the present economy, not stellar. In the past, Clint would have perhaps signed on to a factory assembly line and fit right into a collective aimed both at preserving dignity and simultaneously drawing boundaries around appropriate worker exploitation. Given his wage earning capacity, he would, in all likelihood, have begun and sustained a family of his own, under the strictures of both the capital-labor accord and the secret guarantees of earning the family wage: sacrifice, reward, and dignity.

Now, of course, he is simply marginally employed, with no collective surrounding him except that which is aimed at the consumption of alcohol, drugs, car races, dirt bikes, and the like.

The *ethnographic longitudinality* employed here enables us to probe the consequences of varying forms of behavior, given both the potential reworking of self *and* massive changes in the surrounding economy and culture. Without this longitudinal form, the entire set of high school dreams of the Freeway girls, for example, might have been interpreted as just that—a fantasy future, albeit one substantially different from that invoked by the young women in McRobbie's study. The method employed in *Class Reunion* allows me to theorize the rearticulation of a social class fraction, driven in many ways by gender realignment. All too easily a point-in-time ethnography (including my own) could lead one to deposit the young women's initial "moment of critique" into the category of "fantasy future."

I do not claim that the *particular* set of consequences detailed above works inside anything other than the white working-class fraction explored in this volume. The consequences of certain behavior inside youth cultural form are apt to be one thing for white working-class men, for example, and quite another for white men of more affluent background/social class. The latter can perhaps exhibit oppositional behavior in high school, only to remake themselves later on, thereby taking/assuming their "rightful" place as members of the upper middle class in the United States. Their class habitus, social and cultural capital, race, and monetary resources can enable this to happen. Contrast this possibility with that of three African American men whom I interviewed in the mid-1980s (who do not appear in this volume). They were, unfortunately, nowhere to be found in the year 2000, although it is rumored that two of the three are in jail (this could not be confirmed through any search of large databases). Their class/race-linked version of teenage "laddish" behavior in America has very different consequences from that of either the white working-class boys of Freeway or, in the above example, white boys of the upper middle class. My point here is that the actual consequences of youth culture and identity can be understood and fully theorized only when a form of ethnographic longitudinality is engaged. Jay MacLeod (1995) makes this point well in one of the few follow-up studies of youth other than that of Dimitriadis: his African American pro-school (in action as well as attitude) young men landed in the same economic space seven years later as the disengaged and anti-school white boys who, more than anything else, resemble Willis's "lads."

The structure/agency theoretical argument has been raging since the 1970s. It is, though, an argument waged almost entirely in terms of ethnographic studies done at a moment in time—snapshot studies, which "freeze" both a culture and an economic and social context, whether intentionally or not. While it is certainly true that I "freeze" at two points in time, my method implies movement and fluidity—it recognizes, by its very nature, constant change.[2] In order to engage the structure/agency argument further, while offering the complexity it deserves, we need to follow up the same group of people as they leave high school and enter adulthood. In this I make a strong plea for crossing the normal boundaries within which we work. No one lives only in the economic sector; we all live across the public and private spheres. I do not want any more studies of young women and/or men as they go to work from school, irrespective of the broader social context within which they live.

What we need to know is the ways in which individuals/groups engage the entirety of their lives and the ways in which this plays over time. We cannot understand anything about the new white working-class fraction, for example, unless we engage issues of gender, sexuality, and whiteness across public and private sectors, as well as massive shifts in the global economic and cultural context within which this all works. It is under these circumstances that we can probe more fully the structure/agency couplet, focusing carefully on the interplay between and among changing "selves" and changing structural circumstances. Herein lies the power of what I call *ethnographic longitudinality*—a power not duplicated by snapshot ethnographic studies, no matter how brilliant. I exit *Class Reunion*, then, not with the last word, but with a template for future study of the relationships between the production of individual/collective cultures and identities, and the broader economic and social context within which we live.

EPILOGUE
Methods and Reflections

Data for this volume were collected at two points in time; the first data set stems from a full-scale ethnographic investigation of Freeway High. I spent the academic year 1985–1986 in the high school, acting as a participant-observer for three days a week for the entire year. Data were gathered in classrooms, study halls, the cafeteria, and extracurricular activities, and through in-depth interviews with fifty-one juniors (including ten students of color who did not appear in *Working Class Without Work*), virtually all teachers of juniors, the vice principals, social workers, guidance counselors, and others. Data collection centered on the junior class (third year of secondary school), when PSATs, SATs, and the like must be considered if college is a goal. In addition, this was, in the state where Freeway is located, the time when the bulk of a series of state tests must be taken if entrance to a four-year college is being considered (in subsequent years, this has shifted, but this was the case in 1986). Since I sat in on classes across the academic track structure, students were drawn randomly for interviews from across this structure, having been selected from classes which I attended on a regular basis throughout the academic year.

Data in 2000–2001 were collected primarily through in-depth interviews, although some participant observation was employed as I was nestled inside individuals' homes, places of work, donut shops, bars, and the like. As noted in Chapter 3, I contacted individuals through their own networks as well as what I call "walking the streets"—in other words, visiting those community-based institutions where individuals congregate and are likely to know where others are. I frequented the donut shop (which, in this working-class community, is set up like a bar, with soft lighting and an array of beers served along-side coffee and donuts), local bars, the American Legion (and attached bar), gas stations, small convenience stores, and the like in order to find people. It was simply a matter of letting people know that I was interested in locating select individuals. Often the individual's father or mother was sitting there, or an uncle, a friend, or a friend of his/her parents, and I was immediately directed to the adjacent Deltasonic, Home Depot, convenience store, or electrician's shop where I would find either the desired individual or his/her sibling. Using this snowball technique, I was able to locate and interview thirty-five of the original fifty-one cohort students (this includes students of color who do not appear in this volume). Five additional students were found but refused to be interviewed; five more were located but did not respond to my repeated efforts to contact them; two are supposedly incarcerated, although my extensive efforts to locate them in the criminal justice system proved fruitless (both African American men); and four have no apparent address and/or phone number (including one African American man who was in a serious car accident and is reported to be a paraplegic and one Puerto Rican man who has no contact with his family due to alleged drug-related activity out of state).

Although most of the original interviewees ended up in Freeway or the immediately surrounding metropolitan area, eight, including four individuals of color, are confirmed as living outside the broader metro-politan area (Michigan, white woman whom I reinterviewed; New Jersey, Puerto Rican man whom I could not locate; Louisiana, African American woman whom I reinterviewed but who is not included in this volume; Virginia, Puerto Rican woman who did not return my calls; Texas, white man whom I reinterviewed; New Jersey, white woman whom I reinterviewed; South Carolina, African American woman whom I could not locate precisely; and New York, white man whom I re-interviewed and who is completing a degree in veterinary medicine). Among those who live out of town, I reinterviewed all but four.

In 1985–1986 I interviewed a small number of students of color, although their school- and home- based experiences were not discussed in the original volume. So, too, in this volume, where my focus is on the repositioning of the sons and daughters of the white industrial proletariat. Future writing will focus directly on the experiences and practices of students of color as they grow up amid the same massive shift in the world economy.

Upon locating students, I set about interviewing them. I brought their high school yearbook as well as hard copy of their original high school interview, which I left with them. Approximately half of the students remembered the high school interview very well; others somewhat remembered it or did not remember it at all. Those who remembered the interview tended also to remember my interview with their parents (I interviewed parents of half of the students). Those parents whom I reconnected with in 2000 remembered me well, and were happy to put me in touch with their sons and/or daughters. My reconnection with the parents tended to take the form of a party, as hugs and kisses were traded all around. Those students who remembered me were equally happy to reconnect. Even those who did not remember me expressed interest in seeing me fifteen years from now, when they "definitely would remember me." Women tended to remember the original interview in more cases than men. The women wept at passages related to now lost parents and laughed at passages wherein they suggest they would have children but no husband. Groups of women (particularly those discussed in Chapter 6) met and traded their high school interview transcripts, revisiting who they were then and who they are now.

Laughing their way through their own language and ideas, Freeway women thoroughly enjoyed the process of reconnecting with me, inviting me to come back "any time." Men did, too, although they were far more embarrassed by their current lives in many cases. They did not, obviously, enact their fantasy future, thereby enjoying reading their high school transcript far less than the women, especially those men whom I call "hard livers." Comments abounded in this group such as: "We got into lots of trouble back then," "Those were the good times," "I still see them guys and we still do the same things." I sensed nostalgia among the men for a world long lost—an imagined world that never materialized. Among the women I sensed excitement that they had moved so far—"I can't believe that I talked like that," "Oh, my God, I can't believe that I said that." The women are busy—with jobs, family, parents, kids, schools, commitments of all sorts. They have little time for the kind of nostalgia expressed by some of the men, particularly the "hard livers."

Fanning through Freeway, the surrounding white working-class suburbs, the adjacent large city, and locales far from Freeway, I proceeded to interview the men and women in three-to-five-hour sessions conducted in one or two sittings. I conducted all interviews myself, as I quickly concluded that part of the "magic" of the interview lay in the fact that I had worked with them fifteen years earlier. All interviews were tape-recorded following explicit conversations about confidentiality, anonymity, privacy, and informed consent. The tape recorder was fully visible on the table (as it was during their high school years), and all interviewees were invited to turn it off at any time if they wanted information to be "off the record," although few availed themselves of this opportunity. Protocol was followed with respect to Human Subjects Review, and all individuals were apprised of the purpose of the study and informed that their real names would not be used. In accordance with confidentiality, all names were changed, as were certain identifying details of their lives which would obviously compromise their anonymity. All consented to have their words appear as part of future publications.

Upon completion of the individual interviews, all data were transcribed (put into hard copy) and input into Hyperqual, a computer-based analytic program for qualitative data. Using traditional qualitative analysis techniques (Bogdan & Biklen, 1998; Weis & Fine, 2000; Goetz & LeCompte, 1984), I read through over a quarter of the transcripts across gender and established "coding categories"—labels through which the data could be chunked and analyzed. These empirically developed coding categories were added to theoretically driven codes, and included "Family When Growing Up," "Race Relations," "Desire for Future," "Marriage," "Children's Schools," and so forth. These categories stem from the data themselves—as filtered, of course, through my own eyes, but data have to "speak" to a category before it is established as one. Three individuals in Buffalo coded data: myself, Tina Wagle, and Susan Ott, then graduate students.

Discussion took place to establish that there were inter-rater reliability scores of at least 0.80 between raters. We then took the completed codebook and coded each interview on hard copy. Coding was done such that interview segments could be double- or even triple-coded; that is, one interview segment could be coded "Children's Schools," and, at the same time, "Race Relations." After coding on hard copy, the transcripts were coded on screen. Print files were then set up so we could "dump" the data segments into the appropriate data file—for example, "Current Employment, White Male" and "Current Employment, White Female." Data segments were printed out and placed into an appropriately labeled manila file folder, thus enabling me to consider carefully the chunked data. At no time were the original transcripts destroyed, allowing me to move back and forth between coded data snippets and the larger context from which the data segments were drawn.

Once data were printed out and placed into appropriately labeled manila file folders, analysis began. I read and reread all full narratives as well as all folders holding data snippets, ultimately coming to conclusions about the broader themes which swirl through these stories. The coding categories themselves (and embedded data) are constituted of, but not necessarily identical to, the themes, which are embedded in the writing. Coding categories are numerous, and serve as a way of breaking down the data so that they can be looked at systematically and considered. Once data were examined in this way (it is not possible to come to conclusions based on thousands of pages of field notes or interview transcripts without coding), the categories were recombined in order to produce the written research product. This was an extremely painstaking process, one that moved between intense technicality and moments of sheer insight, a point that both Thomas Kuhn (1962) and Abraham Kaplan (1964) made years ago with respect to the logic of scientific inquiry. While coding categories are not established based on the whim of an investigator, and coding itself is not done solely through a series of imaginative moves, it is also the case that without such imagination, scholarship falls flat—in other words, the process outlined here as well as in my other work reflects imaginative thinking in combination with painstaking work with narrative data. It is the simultaneous cutting up and piecing back together of narrative that allows me to weave the final product. Data analysis took up to a year, and I engaged in intense writing and thinking for two additional years before completing this volume.

Reflections

Class Reunion is the most difficult volume I have ever written. Moving between a changing macrolevel context and changing lives (my own included) meant that I had to work on a number of planes simultaneously and, additionally, that no template existed for doing so. While Jay MacLeod's *Ain't No Makin It,* Greg Dimitriadis's *Friendship, Cliques and Gangs,* and Claire Wallace's *For Richer or Poorer* track individual lives over time, thus opening up the specter of what I call *ethnographic longitudinality,* none enacts what Michelle Fine and I have put forward as "compositional studies" (Weis & Fine, 2004), wherein the investigator uses ethnographic inquiry so as to understand how global and national formations and relational interactions seep through the lives, identities, and communities of youth and adults, ultimately refracting back on the larger social formations that give rise to them to begin with. Arguing that "it is relatively easy to write up institutional stories as thick, local qualitative descriptions, without revealing the webs of power that connect institutional and individual lives to larger formations," we seek to push researchers to trace how obviously related and yet seemingly remote structural conditions shape local context, group identities, and individual lives (Weis & Fine, 2004). In *Class Reunion*, I take this further, using data collected at two points in time to trace the continuities and discontinuities of identity, relations, and material lives, enabling us to see the "field of forces" through which structural advances and structural assaults shape how individuals and groups live and narrate their everyday social practices.

As such, *Class Reunion* drives home the point that identities are constructed over time and in relation to the constructed identities of others, as well as dialectically in relation to the broader economy and culture. The ethnographic longitudinality which undergirds this project enables me to track this set of interactions and relationships over time, causing us to shift our eye from pieces drawn at one point in time to those drawn at another, opening ever further the specter of "compositional ethnography" (Weis & Fine, 2004). In so doing, I chart new theoretical and methodological territory. In spite of the few excellent longitudinal studies noted above, I needed to develop a template before engaging the analysis. This was a more dialectical process than indicated here, since templates always emerge in relation to data and vice versa. Nevertheless, my point here is that at the same time I was figuring out how to engage both myself and the reader in movement over time, this very movement served to blast open the "freezing" so characteristic of ethnographies conducted at one point in time. While it can certainly be argued that I "freeze" cultures/identities at two points in time rather than one, as is characteristic of most ethnographic investigations, my method implies fluidity and continued change. In other words, a recognition of motion is built into the method from the very beginning.

In this regard, we invite a rotating position for the writer/researcher; that is, compositional studies, as represented by *Class Reunion*, extend an invitation to the researcher as multiply positioned: grounded, engaged, reflective, well- versed in scholarly discourse, knowledgeable about external circumstances, and able to move between theory and life "on the ground."[1] In so doing, we locate dynamism as a core element of our method, self-consciously embracing movement in relation to large economic and social formations as well as bordering "others." Given the shifting nature of all parts of what we call the "composition," our method enables/encourages us to capture this shifting over place, time, and space (Weis & Fine, 2004).

The operative cut here is not the traversing of the researcher/ researched divide in any simple sense, but rather the ways in which one positions oneself in relation to those studied and the reasons why one chooses to do so. Greg Dimitriadis, for example, runs programs for youth in the site of the community center which he studied (2003), reflecting and writing eloquently on his own "shifting position" as both outsider and outsider/insider, noting that there was a tenor of "mutual manipulation" around his role(s) at the center. In his case, he acted as a "deep insider" in that he ultimately took a position as staff member, offering a variety of programming for poor youth. He reflects poignantly on Michelle Fine's (1994) notion of "working the hyphen"—a form of melding writing about and working with rather than "ripping off" those whom we investigate as we plunge forward in our careers.

What I suggest here is that there are varying ways of working this hyphen—varying ways of working with and giving back that do not necessarily imply the deep participation represented by Dimitriadis's work or the noteworthy work of Michelle Fine and colleagues (2004), excellent though such work may be. Such deep participatory work is indeed *one* way of working the hyphen, but there are others as well. It is the capturing of the experiences of groups and individuals in relation to broader oppressive structures, with an eye toward altering such structures, that is at issue here. Surely investigators need to be deeply embedded within a site (community, school, neighborhood center, or whatever), and must be there for a long enough period of time to learn how to respect and understand those with whom they are working. Also, we must, as investigators give back—we cannot see our role as arrogantly assessing how those "other" than ourselves make the most of their meager circumstances—circumstances with which we do not, on a daily basis, have to live. Having said this, however, we can work the self/"other" divide/hyphen in a variety of ways, including engaging respectfully with the lives of "others" so as to understand what is happening to individuals and communities inside the new world order, ultimately communicating such findings through socially responsible scholarship not wholly driven by our own narrowly constructed career goals. This, too, is "working the hyphen"—engaging with "others" so as to comprehend as fully as possible the ways in which they are surviving and even living in spite of great difficulties at the same time that the "sources" of such difficulties are fully theorized.

I have traversed the self/"other" divide in a number of ways over the years. In *Class Reunion*, I was a relative "outsider." While I gave back to the community by providing lists of names, addresses, and so forth to reunion organizing committees, as well as offering information with respect to schools and colleges in the local area and general knowledge regarding the stratified educational system, I remained an outsider. I moved about the country—seeking individuals whom I had known fifteen years ago, but I did not stay. I was not organically linked to any particular institution, as I have been in past studies. *Class Reunion* represents a further form of "working the hyphen"—a traveling between the lives of people and larger social structures with a deep commitment to social justice.

NOTES

Introduction

I drew this title from a 1980s exhibit of the same name put together by Mia Boynton and Alex Blair. The exhibit was funded by the New York State Council on the Arts.

1. Very little work in English traces carefully the consequences of varying forms of social and cultural capital and habitus. The work of Annette Lareau (1987, 2004), and Horvat, Weininger, & Lareau (2003), looks carefully at these issues in relation to parents and schools.

2. Dennis Carlson and Greg Dimitriadis (2003, pp. 18–21) do an outstanding job of "troubling" identity.

3. This is not to deny the fully and partially independent effects of race in relation to these issues. Rather, it is to suggest that class is a fundamental organizer of social reality, both "objective" and subjective. I agree with Cameron McCarthy (1988) that the experiences and subjectivities of racially subordinated groups cannot be read entirely off class.

4. I also reinterviewed three African American women and one woman of mixed-race international ancestry who were part of a group of ten students of color interviewed in 1985. These students of color were not the subject of the original volume and do not appear here. They will be the subject of future writing.

5. I explore this point at some length in the Theoretical Coda.

6. I talk more specifically about method in the Epilogue in this volume.

Chapter 1

1. The identity of Freeway males has to be understood in light of the history of the American labor movement. As David Hogan (1982, 1985) and others suggest, the history of the American working class is different from that of the English experience, for example. In the American case, the white male working class did not have to develop classwide institutions to achieve political democracy. In contrast to England, the American working class was more defensive, protecting the already existing republican democracy from perceived

foes: monopolists, Catholics, aristocratic impulses, and socialists. In addition, the American experience is linked historically with large-scale immigration and, as I suggest in the Introduction, slavery and subsequent American apartheid. It is, therefore, far more internally divided historically along racial and ethnic lines than is the case in England. As Hogan notes:

> Compared to English working class culture, American working class culture is not as cohesive, thickly textured, or self conscious; it is more diffuse, fractured internally, divided along regional, racial and ethnic lines; its reputation of bourgeois ideology less deep and incisive; its institutional infrastructure—trade unions, political organizations, voluntary associations—less extensive and weaker. (1982, pp. 60–61)

Thus, the working class in America has been fractured historically (especially as compared to that of England) for a variety of reasons. Mike Davis (1986) argues similarly:

> The increasing proletarization of the American social structure has not been matched by an equal tendency toward the homogenization of the working class as a cultural or political collectivity. Stratifications rooted in differential positions in the social labor process have been reinforced by deepseated ethnic, religious, racial and sexual antagonisms within the working class. (p. 16)

In light of the above, it is not surprising that white working-class youth identities differ to some extent in England and America. While there is a form of "laddish" behavior in Freeway, it is not the same as that uncovered by Willis and, later, other investigators.

2. It is important to point out that Freeway students are receiving a particular form of education, what Patrick Finn (1999) calls "domesticating" rather than "empowering education." Domesticating education leads to "functional literacy, literacy that makes a person productive and dependable, but not troublesome" (pp. ix–x). This parallels Jean Anyon's (1981) finding that working-class students receive a form of schooling whose curriculum is highly routinized and aimed at control. Such education prepares students only minimally for college-level work, which partially explains why so many working-class students have difficulty moving from high school to college (London, 1978). Empowering education, in contrast, "leads to powerful literacy, the kind of literacy that leads to positions of power and authority" (Finn, 1999, p. xi), such education being entrenched in schools for Anyon's "executive elite." I discuss the form of education received by Freeway students at great length in *Working Class Without Work* (Weis, 1990). I do not treat this topic in any depth in *Class Reunion*.

3. In spite of the fact that a majority of the students express a desire to continue their education, only 33 percent of juniors took the Preliminary Scholastic Aptitude Test (PSAT), and 27 percent of juniors and seniors combined sat the SAT. This is striking in light of expressed desires to attend college, since the SAT is virtually mandatory for entrance into any four-year school. In addition, even given the relatively low proportion of students, both male and female, who take the PSAT and SAT, results for these students are low. Out of a possible 800 on the math and verbal section of the SAT, the average scores for Freeway youth during the academic year 1985–1986 were as follows: white male verbal, 432; white male quantitative, 493; black male verbal, 395; black male quantitative, 375; white female verbal, 410; white female quantitative,

450; black female verbal, 316; black female quantitative, 374. It can be assumed that one must break 1000 as a combined score in order to obtain entrance to the comprehensive four-year college sector (this is not the university sector), throwing into sharp relief the relatively low nature of these scores. Although I provide data for all students, only 3 percent of students who took the SAT are black (approximately 20 percent of the students in the school are black), and 43 percent of test-takers were female.

In addition, course grades were not high. Grades were gathered from official ninth and tenth grade transcripts for all current juniors during the academic year in which I attended the school. Students do not generally achieve high marks; the marks for whites are generally higher than those for blacks, and white females tend to obtain slightly higher marks than white males. What is striking is the extraordinarily "average" nature of grades. Certainly grades must be seen as "constructed" in some sense, but it is nevertheless noteworthy that they are so low. Grades for whites tend to be in the mid to high 70s, which can be translated into a letter grade of C. Such grades, in combination with low SAT scores, will not enable students to obtain entrance into even the four-year comprehensive college sector in the United States. Statements as to relative status of school (college) are wholly dependent upon the Carnegie Commission classification (1973).

4. The extent to which this "out of control" class is linked to the fact that a black male was the substitute teacher is at least worth pondering here, given the general relations of blacks and whites in this school community. It must also be noted, though, that it was black and Hispanic students who gave him the most trouble. At the very least, this suggests the low esteem in which these young people held this particular man. It is not clear to me that this set of interactions would emerge in relation to *any* teacher of color.

5. Lynch and O'Neill (1994) suggest that this contradictory attitude toward school knowledge and culture is rooted in the fact that if working-class people succeed in the academic realm, they abandon their class background and cease to be working class; they argue that this is unlike the case for other marginal or oppressed groups in education, who will remain "black," for example, even if they embrace schooling. So, too, will a woman remain a woman, whether educated or not. Signithia Fordham and John Ogbu (1986) have raised questions regarding the extent to which one remains "black" if "white" education is embraced. The pivotal role of schooling in relation to identity construction along both race and class lines is highlighted in these formulations.

6. Although there are a number of Hispanics in the school, who are almost entirely Puerto Rican, there were not enough such students to compose a specifically targeted group in 1985.

7. There is some question here as to how much this *specific* set of processes is linked to communities in the United States in which black Americans constitute the primary racial "other." While the processes do, I believe, hold more generally across communities, the "other" may indeed vary, potentially putting into motion a different set of dynamics. Thus communities in Texas may hinge on a Mexican American "other," as brilliant work by Doug Foley (1990) suggests. In other contexts Native American groups and/or groups of Asian descent may play a prominent role, in which case the nature of interactions around race, gender, sexuality, and class will inevitably be different. It must also be remembered that this all plays out in a specific economic

context. The deindustrialization explored here most accurately lies in the northeastern United States—at least it did in the mid-1980s. In later years, the new global economy impacted communities all over the United States, although in different ways, including the increased outsourcing of mid- and upper-level professional positions. Leslie McCall (2001) has written extensively on these latter points.

Chapter 2

1. It must be pointed out here that while this "ideology of romance" may be constructed with the hope of moving out of an oppressive home of origin and is not, therefore, necessarily "homebound," as has been seen by some investigators, it does, nevertheless, continue to tie women to the home of their future husband in much the same way their mothers are tied. While homebound, then, the identity uncovered by previous investigators may not reflect any particular attachment to the home of their father, but rather a generally ill-founded hope that their future home will be less oppressive than the one they grew up in.

2. See also Kessler-Harris (1975), as cited in Brodkin Sacks, p. 18.

3. An early classic on this subject is Douvan and Adelson (1966). On the basis of research conducted by means of two national interview studies in 1955 and 1956, they suggest that most boys are concerned about choosing jobs and making work decisions. The adolescent girl, on the other hand,

   > does not look at the occupational sphere as a source of a life meaning or life work. Her life plan is contained in her feminine goals of marriage and motherhood and her education and work are conceived as providing access to these goals or making her more competent and well-rounded in the roles of wife and mother. She will work for a while and then marry. She will help out with family finances, particularly in the early years before she has children. And her education and work experience before marriage will increase her efficiency in meeting the complex demands of an active family life. (p. 233)

4. Jennifer is the only daughter of professional parents. As one of the central school district office workers put it, "He [Jennifer's father] was almost too smart in high school, you know what I mean?" (She had gone to school with him.)

5. One of the machine shop teachers also had a daughter in engineering. He was the person who initially pointed out to me that a number of students from manual-laboring families who do become professionals go into engineering.

6. Center for Education Statistics (1985–1986, 1986–1987).

7. This does not mean that blacks never worked in unionized positions under the industrial economy, but rather that they obtained such positions far less frequently relative to their overall availability than white men did.

8. I take seriously the fact that students construct identities within the site of the school—identities that may be encouraged and/or blocked by a variety of interactions within the school itself, since schools sit at the very nexus of contradictory tendencies emanating from the demands of the state, the economy, and a semiautonomous cultural level (lived as well as commodified). In this case, the young women's "glimmer of critique" was partially encouraged but predominantly blocked at the level of the school (see Weis, 1990). The contradictory pressures on schools are still best laid out theoretically by Martin Carnoy and Hank Levin (1985).

Chapter 4

1. One additional man, Greg, fits the profile of men I am calling class "border crossers." He and his wife are at the very beginning stages of careers in marketing for an architectural firm. They each have a B.A., and they are living in a middle-class white suburb. Their situation feels more precarious to me, however, than that of Jerry and Bob, who are further entrenched in their new class status.

2. For this to work, the "partner" need not necessarily be a lover, although in all likelihood, such partner would be a lover. Marriage is obviously not a prerequisite here; however, again, most of the men who fall in the "settled" category are married to their partner. A more complicated question involves the necessity of heterosexual coupling. In principle, my argument does not rest upon heterosexual coupling, since same-sex partners could behave in exactly the same way as outlined here and still "accomplish" settled living. The reality, though, is that same-sex partnerships may not easily be accepted in this particular class/cultural community at this moment in time, and that same-sex partners would be more likely to be absorbed by broader gay and lesbian communities located outside the bounds of the specifically white working-class fraction explored here. None of those reinterviewed in 2000 currently live a gay or lesbian lifestyle.

3. Here it can be argued that the men and women of the white working class are behaving as neoliberal subjects; I take up the complexities of this status in Chapter 7.

4. By the 1970s African American men constituted a noticeable portion of the industrially based proletariat. In Freeway, however, it was well known that there were still jobs for "white guys" and jobs for "black guys." My thanks to Stanley Aronowitz for pressing the point related to racial diversity.

Chapter 5

1. Investigations since *Working Class Without Work* (1990) probe carefully the remaking of femininity and the female subject across race and social class lines. See Raissiguier (1994), Proweller (1998), Best (2000), and Weiler (2000) for excellent recent examples. Weiler suggests that in an economic context where fathers are still providing for their families, white working-class girls adopt more traditional notions of femininity and romance. This is an important recent finding, one that differs from that in my original study, thereby underlining the economic context within which cultures and identities are produced.

2. Jennifer Johnson (2002) has recently focused on those working-class women who "get by on the minimum." The women discussed here exemplify a more "settled" version of working-class family life.

3. Diane Reay (2002) recently took me to task for my apparent "homogenization" of white working-class male forms, suggesting that such homogenized accounts of white working-class masculinities not only ignore differences within masculinities but also leave this class to "bear the weight of White racism and male sexism" (p. 222). I agree with her latter point wholeheartedly. When we point fingers at this group and locate racism and sexism within it, we ignore the differently coded but nonetheless real racism and sexism within the middle and upper-middle classes, for example, as well as racism and sexism

embedded within economic and state policies, which are most definitely not crafted by the white working class (but may, nonetheless, benefit them as "whites"). This is obviously not my intent, but I recognize that a focus on one group inadvertently tends to "black out" the ways in which these same characteristics may be embedded within another group or broad-based policies (Pollack, 2004). Michelle Fine and I have taken up this point elsewhere (Fine & Weis, 1998), arguing strongly that white working-class men and women, and particularly men, often bear the brunt of broad class-based racism and sexism simply because they speak out, whereas others offer more coded versions of similar sentiments.

With respect to Reay's point about homogenization, I do not mean to imply that all men and women from the white working class live out the stories presented in any of my writing or *necessarily* exhibit the range of characteristics embedded within the stories. However, I do suggest that these are *modal* stories—that a *significant* proportion of the specified group could tell a similar story, as evidenced by Reay's admission that "my own childhood and adolescent experience of white working-class masculinities was one scarred by violence, both physical and verbal abuse plus the more symbolic but equally damaging violence of deeply entrenched sexism and racism within the male dominated coal mining community I used to be part of" (p. 222). Again, then, I do not mean to imply that there are not varying masculinities or femininities within this class cultural group. Obviously there are. What I do suggest, though, in line with a range of scholars such as R. W. Connell (1995), Kenway and Fitzclarence (1997), and others, is that particular masculinist constructions are highly valued—or hegemonic—thereby providing the center with which and against which all other competing masculinities (or femininities) must emerge. My point in this chapter, then, is not that every white working-class woman has the experience outlined here, but rather that my data suggest its very typicality, a typicality that should not be ignored as we focus on the adult "living out" of culturally rooted "penetrations" observed during teenage years (metaphorically ours and actually theirs).

Chapter 6

1. The white women in *The Unknown City* (Fine & Weis, 1998) were less often the descendants of the white industrial proletariat. They more obviously approximate those women interviewed by Jennifer Johnson (2002).

2. Data reported in this chapter regarding housing values are based on blacks and whites. It is not totally clear, of course, how a group such as "Arabians" will affect housing values of the future. It is fair to assume, though, that the patterns will be similar. This set of processes will perhaps play somewhat differently, depending on the bordering "other" of color, a point that I have stressed repeatedly in this volume.

3. Hank Levin (personal communication) stresses that we cannot know for certain the lived outcome of changes in the economy. What looks potentially devastating for certain groups, at times turns out not to be. A key example here is the uproar over the spotted owl in the northwestern United States (Niemi, Whitelaw, & Grossman, 2000). My thanks to Hank for engaging this discussion at length.

Chapter 7

1. A related and critically important question, although it is not addressed in this volume, involves the extent to which schooling can lessen existing social inequalities. Hank Levin and Carolyn Kelley (1994) have authored an extremely important piece that addresses this set of issues

2. A related question, although one not probed here, involves the voting patterns of this group and the extent to which they vote their "class" interests. While it is not my intention to examine this issue extensively, it is worth noting that the voting patterns of unskilled workers in the "past four elections reflect a decline in traditionally high levels of support for Democratic candidates." Nevertheless, unskilled workers remain the most Democratic of the seven categories in recent analyses. Brooks and Manza (1997) argue that such trends do not suggest greater feelings of political alienation since 1980:

    > Instead, this political shift among unskilled workers is the outgrowth of higher levels of economic satisfaction under Republican administrations (and particularly high levels of dissatisfaction in 1980 under a Democratic President) coupled with declining support for the welfare state. This form of conservative class politics is very similar to the forces realigning the self-employed. Moreover, its presence among the working-class cuts against an expectation common among class analysts and political commentators alike that the growing immiseration of the working-class in postindustrial societies will by itself eventually compel them to support liberal or left political alternatives. (p. 397)

    A second shift worth noting here is the "increasingly volatility" of the voting behavior of skilled workers (Hout, Brooks, & Manza, 1995, p. 825). Analysts suggest that no other group in the population evidences the dramatic election-to-election shifts of this particular group, a group that was the bedrock of the New Deal coalition in the United States (Brooks and Manza, 1997, p. 397). It is worth speculating that as long as the white working class can carve itself as a distinct class fraction, as I suggest in this volume—one always seen and understood to be above other groups, particularly other groups of color—this swing to conservative politics will intensify over the years.

3. This unmooring is contradicted at the same time by the "fixing" of racial identities worldwide, particularly the current fixing of "Arabs," "Muslims," and people of Middle Eastern descent in general.

4. At the same time that whites are instantiating and stabilizing whiteness, Guinier and Torres (2002) suggest that there is some "promise of a cross-racial and democratically committed alliance whose leaders are people of color but who struggle together against hierarchies of power at the right historical time" (p. 252). There is some movement, then, toward a multicultural coalition (including some whites) that could challenge the existing racial hierarchy at the same time that groups such as the white working-class fraction are attempting to stabilize whiteness. While not being overly romantic about this possibility, Guinier and Torres suggest that Hispanics/Latinos who already live at the hyphen of the black–white binary could spearhead such a multiracial movement.

5. Yemenites assume particular importance in this community as a way both of "stretching" processes surrounding the production of whiteness and of establishing the "goodness" of whiteness itself. Given an increasingly diverse

America, I am quite certain that other groups of color in a wide variety of communities serve this very same function for the newly articulated white working-class fraction. This is a subject for future research in other communities.

6. Again, the fact that Yemenites live in Freeway serves a day-to-day function for these particular white men. I am certain, though, that media images that surround a now well-established international "enemy" help white working-class men across America swallow, to some extent at least, their own devalued and feminized positions in both home and workplace. Obviously the politically motivated and linked representations of "others" are far more complex than indicated here; I raise this issue only in relation to the rearticulation of gender in the United States and its meaning for the white working-class fraction.

Theoretical Coda

1. My thanks to Greg Dimitriadis for pushing me on this set of issues.
2. My thanks to Alan Sadovnik for pushing me on this set of points.

Epilogue

1. These ideas were forged in tandem with Michelle Fine. The framework is fully elaborated in Weis and Fine (2004).

REFERENCES

Adkins, L. (2001). Cultural feminisation: "Money, sex and power" for (wo)men. *Signs, 26* (3), 31–57.

Adonis, A., & Pollard, S. (1997). *A class act: The myth of Britain's classless society.* London: Penguin.

Althusser, L. (1971). Ideology and ideological state apparatus. In L. Althusser (Ed.), *Lenin and philosophy and other essays.* London: New Left Books.

Amadiume, I. (1987). *Male daughters, female husbands: Gender and sex in an African society.* London: Zed Books.

Anonymous. (2003) County survey on women. Specific information about this source is purposefully withheld to ensure confidentiality.

Anyon, J. (1997). *Ghetto schooling: A political economy of urban educational reform.* New York: Teacher's College Press.

Anyon, J. (1980, Winter). Social class and the hidden curriculum of work. *Journal of Education, 162* (1), 67–92.

Anyon, J. (1981). Social class and school knowledge. *Curriculum Inquiry, 11* (1), 3–42.

Appadurai, A. (1996). *Modernity at large: Cultural dimensions of globalization.* Minneapolis: University of Minnesota Press.

Apple, M. (1982). *Education and power.* Boston: Routledge and Kegan Paul.

Apple, M. (1986). *Teachers and texts: A political economy of class and gender relations.* Boston: Routledge and Kegan Paul.

Apple, M. (2001). *Educating the "right" way: Markets, standards, God and inequality.* New York: RoutledgeFalmer.

Apple, M. (2004). Introduction. In M. Apple (Ed.), *Ideology and curriculum* (Rev. ed.). New York: Routledge.

Arnot, M. (2002). *Reproducing gender? Essays on educational theory and feminist politics.* London: RoutledgeFalmer.

Arnot, M. (2004). Male working class identities and social justice: A reconsideration of Paul Willis's *Learning to Labour* in light of contemporary research.

In N. Dolby & G. Dimitriadis (Eds.), *Learning to labor in new times* (pp. 17–40). New York: Routledge.

Arnot, M., M. David and G. Weiner (1999). *Closing the gender gap*. Cambridge, U.K.: Polity Press.

Aronowitz, S. (1992). *The politics of identity: Class, culture and social movements*. New York: Routledge.

Aronowitz, S. (2004). Preface. In N. Dolby & G. Dimitriadis (Eds.), *Learning to labor in new times* (pp.). New York: Routledge.

Aronowitz, S., & DiFazio, W. (1994). *The jobless future: Sci-tech and the dogma of work*. Minneapolis: University of Minnesota Press.

Bensman, D., & Lynch, R. (1987). *Rusted dreams: Hard times in a steel community*. Berkeley: University of California Press.

Bernstein, B. (1990). *The structuring of pedagogic discourse*. New York: Routledge.

Best, A. (2000). *Prom night: Youth, schools, and popular culture*. New York: Routledge.

Bettie, J. (1995, Winter). Class dismissed? Roseanne and the changing face of working-class iconography. *Social Text 45*, 14 (4), 125–149.

Bettie, J. (2003). *Women without class: Girls, race and identity*. Berkeley: University of California Press.

Bluestone, B., & Harrison, B. (1982). *The de-industrialization of America*. New York: Basic Books.

Bogdan, R., & Biklen, S. (1998). *Qualitative research for education: An introduction to theory and methods*. Boston: Allyn and Bacon.

Borman, K. (1991). *The first "real" job: A study of young workers*. Albany: State University of New York Press.

Bourdieu, P. (1979). *La distinction, critique sociale du jugement*. Paris: Editions de Minuit.

Bourdieu, P. (1980). *Le sens pratique*. Paris: Editions du Seuil.

Bourdieu, P. (1994). *Raisons pratiques: Sur la théorie de l'action*. Paris: Editions du Seuil.

Bourdieu, P., & Passeron, J. C. (1970). *La reproduction: Éléments pour une théorie du système d'enseignement*. Paris: Editions de Minuit.

Bowles, S., & Gintis, H. (1976). *Schooling in capitalist America*. New York: Basic Books.

Brodkin Sacks, K. (1984). *My troubles are going to have trouble with me*. New Brunswick, NJ: Rutgers University Press.

Brooks, C., & Manza, J. (1997, December). Class politics and political change in the United States, 1952–1992. *Social Forces*, 76 (2), 379–408.

Carlson, D., & Dimitriadis, G. (Eds.). (2003). *Promises to keep: Cultural studies, democratic education, and public education*. New York: RoutledgeFalmer.

The Carnegie Commission on Higher Education: A classification of institutions of higher education. (1973). Berkeley, CA: The Carnegie Foundation.

Carnoy, M., & Levin, H. (1985). *Schooling and work in the democratic state*. Palo Alto, CA: Stanford University Press.

Centrie, C. (2004). *New lives, new freedoms: The identity formation of Vietnamese immigrant youth in an American high school*. New York: LJB Scholarly Press.

Charlip, J. (1995). A real class act: Searching for identity in the "classness" society. In C. L. Barney Dews & C. Leste Law (Eds.), *This fine place so far from home.* Philadelphia: Temple University Press.

Cohen, P., & Ainley, P. (2000). In the country of the blind? Youth studies and cultural studies in Britain. *Journal of Youth Studies, 3* (1), 79–93.

Connell, R. W. (1993). Disruptions: Improper masculinities and schooling. In L. Weis & M. Fine (Eds.), *Beyond silenced voices: Class, race and gender in United States schools* (pp. 191–208). Albany: State University of New York Press.

Connell, R. W. (1995). Cool guys, swots and wimps: the interplay of masculinity and education. *Oxford Review of Education, 15*(3), 291–303.

Connell, R. W. (1995). *Masculinities.* Cambridge: Polity Press.

Connell, R. W. (2000). *The men and the boys.* Berkeley: University of California Press.

Corcoran, M., Datcher, L., & Duncan, G. (1980, August). Most workers find jobs through word of mouth. *Monthly Labor Review, 103* (8), 33–35.

Cornbleth, C. (2003). *Hearing America's youth: Social identities in uncertain times.* New York: Peter Lang.

Crenshaw, K. (1988). Race, reform and retrenchment: Transformation and legitimation in antidiscrimination law. *Harvard Law Review, 101*, 1356–1387.

Crenshaw, K. (1989). *Demarginalizing the intersection of race and sex: A Black feminist critique of antidiscrimination doctrine, feminist theory and anti-racist politics* (pp. 139–167). Chicago: University of Chicago Legal Forum.

Davis, M. (1986). *Prisoners of the American dream.* London: Verso Press.

Dimitriadis, G. (2003). *Friendship, cliques and gangs: Young black men coming of age in urban America.* New York: Teachers College Press.

Dolby, N. (2001). *Constructing race: Youth, identity and popular culture in South Africa.* Albany: State University of New York Press.

Dolby, N. and Dimitriades G., eds. (2004). *Learning to labor in new times.* New York: RoutledgeFalmer.

Douvan, E., & Adelson, J. (1966). *The adolescent experience.* New York: John Wiley.

Edwards, R. (1979). *Contested terrain: The transformation of the workplace in the twentieth century.* New York: Basic Books.

Eisenstein, Z. (1984). *Feminism and sexual equality.* New York: Monthly Review Press.

Elder, G. (1974). *Children of the Great Depression.* Chicago: University of Chicago Press.

Everhart, R. (1983). *Reading, writing and resistance.* Boston: Routledge and Keagan Paul.

Fine, M. (1991). *Framing dropouts: Notes on the politics of an urban public school.* Albany: State University of New York Press.

Fine, M. (1994). Working the hyphens: Reinventing self and other in qualitative research. In N. Denzin & Y. Lincoln (Eds.), *Handbook of qualitative research* (pp. 70–82). Thousand Oaks, CA: Sage.

Fine, M., & Weis, L. (1998). *The unknown city: The lives of poor and working class young adults.* Boston: Beacon Press.

Fine, M., Weis, L., Powell, L., & Wong, M. (1997). *Off white: Readings on race, power and society*. New York: Routledge.

Fine, M., Weis, L., Pruitt, L., & Burns, A. (2004). *Off white: Readings in power, privilege and contestation*. New York: Routledge.

Fine, M., & Zane, N. (1989). Bein' wrapped too tight: When low income African American women drop out of high school. In L. Weis, E. Farrar, & H. Petrie (Eds.), *Dropouts from school* (pp. 23–24). Albany: State University of New York Press.

Fine, M., Bloom, J., Burns, A., Chajet, L., Guishard, M., Perkins-Munn, T., and Torne, M. (2004). Dear Zora: A letter to Zora Neale Hurston fifty years after Brown. In L. Weis and M. Fine, eds., *Working method: Research and social justice*. New York: Routledge.

Finkelhor, D. (1983). Common features of family abuse. In D. Finkelhor, R. Gelles, G Hotaling, & M. Strauss (Eds.), *The dark side of families: Current family violence research* (pp. 17–28). Beverly Hills, CA: Sage.

Finkelhor, D., Hotaling, G., & Yllo, K. (1988). *Stopping family violence: Research priorities for the coming decade*. Beverly Hills, CA: Sage.

Finn, P. (1999). *Literacy with an attitude: Educating working-class children in their own self interest*. Albany: State University of New York Press.

Foley, D. (1990). *Learning capitalist culture: Deep in the heart of Texas*. Philadelphia: University of Pennsylvania Press.

Fordham, S. (1996). *Blacked out: Dilemmas of race identity and success at Capital High*. Chicago: University of Chicago Press.

Fordham, S., & Ogbu, J. (1986). Black students' school success: Coping with the "burden of acting white." *The Urban Review, 18* (3), 176–206.

Frankenberg, R. (1993). *White women, race matters: The social construction of whiteness*. Minneapolis: University of Minnesota Press.

Gaskell, J. (1984, March). Gender and course choice. *Journal of Education, 166,* 89–102.

Gaskell, J. (1992). *Gender matters from school to work*. Philadelphia: Open University Press.

Giddens, A. (1991). *Modernity and self identity: Self and society in the late modern age*. Oxford: Polity Press.

Giddens, A. (1998). *The third way*. Malden, MA: Polity Press.

Giddens, A. (2003). *Runaway world*. New York: Routledge.

Gilmore, G. E. (1996). *Gender and Jim Crow: Women and the politics of white supremacy in North Carolina, 1896–1920*. Chapel Hill: University of North Carolina Press.

Giroux, H. (1997, Summer). Rewriting the discourse of racial identity: Towards a pedagogy and politics of whiteness. *Harvard Educational Review, 67* (2), 285–320.

Goetz, J., & LeCompte, M. (1984). *Ethnography and qualitative design in educational research*. Orlando, FL: Academic Press.

Golden, M., & Shreve, R. (Eds.). (1995). *Skin deep: Black and white women write about race*. New York: Nan A. Talese.

Gorz, A. (1982). *Farewell to the working class: An essay on post-industrial socialism* (M. Sonenscher, Trans.). London: Pluto Press.

Guinier, L., & Torres, G. (2002). *The miner's canary: Enlisting race, resisting power, transforming democracy.* Cambridge, MA: Harvard University Press.

Hall, S. (1996). Introduction: Who needs identity? In S. Hall & P. DuGay (Eds.), *Questions of cultural identity* (pp. 1–17). London: Sage.

Halle, D. (1984). *America's working man.* Chicago: University of Chicago Press.

Hine, D. C. (1989). *Black women in white: Racial conflict and cooperation in the nursing profession, 1890–1950.* Bloomington: Indiana University Press.

Hogan, D. (1982). Education and class formation: The peculiarities of the Americans. In M. Apple (Ed.), *Cultural and economic reproduction in education* (pp. 32–78). London: Routledge and Kegan Paul.

Hogan, D. (1985). *Class and reform: School and society in Chicago, 1880–1930.* Philadelphia: University of Pennsylvania Press.

hooks, b. (1990). *Yearning: Race, gender and cultural politics.* Boston: South End Press.

Horvat, E. M., Weininger, E., & Lareau, A. (2003, Summer). From social ties to social capital: Class differences in the relations between schools and parent networks. *American Educational Research Journal, 40* (2), 319–351.

Hout, M., Brooks, C., & Manza, J. (1995, December). The democratic class struggle in the United States, 1948–1992. *American Sociological Review, 60* (6), 805–828.

Howell, J. (1973). *Hard living on Clay Street.* Garden City, NY: Anchor Books.

Hunter, A. (1987). *The politics of resentment and the construction of Middle America* (p. 9). Unpublished paper, Havens Center for Social Structure and Social Change, University of Wisconsin at Madison.

Jackson, C. (2002). "Laddishness" as a self-worth protection strategy. *Gender and Education, 14* (1), 37–51.

Jensen, J., and Davidson, S. (1984). *A needle, a bobbin, a strike: Women needle-workers in America.* Philadelphia: Temple University Press.

Johnson, J. (2002*). Getting by on the minimum: The lives of working class women.* New York: Routledge.

Kaplan, A. (1964). *The conduct of inquiry.* Scranton, PA: Chandler.

Karabel, J. (1972). Community colleges and social stratification. *Harvard Educational Review, 42* (4), 521–562.

Katz, M. (2001). *The price of citizenship.* New York: Metropolitan Books.

Kefalas, M. (2003). *Working-class heroes: Protecting home, community, and nation in a Chicago neighborhood.* Berkeley: University of California Press.

Kelley, R. (1994). *Race rebels: Culture, politics and the black working class.* New York: Free Press.

Kenway, J., & Fitzclarence, L. (1997). Masculinity, violence and schooling— Challenging "poisonous" pedagogies. *Gender and Education, 9*(1), 117–133.

Kessler-Harris, A. (1975). Where are the organized women workers? *Feminist Studies, 3* (1), 92–110.

Kessler-Harris, A. (1982). *Out to work: A history of wage earning women in the United States.* New York: Oxford University Press.

Kimmel, M. (1996). *Manhood in America: A cultural history.* New York: Free Press.

Kincheloe, J., Steinberg, S., Rodriguez N., Chennault, R. (Eds.). (1998). *White reign: Deploying whiteness in America.* New York: St. Martin's Press.

Kuhn, T. (1962). *The structure of scientific revolutions.* Chicago: University of Chicago Press.

Kurz, D. (1995). *For richer for poorer: Mothers confront divorce.* New York: Routledge.

Lamont, M. (2000). *The dignity of working men: Morality and the boundaries of race, class and immigration.* Cambridge, MA: Harvard University Press.

Langston, D. (1993). Who am I now? The politics of class identity. In M. Tokarczk & E. Fay (Eds.), *Working-class women in the academy: Laborers in the knowledge factory* (pp. 60–72). Amherst: University of Massachusetts Press.

Lareau, A. (1987, April). Social class differences in family–school relationships: The importance of cultural capital. *Sociology of Education, 60,* 73–85.

Lareau, A. (1989). *Home advantage: Social class and parental intervention in elementary education.* New York: Falmer Press.

Lareau, A. (2004). *Unequal childhoods: Class, race and family life.* Berkeley: University of California Press.

Lather, P. (1991). *Getting smart: Feminist research and pedagogy with/in the postmodern.* New York: Routledge.

Lee, S. (1996). *Unraveling the "model minority" stereotype: Listening to Asian youth.* New York: Teachers College Press.

Levin, H. and Kelley, C. (1994). Can education do it alone? *Economics of Education Review, 13*(2), 97–108.

Levin, H., & Rumberger, R. (1987). Education requirements for new technologies: Visions, possibilities, and current realities. *Educational Policy, 1* (3), 333–354.

Lombardo, S. (2000). *Ties that bind: Irish (Americans) within the spaces of an Irish community center. An ethnography.* Unpublished doctoral dissertation, State University of New York at Buffalo.

London, H. (1978). *The culture of a community college.* New York: Praeger.

Lopez, N. (2003). *Hopeful girls, troubled boys: Race and gender disparity in urban education.* New York: Routledge.

Luttrell, W. (1997). *Schoolsmart and motherwise: Working-class women's identity and schooling.* New York: Routledge.

Lynch, K., & O'Neill, C. (1994). The colonisation of social class in education. *British Journal of Sociology of Education, 15* (3), 307–324.

Mac an Ghaill, M. (1991). Schooling, sexuality and male power: Towards an emancipatory curriculum. *Gender and Education, 3*(3) 291–309.

Mac an Ghaill, M. (1994). *The making of men: Masculinities, sexualities and schooling.* Buckingham, UK: Open University Press.

MacLeod, J. (1995). *Ain't no makin it: Aspirations and attainment in a low-income neighborhood.* Boulder, CO: Westview Press.

Marable, M. (1997). *Black liberation in conservative America.* Boston: South End Press.

Martino, W. (1999). "Cool boys," "party animals," "squids" and "poofters": Interrogating the dynamics and politics of adolescent masculinities in school. *British Journal of Sociology of Education, 20* (2), 239–263.

Martino, W., & Meyenn, B. (2001). *What About the Boys?* Buckingham, UK: Open University Press.

Massey, D., & Denton, N. (1993). *American apartheid: Segregation and the making of the underclass.* Cambridge, MA: Harvard University Press.

May, M. (1987). The historical problem of the family wage: The Ford Motor Company and the five dollar day. In N. Gerstel & H. Engel Grass (Eds.), *Families and work* (pp. 111–131). Philadelphia: Temple University Press.

McCall, L. (2001). *Complex Inequality: Gender, Class, and Race in the New Economy*. New York: Routledge.

McCarthy, C. (1988). Marxist theories of education and the challenge of a cultural politics of non-synchrony. In L. Roman, L. Christian-Smith, & E. Ellsworth (Eds.), *Becoming feminine: The politics of popular culture* (pp. 185–204). Philadelphia: Falmer Press.

McCarthy, C. (1990). *Race and curriculum*. Philadelphia: Falmer Press.

McCarthy, C. (1993). Beyond the poverty of theory in race relations: Nonsynchrony and social difference in education. In. L. Weis & M. Fine (Eds.), *Beyond silenced voices: Class, race and gender in U.S. schools* (pp. 325–346). Albany: State University of New York Press.

McCarthy, C. (2003). *Race, identity and representation in education*. Unpublished manuscript.

McCarthy, C., Critchlow, W., Dimitriadis, G., & Dolby, N. (Eds.). (2004). *Race, identity and representation in education* (Vol. 3). New York: Routledge.

McCarthy, C., Rodriguez, A., Meecham, S., David, S., Wilson-Brown, C., Godina, H., Supriya, K., and Buendia, E. (1997). Race, suburban resentment and the representation of the inner city in contemporary film and television. In M. Fine, L. Weis, L. Powell, & M. Wong (Eds.), *Off white: Readings on race, power and society* (pp. 229–241). New York: Routledge.

McChesney, R. (1999). Introduction. In N. Chomsky (Ed.), *Profit over people: Neoliberalism and the global order* (pp. 7–16). New York: Seven Stories Press.

McIntyre, A. (1997). *Making meaning of whiteness: Exploring racial identity with white teachers*. Albany: State University of New York Press.

McLaren, P. (1994). Collisions with otherness: Traveling theory, postcolonial criticism, and the politics of ethnographic practice—The mission of the wounded ethnographer. In P. McLaren & J. Giarelli (Eds.), *Critical theory and educational research* (pp. 271–300). Albany: State University of New York Press.

McNeil, L. (1986). *Contradictions of control*. New York: Routledge and Kegan Paul.

McNeil, L. (2000). *Contradictions of school reform: Educational costs of standardized testing*. New York: Routledge.

McRobbie, A. (1978). Working class girls and the culture of femininity. In Women's Studies Group (Ed.), *Women take issue*. London: Huchinson.

Milkman, R., ed. (1985). *Women, work and protest: A century of U.S. women's labor history*. London: Routledge and Kegan Paul.

Metro News. (2000, October 13). Test scores show pupils far short of proficiency, p. A1. [This reference is purposefully vague to ensure anonymity.]

Morrison, T. (1992). *Playing in the dark: Whiteness and literary imagination*. Cambridge, MA: Harvard University Press.

Mullings, L. (1997). *On our own terms: Race, class and gender in the lives of African Americans*. New York: Routledge.

National Center for Education Statistics. (1985–1986). *Digest of educational statistics*. Washington D.C.: U.S. Department of Education.

National Center for Education Statistics. (1986–1987). *Digest of educational statistics*. Washington D.C.: U.S. Department of Education.

Nayak, A. (2001). *Ivory lives: Race, ethnicity and the practice of whiteness in a northeast youth community*. Paper presented at the Economic and Social Research Seminar Series, Interdisciplinary Youth Research: New Approaches, Birmingham University, UK.

Newman, K. (1988). *Falling from grace*. New York: Free Press.

Niemi, E., Whitelaw, E., & Grossman, E. (2000, Fall). Bird of doom ... or was it? *The Amicus Journal, 22* (3), 19–30.

Oakes, J. (1985). *Keeping track: How schools structure inequality*. New Haven, CT: Yale University Press.

Ogbu, J. (1974). *The next generation*. New York: Academic Press.

Ogbu, J. (1988). Class stratification, racial stratification and schooling. In L. Weis (Ed.), *Class, race and gender in American education* (pp. 163–182). Albany: State University of New York Press.

Ogbu, J. (2002, Winter). Black American students and the achievement gap: What else you need to know. *Journal of Thought, 37* (4), 9–33.

Ogbu, J., & Simons, H. (1998). Voluntary and involuntary minorities. A cultural–ecological theory of school performance with some implications for educators. *Anthropology and Education Quarterly, 29* (2), 155–188.

O'Farrell, B. and Kornbluh, J., eds. (1996). *Rocking the boat: Union women's voices, 1915–1975*. New Brunswick: Rutgers University Press.

Olivas, M. (1979). *The dilemma of access: Minorities in two year colleges*. Washington, DC: Howard University Press.

Oliver, M., & Shapiro, T. (1995). *Black wealth/white wealth: A new perspective on racial inequality*. New York: Routledge.

Omi, M., & Winant, H. (1994). *Racial formation in the United States: From the 1960s to the 1990s*. New York: Routledge.

Overall, C. (1995). Nowhere at home: Toward a phenomenology of working-class consciousness. In C. L. Barney Dews and C. Leste Law (Eds.), *This fine place so far from home*. Philadelphia: Temple University Press.

Pollack, M. (2004). *Colormute: Race talk dilemmas in an American school*. Princeton, NJ: Princeton University Press.

Proweller, A. (1998). *Constructing female identities: Meaning making in an upper middle class youth culture*. Albany: State University of New York Press.

Raissiguier, C. (1994). *Becoming women, becoming workers: Identity formation in a French vocational school*. Albany: State University of New York Press.

Reay, D. (1997a). Feminist theory, habitus, and social class: Disrupting notions of classlessness. *Women's International Forum, 20* (2), 225–233.

Reay, D. (1997b). The double-bind of the "working-class" feminist academic: The failure of success or the success of failure. In P. Mahony & C. Zmroczek (Eds.), *Class matters: Working class women's perspectives on social class*. London: Taylor and Francis.

Reay, D. (1998). Surviving in dangerous places: Working-class women, women's studies and higher education. *Women's Studies International Forum, 20* (1), 11–19.

Reay, D. (2002). Shaun's story: Troubling discourses of white working-class masculinities. *Gender and Education, 14* (3), 221–234.

Reich, R. (1991). *The work of nations: Preparing ourselves for 21st-century capitalism*. New York: Alfred A. Knopf.

Reich, R. (2001). *The future of success*. New York: Alfred A. Knopf.

Riley, L., & Glass, J. (2002, February). You can't always get what you want— Infant care preferences and use among employed mothers. *Journal of Marriage and Family, 64*, 2–15.

Rodriguez, C. (1990). Racial identification among Puerto Ricans in New York. *Hispanic Journal of Behavioral Sciences, 12*, 366–379.

Rodriguez, C. (1992). Race, culture and Latino "otherness" in the 1980 census. *Social Science Quarterly, 73* (4), 930–937.

Rodriguez, C. (1994). Challenging racial hegemony: Puerto Ricans in the United States. In S. Gergory & R. Sanjek (Eds.), *Race*. New Brunswick, NJ: Rutgers University Press.

Rogers, J., & Teixeira, R. (2000). *America's forgotten majority: Why the white working class still matters*. New York: Basic Books.

Roman, L. and Christian-Smith L., eds. (1988). *Becoming feminine: The politics of popular culture*. Philadelphia: Falmer Press.

Rosenbaum, J. (1976). *Making inequality: The hidden curriculum of high school tracking*. New York: John Wiley.

Rubin, L. (1976). *Worlds of pain*. New York: Basic Books.

Said, E. (1979). *Orientalism*. New York: Vintage Books.

Seller, M., & Weis, L. (1997). *Beyond black and white: New Faces and voices in U.S. schools*. Albany: State University of New York Press.

Sennett, R., & Cobb, J. (1972). *The hidden injuries of class*. New York: Vintage Books.

Smith, D. (1987). Women's inequality and the family. In M. Fainsod Katzenstein & C. McClurg Mueller (Eds.), *The women's movements of the United States and Europe*. Philadelphia: Temple University Press.

Solomon, P. (1992). *Black resistance in high school*. Albany: State University of New York Press.

Spelman, E. (1988). *Inessential woman*. Boston: Beacon Press.

Stacey, J. (1990). *Brave new families: Stories of domestic upheavalin late twentieth century America*. New York: Basic Books.

Strohmeyer, J. (1994). *Crisis in Bethlehem: Big steel's struggle to survive*. Pittsburgh, PA: University of Pittsburgh Press.

Tentler, L. (1979). *Wage earning women: Industrial work and family life in the United States, 1900–1930*. New York: Oxford University Press.

Thévenon, E. (Juillet 2002). Pierre Bourdieu: Un regard neuf sur le monde social. *Label France, le magazine*, 47 (2) 1–5. http://www.france.diplomatie.fr/label_france/47/fr/20.html

Thompson, E. P. (1966). *The making of the English working class*. New York: Vintage Books.

U.S. Bureau of the Census. (1960). Washington, DC: Government Printing Office.

U.S. Bureau of the Census. (1970). Washington, DC: Government Printing Office.

U.S. Bureau of the Census. (1980). Washington, DC: Government Printing Office.

U.S. Bureau of the Census. (1990). Washington, DC: Government Printing Office.

U.S. Bureau of the Census. (2000). Washington, DC: Government Printing Office.

Valenzuela, A. (1999). *Subtractive schooling: U.S. Mexican youth and the politics of caring*. Albany, NY: State University of New York Press.

Valli, L. (1986). *Becoming clerical workers*. Boston: Routledge and Kegan Paul.

Wacquant, L. (1992). Toward a social praxeolgy: The structure and logic of Bourdieu's sociology. In P. Bourdieu & L. Wacquant (Eds.), *An invitation to reflexive sociology* (pp. 1–59). Chicago: University of Chicago Press.

Walker, J. C. (1988). The way men act: Dominant and subordinate cultures in an inner-city school. *British Journal of Sociology of Education, 9* (1), 3–18.

Walkerdine, V., Lucey, H., & Melody, J. (2001). *Growing up girl: Psychosocial explorations of gender and class*. New York: New York University Press.

Wallace, C. (1987). *For richer, for poorer: Growing up in and out of work*. New York: Tavistock.

Ware, V. (1992). *Beyond the pale: White women, racism and history*. New York: Verso.

Weiler, J. (2000). *Codes and contradictions: Race, gender identity, and schooling*. Albany: State University of New York Press.

Weis, L. (1985). *Between two worlds: Black students in an urban community college*. Boston: Routledge and Kegan Paul.

Weis, L. (1990). *Working class without work: High school students in a de-industrializing economy*. New York: Routledge.

Weis, L. (2001, Autumn). Race, gender and critique: African American and white women in the 1980s and 1990s. *Signs, 27* (1), 139–169.

Weis, L., & Fine, M. (1997). Narrating the 1980s and 1990s: Voices of poor and working-class white and African-American men. *Anthropology and Education Quarterly, 27* (4), 1–24.

Weis, L., & Fine, M. (2000). *Speed bumps: A student friendly guide to qualitative research*. New York: Teachers College Press.

Weis, L., & Fine, M. (2004). *Working method: Research and social justice*. New York: Routledge.

Weis, L., & Hall, J. (2000, March). I had a lot of black friends that my father didn't know about: An exploration of white working class and poor female racism. *Journal of Gender Studies, 10* (1), 43–66.

Wexler, P. (1987). *Social analysis of education*. New York: Routledge.

Willis, P. (1977). *Learning to labour: How working class kids get working class jobs*. Westmead, UK: Saxon House Press.

Willis, P. (2000). *The ethnographic imagination*. Malden, MA: Polity Press.

Wilson, W. J. (1996). *When work disappears*. New York: Alfred A. Knopf.

Wolpe, A. M. (1978). Education and the sexual division of labour. In A. Kuhn & A. M. Wolpe (Eds.), *Feminism and materialism: Women and modes of production* (pp. 290–338). London: Routledge and Kegan Paul.

Zinsser, C. (1991). *Raised in East Urban: Child care changes in a working class community*. New York: Teacher's College Press.

INDEX